Studies in Computer Science

In Honor of Samuel D. Conte

Software Science and Engineering

Series Editor: **Richard A. DeMillo**
Purdue University, West Lafayette, Indiana

High-Integrity Software
Edited by C. T. Sennett

Software Reuse: Guidelines and Methods
James W. Hooper and Rowena O. Chester

Studies in Computer Science: In Honor of Samuel D. Conte
Edited by John Rice and Richard A. DeMillo

A Continuation Order Plan is available for this series. A continuation order will bring delivery of each new volume immediately upon publication. Volumes are billed only upon actual shipment. For further information please contact the publisher.

Studies in Computer Science

In Honor of Samuel D. Conte

Edited by

John Rice and **Richard A. DeMillo**

Purdue University
West Lafayette, Indiana

Springer Science+Business Media, LLC

Library of Congress Cataloging-in-Publication Data

Studies in computer science : in honor of Samuel D. Conte / edited by
   John Rice, Richard A. DeMillo.
      p.   cm. -- (Software science and engineering)
   Includes bibliographical references and index.
   ISBN 978-1-4613-5723-0   ISBN 978-1-4615-1791-7 (eBook)
   DOI 10.1007/978-1-4615-1791-7
   1. Computer science. 2. Conte, Samuel Daniel, 1917-   .
I. Conte, Samuel Daniel, 1917-   . II. Rice, John Rischard.
III. DeMillo, Richard A. IV. Series.
QA76..S848 1994
004--dc20   94-34693
                                                               CIP

ISBN 978-1-4613-5723-0

© 1994 Springer Science+Business Media New York
Originally published by Plenum Press New York in 1994
Softcover reprint of the hardcover 1st edition 1994

Contributors

Chandrajit L. Bajaj • Department of Computer Sciences, Purdue University, West Lafayette, Indiana

Samuel D. Conte • Department of Computer Sciences, Purdue University, West Lafayette, Indiana

C. de Boor • Center for Mathematical Sciences, University of Wisconsin–Madison, Madison, Wisconsin

Peter J. Denning • George Mason University, Fairfax, Virginia

Norman E. Gibbs • Software Engineering Institute, Carnegie Mellon University, Pittsburgh, Pennsylvania

Felix Haas • School of Science, Purdue University, West Lafayette, Indiana

Alan R. Hevner • Information for Systems Research, University of Maryland, College Park, Maryland

Thomas I. M. Ho • Information Networking Institute, Carnegie Mellon University, Pittsburgh, Pennsylvania

Joseph E. Hollingsworth • Indiana University at New Albany, New Albany, Indiana

Sang-Ha Kim • Korea Institute for Science and Technology, Cheongryang, Seoul, Korea

Harlan D. Mills • Information for Systems Research, University of Maryland, College Park, Maryland

L. Duane Pyle† • Department of Computer Science, University of Houston, Houston, Texas

John R. Rice • Department of Computer Sciences, Purdue University, West Lafayette, Indiana

Saul Rosen† • Department of Computer Sciences, Purdue University, West Lafayette, Indiana

Bi Roubolo Vona • Center for Numerical Analysis, University of Texas at Austin, Austin, Texas

David M. Young, Jr. • Center for Numerical Analysis, University of Texas at Austin, Austin, Texas

R. V. M. Zahar • Département d'Informatique et de Recherche Operationelle, Université de Montréal, Montréal, Québec, Canada

† Deceased.

Preface

This book is the proceedings of a conference held November 1–3, 1989, to honor Samuel D. Conte for his many contributions to computer sciences at Purdue University and to the profession as a whole. The computer sciences program reflected the breadth of Conte's interests and accomplishments; there were tributes to Conte, perspectives on computer science itself, and research papers.

The first part of these proceedings chronicles the career and contributions; much of it is based on Conte's remarks made at the conference banquet. The second part of the proceedings starts with one vision of the future of computer sciences given in Peter Denning's keynote address. Historical accounts of building successful educational programs in computer sciences follow. The third part consists of seven research contributions, primarily from past or present colleagues. These include Conte's numerical analysis, computational geometry, and discussions of software engineering.

The conference was organized by the Purdue University Department of Computer Sciences and the Software Engineering Research Center at Purdue. Both of these organizations were founded by Conte, so is fitting for them to recognize their founder's achievements in such a concrete way.

John R. Rice

West Lafayette, Indiana

When I first met Sam Conte, he was at the height of his career. He had been head of the first academic department of computer sciences in the world—a department he founded—for 10 years. He would hold this position for another 7 years. I was not at the height of my career. It was January 1972, and I was visiting Purdue as a candidate for a junior faculty position in computer sciences.

The interview at Purdue was my first as a Ph.D., and I was visibly nervous. Purdue was after all a famous place among computer scientists. It had been home to Alan Perlis at the start of his career. The computer sciences department numbered among its faculty many of the luminaries in the field. Richard Buchi, Paul Young, John Rice, Saul Rosen, Carl de Boor, Walter Gautschi, Maurice Halstead, Bob Lynch, and of course Conte were already senior faculty members. These were people who heretofore had been names on influential articles and textbooks—required reading for graduate students. Conte did his best to put me at ease, but he did not entirely succeed.

Purdue did not hire me that year (they hired Michael Machtey after whom the Machtey prize in theoretical computer science is named, and Peter Denning, who succeeded Conte as head of the department), but Conte and I became lifelong friends as a result of that interview.

Fifteen years later Purdue did hire me. One afternoon in late 1985, Conte rushed unannounced into my office at Georgia Tech, and asked me what I had been doing. I told him that I was forming a software engineering research center at Georgia Tech, and I spent some time describing how it was going to work. I also wanted to tell him about some technical results, but he left before I had a chance. In 1986 Conte invited me to visit Purdue as a speaker in their Distinguished Speaker program. When I arrived to give my talk, Conte said that Purdue wanted to hire me. In 1987 I joined the faculty as professor of computer sciences and director of the Purdue Software Engineering Research Center, succeeding Conte, who had been the center's founding director.

Shortly after my arrival at Purdue, Rice suggested that we organize a symposium in honor of Conte's seventieth birthday. The symposium would very nearly coincide with another anniversary of note: the twenty-fifth anniversary of the forming of the computer sciences department at Purdue University. The present volume comprises the proceedings of that symposium. Papers were contributed by Conte's friends and colleagues as the result of a call for papers, and these were selected by a program committee composed of computer sciences faculty members. These papers represent work in the technical disciplines that Conte's career has spanned: numerical analysis, software engineering, and computer science education.

Conte received his doctorate in mathematics from the University of Michigan in 1950. His first academic position was as associate professor of mathematics at Wayne State University. In 1956 Conte began the industrial phase of his career, first at TRW's Space Technology Labs, then at the Aerospace Corporation. TRW's Dr. Hal Hart recalls Conte's contributions:

> TRW wishes to join in honoring Samuel D. Conte on the occasion of the Symposium in his honor at Purdue. We are proud that former employee Conte is our continuing link to the history-making establishment of the first academic Computer Sciences department at Purdue. Scores of former colleagues here from the "early days" and former Purdue CS students send their greetings and congratulations to Dr. Conte.

> None of us here who know him doubt Sam Conte's contributions to TRW's rise from a small upstart aerospace systems house to the world's second largest developer of software systems! His pioneering software activities here in the 1950's and 60's and the steady flow of highly educated software professionals he has steered from Purdue to TRW for the past quarter century are no small part of TRW's success. Of course, Sam's legacy is shared by software institutions all over the world—how many believed in 1962 the insatiable future requirements for software education that would dominate the following decades and the unavoidable need Sam Conte and Purdue were first filling then?

> Careers are measured by positive accomplishments. Lives are measured by the quality of friendships. Sam Conte's life and career can only be judged "A+" based on the many fond memories of friends everywhere who have been touched by Sam. He has contributed substantially to the rise of TRW, academic computer sciences and the still-continuing advent of the true profession of software engineering.

This helps explain Conte's return nearly 20 years later from research in numerical analysis to software engineering.

Since 1962 when he joined the faculty at Purdue as director of the Computer Center and professor and first head of the new computer sciences department, Conte divided his energies among research, building the department, and advancing the discipline of computer science.

In the sixties and seventies, Conte's research interests centered around numerical mathematics. The dinner remarks by Felix Haas and Rice, transcribed elsewhere in this volume, help give the reader a flavor of Conte's contributions in this area. I am not a numerical analyst, but I was of course familiar with the classic text on the subject by Conte and de Boor.

I found it fascinating therefore that for his contribution to this volume, de Boor chose to report on a long-sought solution to a problem whose importance (and difficulty) is raised in the Conte–de Boor text: multivariable polynomial interpolation.

Building the computer sciences department at Purdue spans nearly 30 years. Rosen was at Purdue to see and participate in most of it. Rosen and Rice have contributed a historical perspective of the department to this volume. One story that does not appear in the Rosen–Rice chapter sheds light on how Conte was able to be so effective at recruiting. Denning relates that Conte walked into his Princeton office one afternoon unannounced and offered him a full professorship at Purdue. This is like the approach that Conte used to attract me to Purdue, so I can only conclude that much of the recruiting during this period was carried forward by the force of Conte's personality. In any event the result of Conte's tenure as leader of this extraordinary collection of scholars was the emergence of Purdue's Department of Computer Sciences as one of the premier academic and research programs in this new and vital discipline.

Rosen, who contributed much to the preparation of these proceedings and who contributed enormously to the birth and development of computer sciences at Purdue University, passed away suddenly in June 1991 before this book went to press. Rosen's anthology on languages, compilers, and machines was one of the first textbooks on computer science. It was exactly the first that I read—cover to cover—as an undergraduate. I trace my interest in becoming a computer scientist to Rosen.

During the sixties and early seventies, Conte was a leading member of an informal group of heads of computer sciences departments from Midwestern universities. This group was primarily responsible for setting goals and directions for the field in the early years. The Computing Research Association, which now represents the policy interests of all Ph.D.-granting computer sciences departments in Washington developed from this group. It was also responsible for launching the first national computer sciences research conference: the Computer Science conference. For the symposium Marshall Yovitz, chairman of the information and computer science department at Ohio State University for many years, recalled his experiences with Conte during these formative years.

In the late seventies Conte's interests returned to software development. He began a collaboration with Halstead—a pioneer in the new field of software engineering—and a number of more junior colleagues, including Vincent Shen and H. E. Dunsmore, aimed at providing scientific foundations for developing and engineering large and complex software systems.

In 1985 Conte and his Purdue colleagues teamed up with a group of junior scientists at the University of Florida in Gainesville, Florida, to establish the Software Engineering Research Center, or SERC, as it was to be called. The SERC was chartered as one of the National Science Foundation's (NSF) Industry/University Cooperative Research Centers—consortia established by NSF to foster and support university research on problems of industrial relevance. The SERC was launched at a time when software engineering consortia were multiplying. Most (like the Micro-electronics and Computer Research Consortium in Austin, Texas, and the Software Productivity Consortium in Reston, Virginia) were much larger and more well-endowed than SERC. However Conte and Roger Elliott, his counterpart at the University of Florida, were passionately convinced that universities were the best place to carry out this sort of work. At the first meeting of its industrial advisory board in October 1986, SERC had 12 industrial sponsors and NSF and the Florida High Technology and Industry Council. The annual research budget of the center quickly rose to nearly $1 million per year. SERC has continued to prosper. To date, nearly 20 industrial affiliates have signed agreements with SERC, which has supported the research of 30 faculty researchers at seven institutions. The SERC research products have included software technology that is actively being transitioned to practical use by member companies. As other larger consortia falter, SERC with its visionary approach to teaming university-based scientific talent and industrial collaborators continues to thrive. Conte's career had indeed come full circle—from his early industrial software experience at TRW to establishing an industry-university research center in software technology.

In the summer of 1987, Conte turned 70 and retired from the faculty at Purdue to become Professor Emeritus. I became the second director of SERC at Purdue. When I arrived, Conte's wife, Peggy, herself a retired dean at Purdue, said that she thought now maybe her husband would take his retirement seriously. Conte admitted that he might take an occasional afternoon off.

In the past few years, Conte has directed a highly successful SERC research project, been a visiting professor at the University of Florida, and spent a year in Washington, D.C., managing a large program in the Computer and Information Sciences and Engineering Directorate at NSF. He is currently designing a master's program in software engineering at Purdue. Conte is still at the height of his career.

Richard A. DeMillo

West Lafayette, Indiana

Contents

SAMUEL D. CONTE

Welcome*

John R. Rice

I want to start off with some material that we received today from people at TRW Corporation. At lunch time, where there were many fewer people, Rich read the official communications from them, but they also sent along a number of personal messages from former colleagues and students at TRW Corporation. For those of you who are not aware of it, Sam was at a predecessor of TRW before he came to Purdue in 1962. I think it was Aerospace Corporation at that time. Let me read a few of these.

From Bob Burnett: "Not only am I from Purdue, but I knew Sam when he was an arbor vitae in the early days of Ramo Woolridge and the ICBM programs. I am glad to hear that he is still productive at Purdue. I have lost track of him, and [I] have had no contact with him for a number of years. Please pass on my regards and my congratulations for an outstanding career and my hope that he continues to have a major positive impact on Purdue and the students."

Another message is from Don Routh: "Dear Dr. Conte. Congratulations to you on this special occasion. I had not heard that you had retired and wanted to wish you the best in all your plans for the years ahead.

---

* This speech was given at the Samuel D. Conte dinner.

John R. Rice • Purdue University

Studies in Computer Science, edited by John R. Rice and Richard A. DeMillo. Plenum Press, New York, 1994.

[Actually he hasn't retired.] The contributions that you made to STL/RW [that must be Space Technology Laboratories in Ramo-Wooldrige] in those early years were certainly noteworthy. I also have pleasant memories of college recruiting at Purdue in the late sixties and early seventies and being able to obtain such qualified employees from you and your computer science department. It has been over 10 years since I've had any contact with you and your son, Bob, and would like to extend best wishes to you, Bob, and your entire family."

The next message is from Mike Bouton: "Sam Conte was at STL during my first 4 years there, and I had a fair amount of interaction with him because of my continuing business with the computing center and the mathematics department. Please convey my best wishes to him and tell him that Hawaii is a great place to consider if the winters in Lafayette get to be too much. While I knew him [Sam Conte] on an occasional basis, Bob Page, who was my boss at the end of that period, knew him better, and Aubry Mickelwaite better still, as I remember it. If you haven't contacted Mick, it might be worth the effort. He might still be on the consultant rolls at TRW, and if not, he may be in the South Bay phone book. It is possible that Sam may not know that Bob Page, and his wife also, died some years ago."

From Richard Blue: "Sam, Good Luck! I certainly do appreciate all the help you gave me in the past. Particularly you were an invaluable reference for all the applicants from Purdue when I was a hiring manager. Thanks again."

Other people, colleagues of Sam's TRW, STL/RW days who want to be remembered but did not send special messages are Bob Beach, Bill Mancina, Ed Blum, Don Gantner, Herb Ashbury, Eldred Nelson, Bob Rector, and Ed Goldberg.

We now have some messages from former students.

Steve J. Whitson: "I was a student for one semester. Really enjoyed his [Sam Conte's] class and his personal style. Happy to sign a letter or whatever you have in mind." This, it turns out, is in response to a message from Hal Hart, who some of the old-timers at least remember. He is at TRW and orchestrated all of these messages.

From Beth and Bill Allendorfer: "You will of course remember that Bill and I were there when Sam was department head. Bill also said to tell you that Mike Burgin knew him. Dr. Conte got Bill in an elevator and wouldn't let him out until he promised to interview at TRW. I guess TRW owes us for him."

From Ruth Hart: "I (laughingly) recall Dr. Conte's apparent tolerance of all the inbreeding going on in graduate computer science in the late sixties and early seventies. Ten interdepartmental marriages in 3 years. You see that at least the two couples that came to TRW are still together, and we keep in touch with some of the others. Unfortunately not all of them made it."

From Hal Hart: "I recall the ready willingness of Dr. Conte to take onto the faculty as an instructor in 1969 a teaching assistant just finishing his MS and badly wanting a draft deferment. Perhaps not ultimately the most important thing in my life, but it seemed close to it at the time, and it is probably unique among the many things for which Sam Conte is credited. I'm glad that we finally recruited Dave Capsum to TRW. Before that we had no Purdue CS Ph.D.s but four of us Ph.D. dropouts. More professionally I think part of Dr. Conte's legacy is revealed in perusing the names of those elected to office in the Association for Computing Machinery and its subunits during the past two decades. I'm always proud to note the unusually high percentage of names, both contemporary students and faculty, from my era in Purdue computer sciences."

Other former students, now at TRW, who sent best wishes but did not send special messages are Don Andres, Frank Beltz, Mike Bergen, Dave Capp, Greg Ferguson, Jackie Garnet Smith, Kathy Mapes, Rich Messenger, Maxine Villar, Anna Qualessa, and Dick Smith.

I will give these to you, Sam, to keep. I also have a plaque here that only I can read at this moment. At the top it has three symbols representing software engineering, computer sciences education, and numerical analysis, and reads, "To Samuel D. Conte, in honor of your outstanding accomplishments and continuing distinguished career in the areas of computer science education, numerical analysis, and software engineering. Presented by the Software Engineering Research Center and the faculty of the Department of Computer Sciences at Purdue University, November 1989."

Introduction*

Felix Haas

I've been given the pleasant task of introducing tonight's speaker. One of the clichés that is often used by people who have been asked to introduce a speaker, especially if the person is lazy, is the statement describing the speaker as someone who needs no introduction. That statement is valid to varying degrees, depending of course on the speaker and the audience. It is certainly true tonight, given the reputation of the speaker and this gathering of friends.

The conference you have just had for the last 24 hours is ample evidence that Sam's colleagues and friends not only know (he is not an easy man to know), but respect and admire Sam. Sam the man, Sam the scientist, and Sam the administrator. Please note the order. This would be an appropriate place for me to stop, actually, because I have done the formal task of introducing Sam, but I'm not going to stop, and in about 3 or 4 minutes, you will know why.

Sam grew up in upstate New York; he has bachelor's and master's degree[s] from the University of Buffalo, and except for the Second World War, he might have ended up as a high school teacher of mathematics,

---

* This speech was given at the Samuel D. Conte dinner.

Felix Haas • Purdue University

Studies in Computer Science, edited by John R. Rice and Richard A. DeMillo. Plenum Press, New York, 1994.

possibly a bank president, or a professional gambler: areas in which Sam has some interest. But the Second World War changed Sam's life as it changed the life of so many of his contemporaries. Soon after the end of the war, Sam was stationed in France and met a man by the name of Al Nelson, who happened to be chairman of the mathematics department at Wayne State University. Al Nelson convinced Sam to go back to graduate school, get a Ph.D. at Michigan, and then join the Wayne State faculty. After more or less 10 years at Wayne State, Sam entered industry. I think he entered industry in the second generation of computer professionals . . . people who were still pioneers, but of the second generation. The real dividing line between the first and second generation was the invention of magnetic memory, which shows how far back Sam really goes.

In 1962 Sam came to Purdue, where he was in charge of the Department of Computer Science from 1962 to 1979. Between 1962 to 1968 he was also responsible for the Purdue University Computing Center. It was during this period that I learned to appreciate our speaker's integrity and ability. Now integrity in the case of someone who's in charge of an organization, a not-for-profit organization, I think translates into trying to provide the best service to the public that your resources permit. Add to that trying to get more resources, of course. Ability translates in such a situation into defining what services best to provide in your particular environment and having the natural and necessary intellectual quality to approximate this optimization goal. I want to give you a few examples of Sam's past activities that exhibit his integrity and his ability. I will switch back and forth between talking about the speaker and Sam because I just can't get myself to refer to him as Dr. Conte.

When Sam first came to Purdue, he very rapidly brought us Saul Rosen and John Rice. In the first 2 or 3 years, he attracted Walter Gautschi, Maury Halstead, and a number of other people of distinction. A few years later we got Peter Denning.

Sam was in no way naive during those years, financially. I remember again and again in making important appointments, he used funds that had been given to the computing center to hire people who were actually needed for the computer science department because it was easier to get resources for the computing center than for the department.

But you know, the appointments that I have mentioned . . . I see Carl de Boor here for instance . . . were real evidence of Sam's dedication to strive for quality. And during all the years Sam was department head, I think he could never get himself to appoint someone who did not measure up to his standards of scholarship. But his record of recruitment didn't just reflect quality, it also reflected the changing nature of the computer science field. When your discipline is really being defined, it may be defined several times. And what is noticeable is that Sam was always just a few steps ahead, well maybe a few miles ahead, of the community consensus of what represented computer science at that particular time. So the nature of his appointments changed over the years as the discipline changed, and he was able to reflect these changes. In the early years Sam was also responsible for the equipment that we had at Purdue. He sought the advice of many experts and just as in the case of appointments, I cannot think of a single mistake that Sam made.

By now you can probably guess why I wanted to say a few words. You know in a university environment, there are those who are loud, those who are given to histrionics, those who threaten to leave all the time and are repeatedly assured of how valuable and important they are to the institution (in many cases it's even true), but a quiet and unassuming giant like Sam Conte tends not to get the accolades that he has deserved. So this introduction gave me an opportunity to belatedly undo some of our earlier omission. Sam, I have enjoyed working with you; I look forward to hearing your talk.

Address to Guests*

Samuel D. Conte

First of all I want to express my deep appreciation to all of you former students, faculty, colleagues, and friends for attending this symposium. I want to especially thank those of you who contributed invited papers, particularly David Young, who worked with me at Aberdeen Proving Grounds in 1951 and later at TRW in California; Carl deBoor, whom I recruited as a faculty member in 1966 and who later coauthored with me a best selling textbook in numerical analysis; Peter Denning, who joined the department in 1972 and later became head of the department; and finally I owe a special thanks to John Rice both for his outstanding contributions to the computer science department as a faculty member and department head and for conceiving and organizing this symposium.

I think of all the students who have graduated from this department as my students, and nothing pleases a professor more than the knowledge that his students have been successful and the feeling that he had some small part in that success. My own life and career were greatly influenced by my parents and by a mathematician named Al Nelson. My parents came to this country as poor, uneducated immigrants and saved,

* This speech was given at the Samuel D. Conte dinner.

Samuel D. Conte • Purdue University

Studies in Computer Science, edited by John R. Rice and Richard A. DeMillo. Plenum Press, New York, 1994.

scrimped, and sacrificed so that I and my brothers could obtain a college degree and share in the American dream. I met Professor Nelson at the American College, which was established by the US army at the end of hostilities in Europe during World War II. He was a civilian professor, and I was assigned there as a GI to teach mathematics. At the end of the war, Dr. Nelson offered me a position at Wayne State University and encouraged me to continue my education toward a Ph.D. Without his guidance and encouragement, I would undoubtedly have remained a high school teacher in my hometown of Lackawanna, New York.

My first contact with computers came in 1951, when after receiving my Ph.D. in applied mathematics from the University of Michigan, I accepted a summer position at the Aberdeen Proving Grounds. The ENIAC and EDVAC computers were housed there at the time. It was there that I first met David Young, Al Perlis, Saul Gorn, and Mario Juncosa. We struggled together to learn the idiosyncrasies of these early computers, and of course all of us went on to become leaders in the new world of computers.

After teaching several years at Wayne State University, I accepted a position at TRW in California in 1956, where our mathematical software group designed and implemented computer programs for satellite and space tracking and for many other scientific problems. It was there in 1961 that Felix Haas, who had been chairman of the mathematics department at Wayne State University and had recently accepted a position as head of the Division of Mathematical Sciences at Purdue, contacted me concerning some ideas he had about initiating an academic program in computer science at Purdue. The situation at Purdue in computing, which was typical of most universities in the early sixties, was not very promising. Academic computing facilities were nonexistent or inadequate; there was no systematic attempt to teach computer science; there were of course no degree programs in computer science; and there were no teaching materials nor textbooks. Nevertheless I accepted a position as professor of mathematics and computer science and arrived at Purdue in July 1962. That summer we put together a program of courses leading to an MS or Ph.D. in computer science; we began to recruit faculty; and we advertised for students even before the program was officially approved by the university. The computer science department was officially approved by the board of trustees in October 1962, thus establishing it as the first university in the country to offer degree programs in computer science. It is fair to say that all of the national leaders, I among them, who struggled for so many years to obtain adequate funding and to gain academic respectability for computer science as a discipline did not foresee the tremendous success that it now enjoys both within the academic community and in the world at large.

No department can be successful without strong, dedicated faculty. I was fortunate in attracting to Purdue some outstanding faculty, including Saul Rosen, Walter Gautschi, Richard Buchi, John Rice, Paul Young, Carl deBoor, Maurice Halstead, Peter Denning, and many others. Recognition of our success as a department came in the early seventies when our department was ranked as one of the top ten best computer science departments in the country. Under the leadership of John Rice, the department has continued to thrive and excel when judged by any of the common measures of success, including the size of the student body, the number of degrees awarded, the funded research base, number of papers published, and faculty excellence.

In conclusion I want to thank all of you again for attending this symposium, which I view more as a celebration of 28 years of successful achievement as a department than as a personal tribute to me as its founder. My special thanks to Rich DeMillo and the Software Engineering Research Center for cosponsoring this symposium. And finally I want to take this occasion to remember those faculty who also contributed, but who have since passed away, including Maury Halstead, Richard Buchi, and Mike Machtey.

Keynote Address*
Worldnet

Peter J. Denning

I chose for my topic "worldnet." The phenomenon I call worldnet is closely wrapped up with the development of computer science as a discipline. We're celebrating here today the birth of computer science as a discipline with the first department in the country for granting Ph.Ds right here at Purdue. Many of the results of the research of this discipline have found their way into practice over the years and are coming together now in this international milieu of networking.

Sam Conte hired me to come to Purdue in 1972. I remember most the speed with which Sam did that. I remember that we met at some conference, and he asked me something like, "How's Princeton treating you?" and I grumbled a little bit. Sam said, "Oh, isn't that interesting," and a few days later I got an offer of a promotion and almost 50% more salary. That was such an attractive offer, I couldn't turn it down.

In 1979 Sam retired after 17 years as department head, and I got the job as department head. That was a very interesting time. The student

---

* This speech was given at the Samuel D. Conte dinner.

Peter J. Denning • George Mason University

Studies in Computer Science, edited by John R. Rice and Richard A. DeMillo. Plenum Press, New York, 1994.

body was growing very large; we had very little space for the enlarged faculty; and our biggest concern was to make a case for more investment of resources by Purdue in computer science. So we developed a 5-year plan and sold it to the provost and the dean. From their action came the building that you now have. I understand that there is a reduction in the student body size now. So it is an honor for me to come here and join with the rest of you to honor Sam, because Sam certainly made a big, a great big, difference in my career. And what happened in my career, I appreciate, and thank Sam for the opportunity to have that happen.

Let me come to the subject of worldnet. I will talk about a variety of phenomena that you've already been witnessing and observing. Nothing that I'm going to say to you should be much of a surprise. I am interested in producing in you a new observer of this phenomenon and showing you that there is something very important going on here that has implications for the future of computer science research. I begin with the observation that business and government are moving very rapidly, almost more rapidly than anybody predicted, into electronic communication. It's part of the everyday way of doing business. Organizations are forming relationships across international boundaries, and that is part of the ordinary way of doing business. Cellular telephones and FAX are taking off like wildfire, not just in this country but all over the world. Science and engineering research now depend on large-scale resources and high-speed networks. So you can see a worldnet emerging right before your eyes. I actually want to turn that around and say the worldnet is here, and what is emerging is our awareness of it. In this context I claim that the research that's going to be associated with worldnet is going to be more relevant than a lot of traditional computer science research—relevant to the concerns of people in the world.

If you start looking for worldnet, you'll first see a lot of hardware. You'll see workstations; you'll see personal computers; you'll see networks; you'll see links of varying speeds. There's even a plan underway to create a gigabit network by 1995. You'll see software on all these computers, hooking them up, making them coherent. All this material forms the components, the observable components, of worldnet, but that's not where I want to look. I want to look somewhere else with you. The effects are much larger than they seem.

You can already see dramatic changes in store in the way people conduct their business. For example it's now a foregone conclusion that markets are global. Few businesses can even think in terms of limited national markets now. New trends in manufacturing are taking advantage of networking and computing. The industrial paradigm of mass production of hundreds of thousands of identical units is shifting to units tailored for the individual needs of the customers. This is going to call on a lot of manufacturing technology. There are some very interesting research problems in manufacturing that we don't even think about in computer science but which we could make giant contributions to if we did. We're already beginning to see new kinds of businesses emerging, which some people are calling network boutiques. They're going to specialize in some particular product or service tailored for the individual. As the owner of a boutique, you can make your offer across the worldwide network. You'll see another phenomenon: The descendant of today's graphic arts firms companies will help people design their network public image.

In science and engineering, we've already begun to see some of these changes. Senator Gore talks about the National Research and Education network as part of the high-performance computing initiative, an initiative to spend close to two billion dollars over the next several years to build up that network. There will be more and more powerful super computers, graphics, radio links, and so on. This is not just the future in science and computer science, but there are all sorts of links to industry coming up. Industry has many very challenging problems. For example drug companies are now looking at using super computers to simulate molecular structures and to help them build and genetically engineer their drugs by doing a lot of the simulation beforehand. If that technology can be mastered, drugs can get to market a lot faster. Drugs are a big business; a good drug that is needed can make a billion dollars in a year. Computer science knows a lot that can help drug companies put algorithms in place to produce new approaches to drugs. I would further claim that many of our students would find research of that kind to be much more relevant to their interests in the world than research, say, in compilers or parallel computers. Another major concern is the global environment. Just the other day, the President reiterated the administration's commitment for the United States to be a leader in the global change arena and research in global change. So in spite of various budget-tightening exercises, global change will fare well. But there are huge opportunities for computer science there, too, ranging from the design of algorithms that will run on parallel computers to solving networking problems to providing technology that allows different groups of scientists working on different parts of the atmospheric and global modeling problem to be interconnected by networks and collaborate with one another. Again I maintain that one would find this more relevant to their concerns in the world than some of the ones we've been engaged in.

All these things are becoming possible because of ubiquitous networking and computing. The whole context of networking, high-speed computing, ubiquitous computers, and personal computing defines a new way of thinking. That's the context that I call worldnet.

The latest issue of the *Kiplinger Newsletter* devoted the last page to some discussion of changes that are occurring in the communications business. These changes are happening inside the context of worldnet. Let me just read you a couple of these things. Listen to this as part of the direction that the world is heading in; listen as an opportunity for new ways of thinking about our research. The newsletter says that magazines will get very specialized, with computerized binding that will let publishers create editions for small groups of readers. Ads in magazines will appeal to individual readers by name. You like that? It may get to the point where they print you your own personal copy of the magazine.

Newspapers are offering new services. Newspapers don't print all the information they collect, but they'll offer it to you by fax or modem. Wake-up news telephone services are coming. Advertisers will soon bind computer disks in magazines; personal messages and offers will be on these disks. There's a new book that just came out about 2 months ago by Pamela Kane called *V-I-R-U-S*. It's about virus and worm attacks on IBM PCs, and it comes with a floppy disk that contains some viral detection and prevention software for your IBM PC. This is starting to happen. Encyclopedias will be sold on compact disks so you can get all sorts of animation and pictures and stuff with them, bringing the encyclopedia to life.

The newsletter talks about interactive television. You watch your television; you dial in on an 800 number; and you can make the plot of the show change by your choices. Audience participation ads are mentioned. You can modify the ad according to your input. And they say, in spite of all this, radio will hold its ground! The newsletter concludes by saying this isn't Star Trek stuff. These changes are already in the works. Now is the time to see how this affects your plans and operations. Where did all this come from? Let me review a little history. I want to review the history in a way that makes you into a new observer of that history so you can appreciate what's going on today. The history that I want to talk about started about 25 years ago. It's called the Arpanet.

The four first nodes of the Arpanet were installed in 1969. In 1971 there were 15 of those nodes, and in 1973 there were 37 nodes. Since that time this network of interconnected computers has expanded becoming Research Internet. This collection of networks now spans over 60,000 nodes. As people connect workstations to these networks, the number of nodes on the network keeps getting larger. This is actually a pretty phenomenal growth of networking, going from four nodes in 1969 to hundreds of thousands of nodes in 1989. If you count telephones, which are getting more intimately connected with computer networking, you're talking about millions and millions of nodes worldwide. So the four-node Arpanet is now so big that nobody knows the exact number of nodes in it.

The story of the Arpanet really begins in the late 1950s with concern about the durability of our communication system in case of (intercontinental ballistic missile) attack. Paul Baran at the Rand Corporation undertook some studies of survivable networks. He came up with the concept of distributed networks with many nodes. He proposed that messages could be broken up into little pieces and routed on what ever path is still functioning in the network. Therefore, if some node or link is taken out, the network can automatically reroute around that hole in the network. Baran's ideas were in internal Rand technical reports that were not released at the time.

But in the meantime, J. C. R. Lickleider, who was then at Advanced Research Projects Agency (ARPA) of the Dept. of Defense (DOD) as the director of the Information Science and Technology office, was speculating about what networks could do. He got Donald Davies of the National Physical Lab in England interested in this question. Davies came up with his own proposal for connecting computers in England, not so much in the context of survivability but to pass information from one computer to another. His proposal was a lot like Baran's. Lickleider noticed this and got these two researchers talking to each other. In the meantime Bob Taylor succeeded Lickleider at ARPA. He brought an interest on the sociological side. He knew that the government had paid for various computer installations around the country, such as at MIT and the University of Illinois. Each center had its own little community of scientists. Taylor was interested in what would happen if these scientists could share information and collaborate with each other over a distance, so he promoted the idea of ARPA getting into a network. Taylor recruited Larry Roberts at MIT Lincoln Labs to come down to ARPA and run this program. In late 1968 a contract was let to Bolt Beranek and Neumann (BBN) to build the first four Interface Message Processors (IMPs), which were delivered in 1969.

Other famous figures participated early on: Len Kleinrock had done some performance studies of distributed networks to determine how much capacity would be needed. Bob Kahn was one of the people who worked on the team building the first IMPs and then went on, as you know, to play a very significant leadership role in networking in the country when he was the director of the ARPA Information Science and Technology office.

One interesting phenomenon: If you go back and look at the original proposals for Arpanet, there was no mention of electronic mail, even though Taylor himself was thinking about having people collaborate. It turned out that by 1971 electronic mail was the major source of traffic on the network. Curiously, as late as 1980, people did not advocate networking for electronic mail. For example when Purdue, Delaware, and Wisconsin Universities and Rand were trying to put together a CSNET (Computer Science Network) proposal, NSF told us very clearly, "Do not base your proposal on electronic mail. It won't fly around here." We wrote the proposal so that it didn't mention electronic mail in any pivotal way, even though we all knew that everybody was going to start using CSNET for electronic mail. Today electronic mail is accepted. You notice the change? Electronic mail is accepted as a reason for doing networking; you don't have to defend it anymore.

Now, around the mid-1970s, it was already becoming clear to ARPA that this one network wasn't going to hold up very well. Other networks were starting, and it was clear that it was necessary to start interconnecting the other networks, so the ARPA devised a new set of protocols to enable internetwork networking. They invented the transport control protocol (TCP) and the internet protocol (IP). These two protocols produced end-to-end, reliable connections spanning multiple networks. Around 1980 we began to see what are now called community networks. These are groups of networks supported by particular communities. One of these networks is CSNET; it is still going. Another is BITNET, built around people who have IBM machines. There are, I understand, discussions about merging the two. Still another is the Usenet, which is all users of the UNIX telephone interconnection network. There are internal networks at IBM and DEC, and others. During this same time we shouldn't forget that there was a lot of networking activity going on in Europe. Networking is part of the plan, as a matter of fact, to create the common united Europe in 1992.

Now I want to start interpreting all these developments in a new way. I want to introduce you to what I call the invention of the new discourse. A discourse is a transparent mode of thinking, speaking, and acting that engage in people and that transcends individuals. It goes on for long periods of time. The Arpanet is the invention of a new discourse in networking. Most of us are unaware of the discourses that we're operating in. As long as we can't see them, we can't take advantage of them; we can't see the opportunities that are there, and more importantly, we can't shift when the realities start shifting. Let me explore this idea of the invention of discourse with a couple of simple examples.

Suppose we brought Henry Ford back to look at automobiles and took him into an automobile showroom. Would he be surprised at what he sees? Chances are he would not be. He'd see a car, and it would have a body, four wheels, a steering wheel, and a transmission. It would have a front-mounted engine and all sorts of things that looked familiar. Of course he'd see power steering and power windows, but I speculate that he wouldn't be very surprised by any of that because they're sort of obvious technological improvements on the basic design. The basic design of the automobile is pretty much the same as when he was working on it. On the other hand, what would happen when you took him out into the street, out of the showroom, and let him look at the world? Well this is where I speculate that Henry Ford would be greatly surprised. He would be surprised by all the practices that have grown up around the automobile. For example there are annual sales of millions of cars; there is the creation and maintenance of the interstate highway system; and there's the whole system of distribution of goods and food based on nationwide trucking. People now look at cars as status symbols. Just watch all the advertising for cars—it's trying to match the car to your own self-image. Cars are not being thought of as purely transportation devices any more. If your kids get a driver's license, they want to have a car, so not only do you have college expenses, you have the expense of cars for your kids. The state got into the act and introduced the driver's license to make sure that people have certain minimal levels of competence and knowledge of the rules when on the road. We also have the traffic helicopter telling you where all the traffic jams are. An examination of human practices since the time the car was invented reveals things that could not have been anticipated by Henry Ford and would genuinely surprise him it he saw what was going on. People who are doing all these things aren't thinking about it; they're just thinking, acting, and speaking inside of a discourse about automobiles.

Let's try the same analysis with Alexander Graham Bell; let's bring him back to look at telephones. I submit that he would not be very surprised by the design of telephones, by the design of telephone switches, by the kinds of links that we transmit over, the technological improvements for transmitting telephone conversations. But the changes in human practices that have grown up around telephones could very well be surprising. For example we have telephones in every home; we have telephones in every hotel room; hotels even advertise that they have telephones to attract customers. We have car phones; we have phone booths all over the place. We have recently gotten the international dial network completely automated so you can call anywhere in the world. We can get news services on the telephone, and such news services as AP or Reuters use the telephone system to move the news around. Multinational corporations routinely conducting business in several countries at once; the banking system now uses telephone systems to do its electronic funds transfers. It's just everywhere, the effects of the telephone system. Then there's the other side of it, like telemarketing: You sit down to eat supper, the phone rings, and somebody tries to sell you something; or there's a computer out there trying to sell you something. You can call almost any business to order something by phone now. And there's the phenomenon that's really taken a lot of people by surprise, the FAX machine; hardly any business now doesn't have a FAX machine. I must mention telephone pornography: Once again you see an invention where the design of the basic elements hasn't changed very much, but the practices that people are engaged in with telephones have changed radically—a new discourse was invented around the telephone.

I invite you to consider a third example: Thomas Edison coming back to look at electricity. He would see light bulbs, electric generators, and power distribution systems. None of that would surprise him; what might be surprising might be the total dependence our society has on electrical power. When power fails, you find you can't do anything; you feel isolated. This is all happening in the developed countries, and it is beginning to spread to the undeveloped countries. Whole industries are built around radio, television, electronics, and computers, but few of these things could have been foreseen when electricity was invented.

Now in each of these examples, you see a certain progression that has five stages. I call these stages declarations, prototypes, tools, industries, and practices. Each of these discourses begins by someone making a declaration. Someone says here's a new invention, then tells other people how this new invention will be useful to them. Stage 2 involves drawings and then a prototype. If the prototypes convince people that this is worthwhile, we see more advanced prototypes and basic tools. And if the tools are found to be useful, we eventually see industries springing up to manufacture the tools in large quantities and to use them in new ways. Finally with the widespread availability of the tools, you see people change the way they live.

Boundaries between these five stages are not clearly identifiable; it is more accurate to describe the process as a drift that starts the moment someone announces the new idea. The process drifts along and eventually passes through these stages and winds up making a big impact on human practices. Another thing to note is that the drift, is constantly perturbed by surprises, so that it's really impossible at the beginning to predict where the idea is going to go. You can't predict what all these people interacting with all those tools are going to do; you literally have to wait until you get there.

The Arpanet illustrates this paradigm; the stages of the drift have lasted about 5 years. Generally from the three examples, you can see that the drift from declarations to practices takes a long time—anywhere from 20 to 50 years. In the microcosm of the Arpanet within the computer science research community, it happened a little faster than that. We see in approximately 1965 the first declarations with Bob Taylor and other people saying, "This is something we're going to do." Five years later in approximately 1970, we have the first prototypes. The first IMPs are now in operation, and people are beginning to see what this little network looks like and what it can do. In approximately 1975 we begin to see the emergence of tools that are based on the network. These are things like the electronic mail as a subsystem, remote login capabilities, and file-transferring capabilities. Around 1980 we see the emergence of little industries—I called these community networks before. And then finally around 1985, we actually see the phenomenon now affects how a lot of people behave, conduct business, and operate even inside the research community.

Along the way there were numerous surprises; one of them I already mentioned: electronic mail. It was not part of the original proposals, and yet it took over as the major source of traffic. Another surprise was the concern for connectivity. Take a network today and slice a link in it and people start going crazy. If your network gateway goes down, whoever is operating it gets thousands of phone calls from the users. A few years ago Usenet was bootlegging links over Arpanet. At that point in time the government didn't sanction such use of ARPAnet, and so every time ARPA found out there was Usenet traffic flowing over a piece of the Arpanet, ARPA chopped the link. And so UUCP would pick up and move someplace else. But perhaps the most dramatic illustration of the concern for connectivity occurred just about a year ago with the Internet worm incident that scared everybody half out of their minds. Fortunately the worm didn't do any harm, but it sure did cause a lot of people to shut down their networks, and that was a major disruption and caused a lot of complaints.

A third surprise was cheap high-speed workstations and personal computers. Many people have powerful computers connected to networks. Most people outside of computer science don't draw a distinction as we do between a computer and a network. They see the computer and the network as being pretty much the same thing. It's important to keep that in mind. Another surprise has been electronic publishing. This is almost an industry itself. It's grown up around networks, the software industry, and some new kinds of graphics.

And perhaps the biggest surprise of all is facsimile transmission. We've seen this just explode in the last few years when the price of the individual units decreased to a few hundred dollars. All of a sudden businesses started buying those things, and now we talk about FAX in the car, FAX on your personal computer. But inside the context of increasing globalization, increasing global markets, FAX makes sense—it facilitates international cooperation. It's possible to do business with somebody without telephone tag: Just send them a piece of paper over the FAX, and later there's your message response to you, so you can actually communicate back and forth effectively using the telephone network. The FAX has also helped people transcend the language barrier because many people can deal with something in another language in the written form, but not the spoken form. Also of course FAX extends the familiar practices of handling and sharing pieces of paper: It's very real to send a piece of paper over the telephone.

Those are my five examples of surprises resulting from the development of computer science: electronic mail, connectivity, ubiquitous personal computers, electronic publishing, and FAX. All have significantly altered the direction of the drift of electronic networking. You can be sure that there will be other surprises that we can't anticipate today.

For those of you interested in design in the context of future networking, let me say a few things. As the network grows, different organizations are coming together and doing business in the network in a routine, everyday fashion. These organizations bring with them discourses from their own communities, so it is apparent that discourses from various communities are starting to mix together on the network. As an example US businessmen have to understand Japanese, French, and Italian cultures. Understanding cultures without passing judgment on them enables the United States to do business better with its foreign counterparts. There are more subtle examples from scientific technology, business, higher education, and government. These four communities have different ways of thinking, but they are now coming into close connect with each other through networking.

Certainly the scientific technology discourse is very familiar to us. Scientific researchers say that by the year 2000 we'll have super computers that produce sustained computational rates of ten teraflops or higher. By the mid-1990s, there will already be the beginnings of a gigabit band-width network, and by the year 2000, it will be widespread. We'll see lots and lots of personal computers in reduced sizes, with more portability, smart cards, and many other phenomena based on personal computing. We'll see new graphics; we'll see a greater use of television and video coupled with our workstations and of course FAX. Speech input and output will be standard. People in research programs are working to produce these things, and there's a consensus that a lot of them will appear on the scene by 1995—2000 at the latest.

The scientific technology discourse also has a darker side. As scientists, we tend to view the world the way we've been brought up historically without ever thinking about it—as a collection of resources to be acquired, optimized, and sometimes discarded when no longer needed. So we view people as resources and talk about enhancing people and optimizing people; we speak as though people were objects. We tend to extend our discourse from engineering and science to problems of the human condition. Using homelessness, hunger, and other phenomena as an example, as scientists we tend to try to bring a scientific point of view to these things. We analyze, produce numbers, decision tables, and invent procedural solutions from these problems. If someone says, "Well, maybe some of these problems are insoluble; maybe the human condition is the way the human condition is, and we just have to accept that and live within it," we don't accept that. We say, "The problem is currently intractable, but it ultimately admits of a solution". That's the darker side of our discourse. We're not open to the possibility in our normal everyday way of talking with each other that there are problems of the human condition that can't be solved by science. We just label those problems as intractable, and we believe that one day we'll have enough knowledge and resources to solve them.

Now the business discourse is one at which we can look more dispassionately as scientists. I know that Tom Ho [Director of Computer Technology Department at Purdue] is intimately involved in that, and sometimes his talk sounds strange. But you can say, "Isn't it interesting that Tom lives in a different discourse and sees the world in a different way from us?" and wonder what kind of opportunities there would be if we could work together. Business discourse is concerned with such things as attitudes and practices in the workplace, global markets, and personalized products. Business success is now viewed as intimately tied to the mastery of workstations and networks. There is also a lot of change going on in business as businesses try to figure out how to manage in an increasingly chaotic world. There is a lot of concern with financial performance, market shares, and quality of products and service.

The government discourse of course depends on which political party is in power. Right now the government talks a lot about international markets, international competition, proving the US position in the world, maintaining a national research lead, and developing better national manufacturing capability. We also hear about the desire to be a world leader in all areas. Also, at least in my listening of the government, I hear a suspicion of multinational ventures, especially with Japan. Well that never gets very far because of the suspicion. Government talks favorably about international cooperation as an abstract entity, but in specific cases, the suspicion comes up.

If you listen to the way we talk to each other in the higher education discourse, you reach the following conclusions. First, we think knowledge encompasses information with structure. Second, instruction is the transmission of some of that knowledge to students. And third, research is the discovery of new facts about the world, discovery of information that already exists but hasn't been seen before. Inside that interpretation of knowledge and education, we've institutionalized a system of rewards that places a very high value on an individual's contribution. We sometimes call that contribution academic freedom. But in our research universities, we have a strong emphasis on research in preference to teaching. Our stated policy says research and teaching are both important, but ask any assistant professors what kind of advice they're getting to get through the tenure committees, and you'll find out that teaching counts against you only if you do it badly; but it never counts in your favor if you do it well. And yet the department's policy, the charter of the department, always says teaching is very important.

This system is always concerned with identifying the unique individual contribution of every person. Just listen to the tenure committees. In a biology paper with ten authors, each author is considered to have contributed one-tenth of the result. This emphasis on the individual leads to a distrust of students collaborating on homework assignments, yet in real-world organizations, people collaborate all the time. Our desire for individual autonomy in the way we teach teaches students to try to be autonomous and alone. Then when students get into organizations, they can't function effectively in teams.

These are all illustrations of the discourse that we're in, and as you can see, I think, there's a little bit of a dark side to that, too; there's a dehumanizing side to it. We forget that we're dealing with human beings. We think that we're dealing with knowledge and the transmission of knowledge from one brain to another.

As these discourses mix in networking, various types of mischief are possible. Let me just give you a couple of examples. One mischief I see coming up very rapidly has to do with FAX and electronic mail. Businesses are now talking about the ability to have electronic mail, but a lot of them aren't familiar with personal computer electronic mail systems. They think of electronic mail as an extension of FAX. They talk about devices to attach your computer to your telephone, using an address protocol like, "Mail, this message to: somebody's name @ phone number." From the point of view of the business world, electronic mail looks like a technology built on FAX. That will in turn accelerate the push for universal phone numbers so that your calls and messages reach you anywhere. Now inside the networking community, we tend to think of FAX in another way: It's the next thing we're going to add to electronic mail. We use fancier terms like multimedia mail, but that's what we're talking about. I think the network designers need to start paying a lot more attention to the business community in this one because business practices based on use of telephones and sharing pieces of paper are much more widespread than business practices based on electronic mail. And as network designers we could easily be surprised by new products that do not take advantage of anything that we know about electronic mail. There's a very real possibility that everything we know about electronic mail is going to take 15 or 20 years to find its way into real products rather than 2–3 years.

Another trouble spot concerns vulnerabilities. As I listen to people talking, I hear a very deep concern for the integrity and privacy of information that we've put inside our computers. This concern heightens with recent incidents involving break-ins, worms, and viruses. Government and business have made some very strong statements recently about these concerns. In contrast statements from universities about these concerns have been much more muted in my assessment. It almost seems to the outsider that we in the universities have a certain lack of willingness to take measures to foster respect in our students for network security. I think there's a recipe for trouble brewing there unless we wake up a little bit, because our discourse is going to come into conflict with a much larger discourse, and higher education will be the loser.

I've given you examples of the development and invention of discourses around networking to show that discourses that never spoke to each other are now talking. Not only are Japanese, Americans, and Europeans talking over networks, but scientist, businesspeople, and government are talking; we have higher education and government talking. A lot of new conversations are going on inside the networks. Unless we begin to see that people in different discourses have different ways of interpreting the world, different priorities, and different values, we will not be as effective. That's my message; that's where we're going. We must not only be scientific designers but observers of the discourses in which people that we want to use our results live.

COMPUTER SCIENCE: PAST AND FUTURE

The Origins of Computing and Computer Science at Purdue University

Saul Rosen† and John R. Rice

1. THE EARLY YEARS: 1950–1961

In 1947 Dr. Carl F. Kossack joined the mathematics department at
Purdue University. He brought with him several research projects that
required extensive computation. He had friends at IBM who offered to
donate some IBM punch card equipment, and Kossack set up a statistical
laboratory in one of the temporary buildings at Purdue. By 1952 the activities of the statistical laboratory had grown considerably, and a decision
was made to install an IBM card-programmed calculator (CPC). The CPC
was not a stored program computer, but it was a general-purpose programmed computer, and the laboratory needed someone skilled in the art
of computing. Kossack was authorized to hire an assistant professor who
would teach part-time in the mathematics department and also be in
charge of the computational division of the statistical laboratory.

On a trip to MIT Kossack tried to recruit Alex Orden for this position. Orden was not interested in coming to Purdue, but he recommended
a recent mathematics Ph.D., Alan Perlis, who was working with Project
Whirlwind at MIT. Project Whirlwind was one of the major early computer projects and the source of many important developments in computer hardware and software. Perlis came to Purdue, and he was probably

† Deceased.

Saul Rosen • Purdue University   John R. Rice • Purdue University

Studies in Computer Science, edited by John R. Rice and Richard A. DeMillo. Plenum Press,
New York, 1994.

as good a person as could have been found anywhere to take charge of the new computing activity at Purdue.

Within a short time Perlis suggested that Purdue needed and should have a more powerful computer. Large computers with magnetic core memory then cost millions of dollars, but a number of companies were introducing medium-sized, medium-priced computers based on magnetic drum storage. A study of what might be available at a reasonable price convinced Perlis that the best computer available for Purdue would be a Datatron computer built by Consolidated Engineering Corporation of Pasadena. Perlis and Kossack went to President Hovde with their proposal that the university spend $135,000 to purchase such a computer. Hovde was very receptive to their proposal and brought in R. B. Stewart, who was then vice president and treasurer of Purdue and also head of the Purdue Research Foundation. Kossack and Perlis were surprised at how quickly a decision was reached to buy the computer and how easily the financing was arranged through the Purdue Research Foundation. A Datatron computer was ordered in the fall of 1953 and delivered in October 1954. Some other universities had much larger computers, but those were usually being run at the university for a major sponsoring agency. The Datatron 204 was then the most powerful computer in its class. Perlis taught a course in numerical analysis where students learned how to program the new computer. Others learned to program in short courses offered by statistical laboratory personnel. At the laboratory Perlis began designing and implementing the Purdue compiler, one of the first algebraic language compilers. One of the graduate students involved was Thomas E. Cheatham, Jr. Cheatham has since had a distinguished career in the computer industry and as a professor of computer science at Harvard University. There were no courses for credit in programming or computer software development in those days. There certainly was nothing like a computer science department, but Purdue was on its way to a position of eminence in the computer field. Plans were being made to obtain a much more powerful computer than the Datatron, and a tentative arrangement had been made with the University of Illinois to obtain a copy of the Illiac II system that was going to be built at Illinois. Unfortunately for the development of the program at Purdue, Perlis decided to leave Purdue in 1956 to accept a position at the Carnegie Institute of Technology (now Carnegie-Mellon University). At Carnegie Perlis rapidly completed the compiler he had started at Purdue and installed it on an IBM 650. The compiler on the 650 called IT (internal translator) is remembered as one of the precursors of the international algorithmic language, Algol. Perlis became very well known as one of the authors of Algol and one of the leading figures in computer science, first at Carnegie and later at Yale University. In 1973 Purdue University conferred an honorary degree on Perlis for his achievements in the area of computer science. At Purdue the work on the compiler languished, but it was eventually finished and used at a number of Datatron installations. Silvia Orgel, Richard Kenyon, and JoAnn Chipps were the principal programmers involved. The Purdue compiler was an important early step in the development of programming languages.

Dr. Paul Brock who had been working for Electrodata Corporation and knew the Datatron computer well was hired as a replacement for Perlis. Brock did not stay very long. He was not happy with his position at Purdue and must have expected something quite different from the situation that he found. Within the year he asked for and was granted leave of absence. While on leave his position remained unfilled, since it was not clear for some time whether he would return. In 1958 the statistical laboratory was renamed the statistical and computing laboratory, and Duane Pyle, a full-time employee who was still a graduate student in mathematics, was made acting head of the computational division. Later in 1960 when Pyle obtained his Ph.D. in mathematics, Pyle became head of the computational division. Kenyon, who had worked in the computational division for a number of years, received his Ph.D. in electrical engineering about the same time and served as assistant head.

Kossack became head of the Department of Mathematics and Statistics in 1956, and Virgil Anderson became head of the Statistical and Computing Laboratory. Anderson himself was not interested in the computing area, and after Brock left, he relied almost totally on Pyle to handle that part of the activity. Pyle was then a relatively junior person, first a graduate student and then a young Ph.D. in a position in which he had to deal with department heads and deans and vice presidents. His efforts and those of Kenyon in maintaining computing services at Purdue may reasonably be described as heroic, but Pyle and Kenyon were not then in a position to provide the kind of leadership that was needed at Purdue in the area of computing and computer science.

Appropriate leadership was lacking, and so a major initiative in computing came from an inappropriate source. Stewart, who was the chief financial officer of Purdue, was a friend of Dawes Bibby, the president of Remington Rand Corporation, whose Univac division was a major computer manufacturer. Stewart knew that Purdue needed to upgrade its computer equipment and that any adequate upgrade would be very expensive. He and his contacts at Univac developed a plan that would upgrade computing at Purdue at little or no cost to the university. Univac would set up a training school for its technical personnel on the Purdue campus. Purdue would provide space and other services (for example, meals), which would be paid for by the training facility, and Univac would install a Solid State (SS) 80 computer at Purdue in the summer of 1960. At least one full shift of time on the SS 80 computer would be available for Purdue use at no cost to Purdue.

In a letter to Executive Dean D. R. Mallet, dated November 18, 1959, the head of training at Univac stated, "You will be assured of having the most advanced equipment at all times because such equipment would be vital to the successful operation of the . . . training center." He points out that as new equipment would be developed by Univac that equipment would be installed at Purdue and Purdue would have the use of it free for one shift. In addition the older equipment that was replaced would be offered to Purdue at a "nominal fee."

On October 9, 1959, President Hovde set up an ad hoc committee on computing. John W. Hicks, assistant to the president, was chairman. It was a high-level committee, which included the head of the agricultural experiment station and the heads of several engineering departments. It included Virgil Anderson and after its first meeting, also Pyle. It included the business manager, Lytle Freehafer, and department heads in the area of business computing, the dean of the graduate school and heads or other representatives from mathematics, agricultural economics, and psychology. The committee's charter was to study and make recommendations concerning the computer needs of the university in academic and research areas and also in student scheduling and business office operations. The first meeting was on October 19, and the committee met frequently and was very active.

In an interview in the fall of 1989, Dr. Hicks stated that President Hovde formed the ad hoc computer committee in the fall of 1959 because of the preliminary negotiations that were then going on between Stewart and Univac and because an agreement of the type suggested by Univac required technical as well as administrative approval. The minutes of the first few meetings and recollections of Pyle suggest that members of the committee were not aware of the projected deal with Univac until the letter from Univac to Dean Mallet was received. The committee then considered that letter, and along with a memo on December 9, 1959 calling for a fourth meeting of the committee, Dr. Hicks included his suggestions for a set of tentative recommendations by the committee. One of these is the recommendation that "the proposal put forth by Remington Rand (that is, Univac) should be accepted."

The Univac proposal was indeed accepted, and a Univac SS 80 system, along with a large complement of Remington Rand 90-column punch card equipment was installed in the Engineering Administration building. On the surface it seemed to be a good deal for Purdue, but it was not so. The SS 80 was more powerful than the 4-year-old Datatron system, but it was still the same class of equipment and did not represent a new generation of computers. It was not the right kind of equipment for a major university to install in 1960.

A number of documents produced in connection with the activities of the ad hoc committee on computing indicate that committee members were aware of the increasing importance that computing and computer science would have for the university in the 1960s. The documents quoted here were provided to the authors by Pyle.

Dr. Harold DeGroff, head of aeronautical engineering volunteered to write concerning university needs in the computing area from the point of view of engineering. In a document dated November 3, 1959 addressed to Dean of Engineering George Hawkins, DeGroff stated that "the staff problem in the computing laboratory is deemed to be a critical item." He stated that as a minimum requirement, the statistical laboratory should employ a full professor with a background in the general field of numerical analysis, "at least two associate professors, three assistant professors, eight to ten instructors and graduate assistants and five to ten coders. . . . The central idea here, of course, is to establish a computer research center with an emphasis on graduate work in this field."

It is clear that what is being suggested here is a graduate Department of Computer Science. Faculty costs were estimated at about $100,000 annually. (Faculty salaries were lower then.)

After the committee had met a number of times during 1960, Stanley Reiter, a professor of industrial management who had a strong interest in computing, offered to write a report for the committee for presentation to the university administration. A meeting was held on February 16, 1961 "to discuss professor Reiter's proposal on the reorganization of the computing laboratory." This quotation is from a memo by John Hicks announcing the meeting to the committee members. Due to suggestions from committee members at that meeting and subsequent to it, some minor modifications were made to the Reiter document. It was forwarded to President Hovde by Hicks on March 28, 1961 with the title "Proposal of ad hoc Committee on Computers to President Hovde." Pyle states that even though the report was written by Reiter, it was based on discussions by the committee and it did indeed represent the views of the committee.

The report recommends establishing a Computer Sciences Center that would be responsible for research computing services and computer education. Reference is made to the need for a strong faculty group that would do research and establish a graduate curriculum in computer science. There would be "A. a strong professional group in numerical analysis and applied mathematics; B. a similar group in mathematical logic and advanced computer programming; C. adequate access to large-scale modern computing equipment; D. a graduate program in computer science." The report also recommends taking steps immediately to find a director for a computer science center reorganized along the lines just set forth. According to the report, the Computer Science Center should be a separate administrative unit with a separate budget. Other universities have such a center report directly to the president, vice president, or a committee of deans, and that type of organization would be appropriate for Purdue.

In his cover letter to President Hovde that accompanied the report of the ad hoc committee on computing, Hicks informed him of the formation of a "hardware" subcommittee that was later called the ad hoc Computing Center Facilities Committee. Thomas F. Jones, head of the School of Electrical Engineering, was chairman of the facilities committee. Its charter was to study and make recommendations concerning computer space and equipment needs of the university.

2. COMPUTING AND MATHEMATICAL SCIENCES: 1960–1962

The 5 or more years prior to 1961 was a period of serious conflict between the mathematics department and William L. Ayres, dean of the School of Science, Education, and Humanities (SEH) in which the mathematics department was located. Kossack was head of the mathematics department from 1956–1959. Kossack states that during that period, he drew up plans and submitted proposals for President Hovde for the establishment of a School or Division of Mathematical Sciences that would be separate from, and independent of, the school of SEH. He changed the name of the mathematics department to the Department of Mathematics and Statistics and states that he administered the department as a number of subdepartments. Computer science was not then sufficiently well developed to qualify as one of the subdepartments. However Kossack was very much interested in the future development of computing instruction at Purdue. In a memo dated March 9, 1959 written by Kossack to President Hovde and a number of department heads and senior faculty at the university, he invited them to a meeting on March 24 to discuss the development of "a long range and comprehensive plan . . . looking toward the introduction of computing science into the several curricula of the university." No record remains of the meeting if it did indeed take place on that date. Kossack left Purdue at the end of that semester, a major reason for his departure was the fact that President Hovde had promised to remove mathematics from the school headed by Dean Ayres and had not done so. Kossack's memo of March 9, 1959 was addressed to many of the people whom Hovde invited to join the ad hoc committee on computing the following October 9. Kossack's memo may have had some effect on Hovde's decision to form such a committee. All of Kossack's statements quoted here are from a telephone interview in the fall of 1989.

Serious dissension between Dean Ayres and the mathematics department continued through 1960 and led to a crisis in early 1961. President Hovde then finally took the drastic steps that were needed to resolve the situation. The mathematics department budget was dramatically increased and the department was removed from the School of SEH and placed in the Schools of Engineering. The major components of the Schools of Engineering, for example, electrical engineering, mechanical engineering, and so forth, were called schools, not departments; however Hovde would not accept a School of Mathematics even though calling mathematics a department seemed inappropriate. A Division of Mathematical Sciences was apparently satisfactory to everyone.

From the point of view of many of the pure mathematicians at Purdue, the Division of Mathematical Sciences was simply the old Department of Mathematics and Statistics with a new name. From the beginning some of the others in the department thought that the division would provide an organizational structure within which such subspecialties as statistics, applied mathematics, and computer science might be able to achieve autonomy and growth.

A document entitled "Proposed Organization of the Division of Mathematical Sciences" dated March 31, 1961 by Virgil L. Anderson, director of the Statistical and Computing Laboratory, suggests organizing the Division of Mathematical Sciences into four departments: mathematics, statistics, computer science, and mathematics education.

Anderson's document points out that there had been much discussion "concerning a separate school for computer science directly under the president," and he argues that establishing an autonomous Department of Computer Science in the Division of Mathematical Sciences would be better for the development of computer science. "There certainly would be strength gained from numerical analysts and other applied mathematicians if it is located in this division. . . ."

Anderson suggests that the computer science department would develop graduate and undergraduate courses and a complete curriculum for advanced degrees. The document points out that the possibility for research projects is almost unlimited, and it also suggests that the department would maintain a computing laboratory that would serve the whole university.

Even though he had been a member of the ad hoc committee on computing, Anderson did not consider the recommendation for a completely independent Computer Science Center to be practical. He felt that his memo described the type of organization that would be acceptable to the very conservative Purdue administration. These thoughts were expressed by Anderson in a conversation with Saul Rosen on September 15, 1989. Anderson did not remember·whether other committee members felt as he did.

Paul Chenea was made temporary head of the new Division of Mathematical Sciences in the spring of 1961. Chenea had served Hawkins in a number of roles in the Schools of Engineering and had established a reputation as an administrator and a troubleshooter, so much so that in the summer of 1961, President Hovde appointed Chenea to the newly established position of academic vice president. Dean Hawkins then served temporarily as the head of the Division of Mathematical Sciences.

The Statistical and Computing Laboratory was moved into the Schools of Engineering along with the Department of Mathematics and Statistics. Hawkins separated the computing laboratory from the statistical laboratory, and the former was renamed the Computer Sciences Center in 1961. That was the name that had been used in the recommendation from the ad hoc committee on computing to President Hovde. For the next 6 months or so, Pyle reported directly to Hawkins. Pyle remembers that Hawkins took great interest in computing and was disturbed by the lack of adequate computing facilities at Purdue, especially when compared with other big ten universities. Hawkins felt that something had to be done to improve the situation, and he supported efforts in this direction. Efforts were made to find a senior person in the computer field to be director of the Computer Sciences Center, and correspondence between Pyle and T. F. Jones mentions Louis Fein and Bernard Galler as possibilities, but the search was not pressed very vigorously until Felix Haas took charge early in 1962.

The Univac SS 80 installed in December 1960 did not have the kind of software that would make it useful for instruction and research. The student-scheduling application was reprogrammed for the SS 80, but the Datatron remained the computer used for instruction along with a number of smaller computers in engineering departments. To provide for research users, Pyle and Kenyon negotiated an agreement with the Allison Division of General Motors in Indianapolis for some use of their IBM 7090 computer. In June 1961 Allison donated 2.5 hours of IBM 7090 time per month to Purdue. Those 2.5 hours soon proved insufficient for satisfying the needs of Fortran users at Purdue, so Hawkins provided funds to purchase additional time. By the end of 1961 usage had increased to 5 hours per month, and Pyle wrote a memo to Dean Hawkins (dated December 27, 1961) recommending the acquisition of an IBM 1401 system. The IBM 1401 would permit input tapes to be prepared and output tapes to be printed locally for jobs to be run on the IBM 7090 at Allison. In that same memo Pyle recommended that Purdue acquire an IBM 7044 system to satisfy its increasing need for large-scale scientific computing. The IBM 7044 was a newly announced IBM computer quite similar to the IBM 7090 but at a lower price and not quite so powerful as the IBM 7090. Both of these recommendations were approved by Dean Hawkins and by President Hovde. An IBM 1401 was ordered almost immediately, and it was installed in March of 1962. A 7044 system was ordered on January 31, 1962 "for delivery in May 1963 at a net lease cost to Purdue of $13,744 per month." The list price of the system was $34,435 per month. The very much lower price to Purdue reflected the generous 60% educational discount that IBM was then offering. Since the 7044 would not be available until May 1963, IBM agreed to install an interim IBM 7072 system on or about September 1, 1962. That never happened, and it now seems to have been a strange idea, since the IBM 7072 was very different from the IBM 7044, so it would have been very difficult to install and use effectively for such a short time. The order for the IBM 7044 contained a clause that gave Purdue the right to cancel up to December 31, 1962.

During the spring and summer of 1961, there was an active search for a permanent head of the Division of Mathematical Sciences. There were negotiations with Dr. F. Joachim Weyl, director of the Naval Analysis Group in the Office of Naval Research. When Weyl withdrew his name from consideration, the position was offered to Felix Haas, who was head of the mathematics department at Wayne State University. Haas accepted the position that summer with the understanding that he would start at Purdue in January 1962.

During the fall semester of 1961, Haas remained at Wayne State but made frequent trips to Purdue. He describes the situation relative to the recently formed division as chaotic. Although his primary responsibility was going to be rebuilding and expanding the mathematics department at Purdue, he had become aware of the importance of computing while at

Wayne State and even before that when he was at MIT. According to Haas the fact that computing and computer science were to be among his responsibilities at Purdue made the position as head of the division more attractive to him.

Dean Hawkins officially turned control of the Computer Sciences Center over to Haas on February 1, 1962. Pyle continued to act as director of the center until the arrival of Sam Conte on July 1, 1962. By the beginning of 1962, many universities, including most of the big ten, had requested, and some had already received, grants from the National Science Foundation (NSF) under a program initiated in 1956 to support institutional computer facilities at universities. That NSF program, which lasted through 1970, was a major factor in expanding the use of computers in research and education.

The most important effort of the Computer Sciences Center under Haas and Pyle in the spring of 1962 was to produce an NSF proposal that requested $920,000 to help finance the acquisition of the IBM 7044 and to support related programs in computer service, research, and instruction.

The ad hoc committee report previously discussed is included as an appendix of the proposal. It is interesting to note that the NSF proposal still refers to the Computer Sciences Center as both a service organization and a center for research and instruction in computer science. Haas's signature appears on the proposal, but there seems to be no doubt that by the May 1962 date on the proposal, Haas was committed to separating the service operation from the instruction and research function.

It is not clear to what extent the report of the ad hoc committee on computing or Anderson's memo influenced Haas's thinking about the future status of computing and computer science at Purdue. Haas recalls a meeting with Hawkins and Hovde, probably before he officially started at Purdue, in which they agreed that the Division of Mathematical Sciences would be internally divided into three academic departments, mathematics, statistics, and computer science and a Computer Sciences Center to provide computing services to the whole university. It was considered only natural then that the head of the Department of Computer Sciences would also be the director of the Computer Sciences Center.

3. THE COMPUTER SCIENCES CENTER AND DEPARTMENT OF COMPUTER SCIENCES: 1962–1964

Having decided that there was going to be a computer sciences department, Haas moved rapidly to recruit a department head. Bill Miller, who was then head of the Division of Applied Mathematics at Argonne, was approached, but when he removed himself from consideration, the position was offered to Conte. Conte had been an associate professor in the mathematics department at Wayne State University up to 1956, before Haas came to Wayne State. Since 1956 Conte had worked for 5 years at Space Technology Laboratories and then at Aerospace Corporation in California, where he was manager of the Department of Programming and Analysis in the Computing Laboratory. At a meeting of the University Executive Council on March 12, 1962, Haas announced that "Samuel Conte, a distinguished scientist currently with Aerospace Corporation, will join the Purdue staff on July 1 to become director of the Computer Sciences Center." It is interesting to note that July 1, 1962 was also the date on which the old Datatron computer, installed in October 1954, was finally turned off and retired from service.

On October 24, 1962, President Hovde asked for and received approval from the board of trustees to change "the internal administrative organization of the Division of Mathematical Sciences . . . effective October 1, 1962." The Department of Computer Sciences and the Computer Sciences Center were listed as components of the division, along with the Departments of Mathematics and Statistics, and a statistical laboratory. Professor Conte was listed as chairman of the Department of Computer Sciences and director of the Computer Sciences Center. The October 24 entry on the board of trustees minutes makes it very clear that a Department of Computer Sciences was officially established in the fall of 1962 and provides a firm basis for the claim that the first computer science department at a U.S. university was established at Purdue.

When Conte arrived at Purdue in the summer of 1962, he faced two major challenges. One was to raise computing services at Purdue to an appropriate level for a major research university. The other was to organize a new computer sciences department, for which no model then existed anywhere.

At the time that Conte was hired, a commitment existed for installing a UNIVAC 1107 computer at Purdue. Pyle was very unhappy with that commitment and recommended installing an IBM 7044 computer instead, and as already mentioned, a 7044 system had been ordered from IBM. The agreement with UNIVAC had been initiated by Stewart, who pushed very vigorously for consummation of that agreement. For a while there existed plans to install both the UNIVAC 1107 and the IBM 7044, which made no sense at all, since the Computer Sciences Center did not have adequate personnel to support even one of these large-scale computers, let alone two of them. Presumably the idea was to phase out the IBM

7044 if and when the UNIVAC 1107 proved to be capable of handling the scientific computing load at Purdue.

The major argument in favor of the UNIVAC equipment was that it would be free to the university. Then it turned out that it was not going to be free after all but would cost the university about $20,000 a month. Support for the UNIVAC 1107 eroded, and the decision was made to install only the IBM 7044—the computer for which support had been subsequently requested in the proposal to the NSF.

Conte had had considerable experience with the IBM 7090, and he felt more comfortable with it than with the IBM 7044. He felt that the IBM 7090 was worth the additional cost and increased computer use at Purdue would soon warrant installing the more powerful system. There was a high-energy physics research group at the university under the late Professor George Tautfest that needed large amounts of computation and had some research money to support such computation. An agreement was reached by Tautfest and Conte whereby the Computer Sciences Center would provide a shift of computer time for use by high-energy physicists, and the more powerful IBM 7090 computer was ordered in place of the IBM 7044.

The proposal to the NSF was modified accordingly, and the NSF gave the Computer Sciences Center $500,000 over the 3-year period starting January 16, 1964. With the aid of this grant from the NSF an IBM 7090 was installed at Purdue in the spring of 1963. Prior to installing the IBM 7090, an arrangement had been made with the University of Chicago to use significant amounts of time on its IBM 7090. A driver trained to operate the IBM 7090 was hired to take to Chicago every evening a load of magnetic tapes produced on the IBM 1401 that represented programs and data for the IBM 7090. The driver ran these programs on the IBM 7090 during the night shift for as many hours as required, then collected the output tapes, and took them back to Purdue where they were listed on the IBM 1401. This was a very effective and economical system even though the turnaround time left something to be desired.

The only change made when the IBM 7090 was installed in the Engineering Administration building at Purdue was to do the IBM 7090 processing locally. During the main day shift, the computer was turned over to the high-energy physics group, which used it as a large personal workstation. The Computer Sciences Center staff was horrified by the inefficient and wasteful use of precious computer time by the high-energy physicists, and Tautfest was horrified because the center staff used precious computer time to run trivial student problems while serious research workers were kept waiting. Within a year or so, the high-energy physics group obtained its own computer and moved from the Computer Sciences Center. Actually the computer the group obtained was the IBM 7044 originally ordered for the Computer Sciences Center and made available at the originally negotiated price. Although both the IBM 7090 and 7044 were obtained at the 60% discount that IBM then offered for university installations, those terms were no longer available by the time the physics computer was ordered.

After Conte the first faculty member hired for the new computer sciences department was Rosen. Conte had known Rosen at Wayne State University before they both left that university in 1956. Rosen then worked in the software area for Burroughs and Philco Corporation and then as an independent consultant. He contacted Conte about possible consulting work on the West Coast, and Conte suggested that Rosen join the new computer sciences department that Conte was forming at Purdue. Another member of the computer sciences department in the fall of 1962 was Robert Korfhage, a young Ph.D. from the Information Sciences program at the University of Michigan; Pyle and Richard Kenyon were the other original members of the computer sciences department. They devoted a major part of their time to the Computer Sciences Center; half of Rosen's salary was also paid by the Computer Sciences Center, and he was always significantly involved in its activities. A major joint activity of the department and the center in those early years was the development of the Purdue University Fast Fortran Translator (PUFFT), a system especially designed for fast and efficient compilation and execution of short programs, typically student assignments, on the IBM 7094. The PUFFT made it possible to run at first hundreds and ultimately thousands of student Fortran jobs each day.

The computer sciences department started out with a number of graduate students, several of whom who had come to Purdue from Aerospace Corporation along with Conte. From the beginning the department recognized three major areas—numerical analysis, systems, and theory. Conte taught the first course in numerical analysis; Rosen taught the first course in computing and programming systems; and Korfhage taught the first course in algorithms and automata. Within the next 2 years, several senior faculty members were added: Richard Buchi in automata theory, Walter Gautschi and then John Rice in numerical analysis. The skeleton of a master's degree program and a Ph.D. program were in place.

The computer sciences department struggled to establish its identity during those first few years. The Division of Mathematical Sciences controlled requirements for the Ph.D. degree, and mathematicians in the division felt that no one should have a Ph.D. from the division without having shown mastery of important parts of the mathematics curriculum. The qualifying examination for the mathematics Ph.D. was designed to eliminate students who did not show promise as researchers in mathematics, and computer science Ph.D. candidates were expected to pass some of these same qualifying exams. One might argue for or against the merits of such policies, but the net result was that a number of promising students, especially in the systems area, were discouraged from trying to obtain the Ph.D. degree in computer science. It took a number of years before the computer sciences department was able to control its own requirements for advanced degrees.

Our thanks to Professor Pyle of the computer science department at the University of Houston who was important in the development of computing and computer science at Purdue. Many documents concerning the history of computing at Purdue before the computer science department was established in 1962 were provided by Professor Pyle who had saved them in his personal files. We believe that in most cases these are the only surviving copies of the documents. Some of the material presented in this chapter is based on personal interviews with participants, including Duane Pyle, Myer Jerison, Felix Haas, Vergil Anderson, John Hicks, Betty Bain, and others. Telephone interviews, especially those with Carl Kossack and Alan Perlis, provided another important source of information.

2

History of the Computer Sciences Department at Purdue University

John R. Rice and Saul Rosen†

1. INTRODUCTION

The previous chapter[1] describes how the first Department of Computer Sciences in the United States was established at Purdue University in October 1962. This chapter describes how the department found its identity and matured into one of the strong departments at Purdue and in the nation. There are three natural phases to this development. In the 1960s the effort was to define courses, degree programs, and indirectly the field itself. The 1970s saw the department's maturation and growth into a typical university department. The 1980s started with a series of crises, some nationwide and some internal to Purdue, which eventually gave the department a considerably different character than it had in the 1970s. Chapter 2 is organized around these three periods.

Table 1 presents a chronology of the principal events and milestones for 1962–1989.

2. THE 1960s: ESTABLISHING THE CURRICULUM

The first task of Samuel Conte as new department head was to hire some faculty and define a graduate program. The course offerings planned

† Deceased.

John R. Rice • Purdue University   Saul Rosen • Purdue University

Studies in Computer Science, edited by John R. Rice and Richard A. DeMillo. Plenum Press, New York, 1994.

Table 2.1.
Milestones and Principal Events in the History of the Computer Sciences
Department at Purdue University, 1962–1989

1962	Department formation, M.S. and Ph.D. programs started
1964	First M.S. degrees awarded (3)
1966	First Ph.D. degrees awarded (2)
1967	Move to Math Sciences building
1968	Undergraduate program started
	First B.S. degrees awarded
	One-hundreth M.S. degrees awarded
	Regular facutly size reaches 10
	Department and Computing Center completely separated
1970	Two-hundredth M.S. degree awarded
1972	Regular faculty size reaches 20
1973	Two-hundred B.S. degree awarded
1977	Five-hundredth M.S. degree awarded
1978	Five-hundredth B.S. degree awarded
	Department acquires first computer facility (VAX 11/780)
1979	Conte retires as head; Denning appointed
1981	Crisis: Enrollment explosion arrives
1982	One-hundred Ph.D. degree awarded
1983	Denning leaves; Rice appointed head
	Crisis: Large loss of key faculty
1984	Crisis: Major growth in facilities and laboratories
	Crisis: No space for faculty, students, or staff
1985	Move to new building
1986	Regular faculty size reaches 30
1987	One-thousandth M.S. degree awarded
1989	Two-thousandth B.S. degree awarded

were not large—enough graduate courses for the M.S. and Ph.D. degrees and an undergraduate service course in programming. In the very first year, there were seven teaching faculty, including Conte, a numerical analyst. Four were already at Purdue: Richard Kenyon, an electrical engineering Ph.D. and assistant professor; L. Duane Pyle, a mathematics Ph.D. and assistant professor; Don Novotny, an industrial engineering Ph.D. candidate and full-time instructor; and Rosemary Stemmler, a full-time instructor. Two new faculty were hired, Robert Korphage in theory and Saul Rosen in programming systems. Although not all of the faculty taught full time, they could offer over 20 courses a year, which was ample to support the planned program.

In 1963 there were three new faculty members: Richard Buchi in theory, Walter Gautschi in numerical analysis, and John Steele in programming systems; Steele worked primarily in the Computer Sciences Center and rarely taught over the years. The following year John Rice was hired in numerical analysis, and this completed the initial phase of hiring.

No new faculty was hired in 1965, and only one, Carl de Boor in numerical analysis, was hired in 1966. De Boor was the first of a number of young Ph.D.s hired who became influential members of the department. Robert Lynch in numerical analysis and Paul Young in theory were hired in 1967; Jay Nunamaker in business applications was hired in 1968; and Victor Schneider and Vincent Shen, both in systems, were hired in 1969. Also hired during this period was Maurice Halstead, a senior person in programming systems who later worked in what is now called software engineering.

The new Mathematical Sciences building was completed in 1967, and the department (along with statistics) moved there from the Engineering Administration building. The Computer Sciences Center occupied the two floors below ground. The department occupied the fourth floor, which was substantially larger than the previous space and also much nicer. In the beginning space was so ample that some graduate students were given faculty offices (with windows!). Fifteen years later even with space on other floors, people were jammed together.

In 1966 Saul Rosen went to SUNY Stony Brook for a year. He returned in 1967 and was soon part of a major management change. Conte had been both director of the Computer Sciences Center, a computing services organization, and head of the computer sciences department, both of which were growing rapidly. In 1968 Rosen was appointed director of the Computer Sciences Center, which was renamed the Purdue University Computing Center (PUCC) in January 1970. Very close ties were established between the computer center and the department while Conte was head of both; this friendly cooperation continued under Rosen's direction and still persists today.

As recounted in Rosen and Rice,[1] the Department of Computer Sciences was a part of the Division of Mathematical Sciences along with the Departments of Mathematics and Statistics. Felix Haas was head of the division and also head of the mathematics department. Initially the three departments were only partially independent within the division: They set degree requirements separately, but there was only one graduate committee and one Ph.D. qualifying exam system. The three departments had separate personnel committees, but not separate budgets. This arrange-

ment was appropriate in view of the small sizes of the computer sciences
and statistics departments, their recent status as departments, and the administrative skill of Haas. This arrangement was of course also a continual
source of friction, and the three departments gradually became truly independent during the next 5 or 6 years. The final step was the complete
separation of budgets in 1968.

2.1. Graduate Program

The M.S. degree was designed as a program to train computer scientists for industry. Students with B.S. degrees in other fields (of course there
were no B.S. graduates in computer sciences at that time) were given a
broad introduction to numerical methods, programming systems, and
theoretical computer science. Ten courses were required for the M.S. degree, with wide flexibility given in selecting them. The only requirement
was that one course must be taken from each of the three main areas.
Students usually took a few related courses from engineering, applied
mathematics, or statistics. This program attracted students immediately,
including some programmers who came from California with Conte. The
first three M.S. degrees were awarded in the spring of 1964. The number
of M.S. graduates per year rose rapidly, reaching 31 from 1965–1966, and
it has been in the 30–60 range (occasionally higher) ever since.

Defining the Ph.D. was not difficult in the areas of numerical analysis
and theory, since there were already well-established research subdisci-
plines in these areas. Furthermore the qualifying exam system was reasonably compatible with these two areas. The Ph.D. qualifying exams
within the Division of Mathematical Sciences were uniform and naturally
very mathematical in nature.

Defining the Ph.D. in programming systems was not so simple. Most
of the research was in industry, not academia; there were no standard
research journals and indeed many important ideas and results were published in ad hoc ways—or even not at all; and there were no textbooks
and very few research monographs. Defining course work and evaluating
theses were difficult, but at least there was an experienced faculty member,
Rosen, for these tasks. The qualifying exam was a particular challenge for
students in this area. The "standard body of knowledge" for this exam
was missing, yet the existing mathematics exams (even the one in applied
mathematics) were far removed from students' needs and interests. Stu-

dents were asked to become expert in these outside areas, which they viewed as both a very difficult task and a waste of time.

The first two Ph.D. graduates were in 1966: Karl Usow, a student of John Rice, and Kenneth Brown, a student of Conte. The following year there were five Ph.D. graduates. The first Ph.D.s in programming systems were not until 1969—Larry Axsom and Edouard Desautels, both students of Rosen. (Table 2.5 gives a complete list of Ph.D. students.) It is not always easy to decide whether some Ph.D. students in the early days were in mathematics or computer sciences for a number of reasons: All the senior computer sciences faculty also had appointments in mathematics; the qualifying exams were the same; and there was a single graduate committee. The Ph.D. requirements, unlike those for the M.S., were essentially the same for all departments, and Ph.D. degrees are not officially labeled by department. Thus there are four Ph.D.s in computer sciences whose advisers were not on the computer sciences faculty, and several computer sciences faculty (for example, Buchi, Gautschi, Lynch, Rice, and Young) had Ph.D. students not listed in Table 2.5.

2.2. Undergraduate Program

The undergraduate program evolved initially from very sparse courses offerings in programming to a computer sciences option in the mathematics department to a separate B.S. degree approved in 1967. Conte was an active member of the Association for Computing Machinery committee that studied and recommended a model B.S. degree program. The result, known as Curriculum '68, was very close to the degree program at Purdue, which was one of the test beds for developing Curriculum '68. B.S. degrees were awarded immediately because many students could and did transfer from the computer science option in mathematics and met the new degree requirements within a year.

The similarities between these B.S. degree curricula are illustrated in Table 2, which compares course requirements for (1) the B.S. degree in computer sciences, (2) the B.S. degree in mathematics within the computer science option, and (3) the model Curriculum '68. The principal difference between the computer sciences major and Curriculum '68 was the increased emphasis on theory and the fact that programming languages material was covered in several courses rather than a single course. The computer sciences option in mathematics simply had lower require-

Table 2.2.
Course Requirements for a B.S. Degree in Computer Sciences, in Mathematics
with a Computer Science Option, and the Curriculum '68 Model B.S. Program

Course	Computer sciences major	Computer sciences option in mathematics	Curriculum '68
Calculus	3	3	3
Advanced calculus	1	1	1
Linear algebra	1	1	1
Programming 1 and 2	2	2	2
Numerical methods	1	1	1
Theory	3	2	1
Computer systems	2	0	2
Programming languages	0	0	1
Electives—Computer Science	2	2	2
Statistics	1	0	0
Electives—mathematics/ computer science/statistics	0	0	2
Total courses	16	12	16

ments, consistent with the requirements of the other mathematics options.

Although a B.S. degree was offered starting in 1967, the department did not have a full range of appropriate undergraduate courses by then. The B.S. program relied heavily on graduate courses, and a typical B.S. degree included three to five courses at the dual graduate/undergraduate level; that is, some of the required B.S. courses were graduate courses or dual-level courses designed for graduate students and special undergraduates. This situation reflected two facts: First the faculty was still not large enough to offer a full range of courses for the B.S., M.S., and Ph.D. degrees and a substantial service program; second material appropriate for undergraduates had to be offered in graduate courses because entering graduate students rarely had a B.S. in computer science. This situation was well recognized by the department, and there was a steady migration of material from the graduate level downward into the undergraduate courses as soon as faculty levels and student backgrounds allowed it. It was not until well into the 1980s that the undergraduate computer science program included the variety of offerings that was common in the other sciences.

There were many lessons learned from the computer science curriculum in these formative years; perhaps the most important was that the rapid evolution of the field renders courses at all levels out-of-date in a few years. In the early days we hoped soon to be able to define courses computer sciences 101, computer sciences 102, and computer sciences 103 that would become semipermanent fixtures analogous to mathematics 101–103 or physics 101–103. That has not yet happened, and it does not seem likely in the near future. Some of the other lessons learned were

- It is unrealistic to teach programming to a mixed class of science, engineering, and business students because business students lack the background to compete.

- It is difficult to keep students, teaching assistants, and even some faculty focused on the principles of computer sciences instead of the mechanics.

- There is never enough money to provide the level of computing facilities that students deserve.

- Programming assignments create new possibilities for student cheating; as soon as one cheating technique is counteracted, another is invented.

3. THE 1970S: MATURATION

By the beginning of the 1970s, the department had completed its pioneering years: Degree programs were established; there was a faculty of 15 and dozens of computer sciences departments at other universities; and Purdue's department was fully independent. The 1970s were to be a decade of consolidation and maturation. But there were still serious challenges; perhaps the most difficult was hiring faculty. By 1970 there was a significant number of computer sciences Ph.D.s, but it did not come close to meeting the demand. Computer sciences departments were being rapidly established; the computing industry was expanding steadily; and several other industries (oil, aerospace, and banking) began to hire significant numbers of Ph.D.s. Throughout the 1970s almost every computer sciences department had unfilled positions for computer sciences Ph.D.s, as did many major industries. The increase in Ph.D.s was slow, almost zero in the latter part of the decade.

The regular faculty at Purdue increased from 15 from 1970–1971 to 22 from 1979–1980, the result of relentless recruiting. Young faculty that was hired and later became important in the department include

- Peter Denning, Michael Machtey, and Herbert Schwetman in 1972

- Douglas Comer, and Christoph Hoffmann in 1976

- Michael O'Donnell in 1977

- Buster Dunsmore in 1978

These gains were offset by losses of key faculty: Four faculty members went to other positions—Pyle, de Boor, Nunamaker, and Schneider; and Halstead and Michael Machtey died suddenly in 1979.

The faculty shortage was compounded by another trend that became widespread in the 1970s: the change from a mathematicslike discipline (using only paper and punched cards) to a sciencelike discipline with a significant experimental science component. Some computer sciences departments originated in engineering and had the experimental component from the beginning, but by the end of the 1970s, most departments, including Purdue's (which originated in mathematics), had started to establish a significant experimental component. As the discipline moved in this direction, it adopted some of the practices of the experimental sciences. In particular teaching loads had to be reduced to compensate for the increased effort needed to operate teaching laboratories and experimental research facilities. The fierce competition for faculty of course accelerated the reduction of teaching loads and the offer of equipment to attract faculty. Although the faculty in 1979 had the same teaching load as in 1970, this did not last for long.

A significant effect of the lack of faculty was the heavy reliance on graduate teaching assistants. Although the department recognized that it was educationally unsound, graduate students sometimes taught other graduate students in the 1960s, and graduate students commonly taught upper division courses in the 1970s. There seemed to be no alternative except not to offer the courses.

A second serious challenge for computer sciences departments everywhere in the 1970s was to establish their scientific respectability. Many science and engineering faculties knew about computing only through contact with Fortran programming, and they assumed that was all there was to computer sciences. Even though the Purdue Department of Computer Sciences was consistently rated in the top ten, it had to reaffirm its permanence and value continually to other parts of the university. While there is still a residual of these feelings even today, by the end of the 1970s, the majority of the university's administrators and faculty believed computer sciences was a serious scientific discipline that was here to stay.

The third serious challenge was the evolution of courses. In spite of repeated reorganizations of courses and the expansion of offerings, it seemed there was always some course that required complete restructuring. The department simply did not have enough faculty to keep all the courses up-to-date at all times, and this situation persists today.

The educational programs were fairly stable in size during the 1970s. From 1970–1979 the number of Ph.D.s awarded annually remained at six, and the number of M.S. degrees increased from 53 to 54. The number of B.S. degrees awarded annually grew from 33 to 92, but 71 had already been awarded from 1973–1974.

The quality of the degree programs improved significantly during this decade. At the graduate level the department required by the end of the decade all entering students to have the equivalent of a B.S. in computer sciences or make up the deficiency. At the undergraduate level the number of courses offered increased significantly, and better text books became available.

The decade ended with Conte stepping down as department head in 1979. In his 17 years as head, he had guided the department from its pioneering infancy to a strong department both nationally and within the university, which was a major achievement. The department also benefited greatly from the foresight and support of Haas, who became Dean of Science soon after the department was formed and later Provost. Already in the early 1960s Haas foresaw that computer sciences would become one of the major scientific disciplines, and he supported Conte's efforts to keep Purdue's department growing and to become one of the best. Conte's successor was Peter Denning, who led the department into the 1980s.

4. THE 1980S: DECADE OF CRISES

The growth and maturation of the 1970s held the seeds for the crises that hit in the first half of the 1980s. These crises stemmed from the numerous major needs and the lack of resources to meet them.

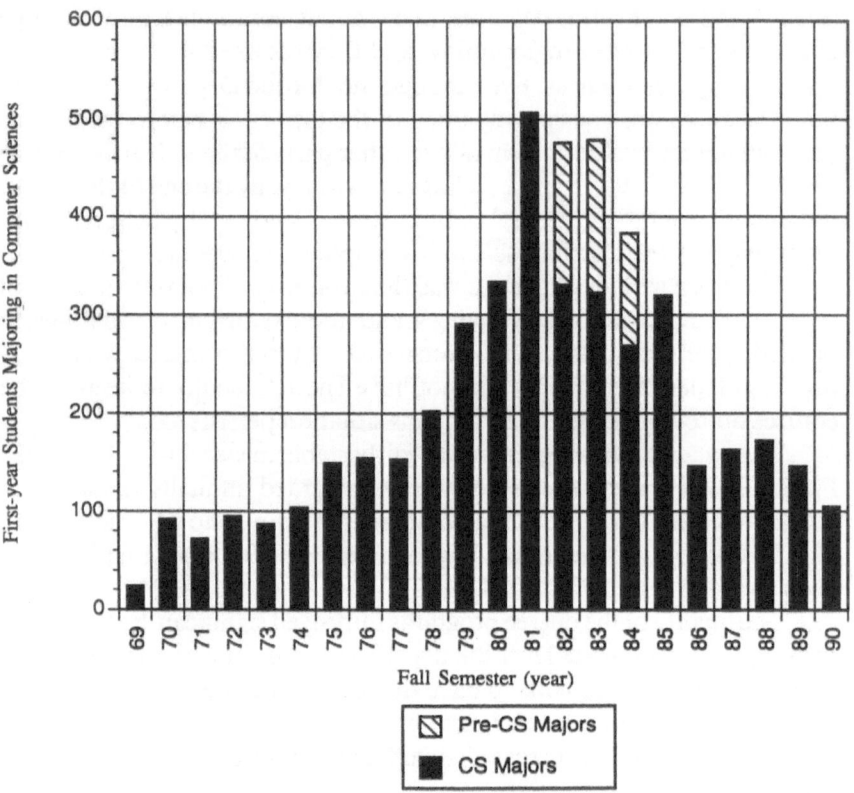

Figure 2.1. Entering freshmen who declared a computer sciences major from 1969–1989. For 1982–1984 the classification of precomputer sciences major is shown on top of the officially declared majors.

4.1. Crisis 1: Student Enrollment Explosion

The number of entering freshmen majoring in computer science during the 1970s did grow some: About 80–100 entered from 1970–1974. Enrollment then increased to 150 a year from 1975–1977. In 1978 and 1979 the number increased to 200, then 300, and the crisis was on us (see Figure 2.1). This growth was nationwide. For one year in the early 1980s, a survey showed that 9% of the high school graduates wanted to study computer science. If this percentage had continued, computer science would have had as many students as all of engineering! By the fall of 1981 there were over 500 freshmen starting out in computer science. Earlier groups of students were advancing through the curriculum, and the undergraduate courses overflowed, new sections were added and then they overflowed again.

Purdue's administration was very reluctant to limit the entering freshmen class in computer sciences, since there was strong pressure to increase the size of the student body. Finally in 1982 a mechanism was agreed on to limit the freshmen class in computer sciences: Higher SAT scores and class rank were required in computer sciences than in the rest of the School of Science. The number of freshmen majors dropped to about 350 in 1982 and stayed there until 1985, but even that number was beyond the capacity of the department.

Sometime after the limit mechanism was put into place, the faculty realized that the administration had quietly created a new category of students, the precomputer sciences classification. Essentially all the students who met the School of Science requirements, but not the computer sciences requirements, were in this classification. Thus there was no reduction in students in computer sciences courses even though the number of official majors decreased. Students in this new classification who made acceptable grades were officially admitted as computer sciences majors when they became upper division students. Such actions are the source of mistrust between faculties and administrations; in this case such an action helped precipitate the 1983 crisis.

The administration did offer to increase the number of positions in the department, but that was completely safe. The department already had unfilled positions and having more of them would not increase the number of faculty. The explosion was handled primarily by increasing class sizes. Examples of the extreme situation during that period were: (1) The senior level course in numerical analysis was taught in a single lecture section with about 150 students and a half-time teaching assistant grader, (2) the first-year graduate course in compilers had over 80 students and no grading assistant, (3) teaching assistants had 160–180 students in lower division courses.

There was a corresponding lack of computing facilities to support the courses. Many courses used VAX 11/780 time-sharing systems and examples of the poor service include: (1) Terminals reserved for "quick fixes" were limited to a 10-minute, use and response was so slow that you could not log on in 10 minutes. (2) Many terminals would automatically disconnect because they did not receive an echo of characters sent to the VAX within 15 seconds and assumed the computer was down rather than merely swamped. (3) Load averages on the VAXes were commonly up to 30, and 60 was sometimes reached. Load averages measure how busy computers are, and most users find the VAX satisfactory with a load average of one, frustratingly slow with a load average of four, and unusable with a load average of ten.)

4.2. Crisis 2: The Space Crunch

Computer sciences started the 1980s in the Mathematical Sciences building where it had been since 1967. The growth of the 1970s had gradually taken up available space in the building for all its occupants—mathematics, statistics, the computing center, School of Science administration, and computer sciences. When computer sciences started changing to an experimental, laboratory-oriented discipline in the 1980s, space was needed for departmental computing, teaching labs, and research labs. A few offices were converted into labs for research projects, but the department was severely constrained by the lack of space. The result was tighter and tighter packing, and most faculty simply could not engage in laboratory work. The following two examples illustrate the extent of the problem.

In 1983 a faculty member asked the department head for a secretary to help support his work. Heads usually reply that they don't have any money for that, but in this case the department head said, "I understand, let's do it. Tell me where you want the secretary to be and I'll hire one." This offer was safe because the head knew that there was no room in the department to put even one more desk. In 1984 the dean of science arranged to borrow space from the chemistry department while the new Computer Science building was being renovated. The plan was to move 20 teaching assistants into a miserable, temporarily abandoned chemistry lab complete with lab bench, sinks, gas, and so forth. The graduate students were so appalled that they created a packing scheme whereby five graduate students could be placed in a 150-square-foot office, each with his/her own desk, chair, and some bookcase space. These offices had been already overcrowded when four students occupied them.

4.3. Crisis 3: Establishing Departmental Computing Facilities

The department acquired its first general purpose computer, a VAX 11/780 in 1978. It was the first VAX to be running VAX UNIX outside

Table 2.3.
Growth of the Computing Facilities from 1979–1989[a]

	1979	1984	1989
Operating budget	$20,000	$150,000	$500,000
Facilities staff	0	3	9
Equipment value	$250,000	$2,000,000	$3,500,000

[a] The operating budget is supported by the university; the people are full-time, and equipment value indicates its current worth, not original cost.

the developer's sites (Berkeley and AT&T Bell Labs). The motivation behind this move was the need for computer scientists to have an interactive, time-shared computing environment. It was not practical for PUCC to provide this service on a widespread basis, and it was unwilling to do so for just one department. It was however inevitable that the department would set up its own facilities as its needs became too specialized and too diverse to be satisfied by a centralized service center. This move was part of the nationwide trend of computer science to become more experimental and laboratory oriented.

This crisis was very real, but it was handled much more smoothly than the others because of the administration's willingness to support this growth. The extent of the changes required is illustrated by Table 3, which gives the operations budget, facilities staff, and installed equipment. In a 10-year period a major new operation was established within the department. The operating budget shown is entirely from university funds; in recent years about 20% more has been received from research grants. A large proportion of the equipment was purchased through government research grants.

While this crisis was handled smoothly, it did have its trying moments. The department, like many others, did not initially realize the necessity of a professional staff to operate the facilities. The early staff (Douglas Comer and his students, then Herbert Schwetman) was regular faculty and students who took on this extra challenge. They did a superb job, but it was not their only job, and more than once the following occurred

- Professor X has a paper that must go out today, and it is being revised on the computer.

- The computer crashes.

- Professor X rushes to the office of Professor Y, who is in charge of the facilities, to demand that the computer be brought up at once.

- Professor Y replies that she has two classes to teach, has not finished preparing for them, and may be able to work on the problem late in the afternoon.

- All the students who might be able to bring up the system are in class, the library, or some place else.

- A heated discussion ensues between Professors X and Y about who is irresponsible, unreasonable, incompetent, and so forth.

These growing pains were on the whole minor, and the department did obtain excellent computing facilities, but such growth did contribute to the space crisis. Fortunately computers were becoming smaller, or the crisis would have been even worse. The professional staff required space that was in very short supply in the mid 1980s, and this group had reached a significant size by 1989, and it continued to grow.

In response to Crisis 3 in January 1984, a building was selected for renovation to house the computer sciences department. The renovation was completed quickly, and the building was occupied in the fall of 1985. The space was of excellent quality, and for a few years, the department enjoyed ample space. However the need for labs, supporting staff, and research assistants grew rapidly, and by 1989 the packing process was being repeated. Fortunately it had not yet reached the extreme situation in 1984.

4.4. Crisis 4: Loss of Key Faculty

The crises already discussed began in the early 1980s to create concern and then alarm among the faculty, who saw that to remain among the top ten departments, Purdue would have to make major investments to create the experimental science facilities needed. This meant more space for laboratories, more support for staff, and more computing facilities. Instead of addressing this challenge, some faculty felt the administration was letting it drown in a flood of students. The faculty realized that it was impossible to hire ten new professors, since they were not available. The faculty did hope however that the administration would help in other ways—more teaching assistants, more lab space, and better computing facilities. Faculty morale dropped steadily as it appeared that little help would be forthcoming.

This crisis should be placed in the context of the national situation: Enrollments were ballooning wherever they were not strictly limited; there was a national awareness that major investments were needed for experimental computer sciences facilities. Many universities were responding with major programs in computer sciences, and it seemed that all the leading departments were receiving $15 million or $30 million for new buildings and 20 new positions. Of course only some universities were, but the Purdue faculty felt it was going to be left behind.

In the summer of 1981 a group (Denning, Rice, Larry Snyder, and Young) from computer sciences met with Provost Haas to discuss the situation. They had prepared a plan[2] to maintain the excellence of the department. The faculty's sense of unease was expressed, and the provost responded by saying that Purdue strongly supported the department and would not let it fall apart. The provost noted that Purdue could not let people like those present become so unhappy that they left Purdue; it would ruin the department. A year-and-a-half later Denning and Young had resigned, and a third (Snyder) resigned about a year after that.

The plan prepared by this group was realistic, since the faculty would receive less than it wanted, and the administration would give more than it wanted. The plan was agreed to in principle, but not as an itemized list of commitments. The plan and resulting actions did not fully disspell the belief that Purdue was willing to settle for a second-tier computer sciences department. In fall 1983 the faculty was systematically surveyed about the department's problems and priorities. Of 22 items, the following were judged to have the highest priority (in the order listed).

1. Large classes
2. Few Ph.D. students
3. Lack of laboratory space
4. University's commitment to maintaining a top-tier department

Overall faculty ratings of the department's and university's performance in attending to these items were, respectively, $D+$, $C-$, D, and $B-$.

In 1983 and 1984 the department lost ten faculty, including many of its key people, as shown in Table 4. This faculty would have constituted one of the better departments in the country, and its loss was clearly a major blow to Purdue. While the departmental crisis was the reason for

Table 2.4.
Loss of Faculty 1983–1984

Year	Person	Rank	New position
1983	Fran Berman	Assistant professor	University of California at San Diego
	Jan Cuny	Assistant professor	University of Massachusetts
	Dorothy Denning	Associate professor	Stanford Research Institute
	Peter Denning	Professor and head	NASA: Research Institute for Advanced Computing Systems
	Mike O'Donnell	Associate professor	Johns Hopkins
	Paul Young	Professor	University of Washington
1984	Richard Buchi	Professor	Died
	Dennis Gannon	Associate professor	Indiana University
	Herbert Schwetman	Professor	MCC
	Larry Snyder	Professor	University of Washington

some of the departures, there was also a certain coincidence. For four of these people, the principal reason for leaving was their spouse's situation, which was also a contributing factor for several others. See Figure 2.2 for data on faculty size from 1963–1990. A regular faculty member is tenured or on the tenure track with principal appointment in computer sciences.

The search for a replacement for Denning as department head was educational. Rice was appointed acting head, and a vigorous search for a new head started. The dean outlined how the candidates would be winnowed out; the department opined that Purdue would be lucky to have any serious candidates to winnow. A year later only three candidates had been found who were both interested and interesting enough to be interviewed. Two were offered the position and turned it down, the third said it would be a wasted effort to make an offer.

As the crisis deepened the administration became more convinced that it was real and efforts should be made to save the department. On January 1, 1983, the entire computer sciences faculty was given a 1% midyear raise as a sign of commitment from the university; Purdue salaries at that time were near the national average. In January 1984, it was decided to completely renovate the Memorial Gymnasium and make it into the Computer Sciences building. Only 3 months later, architects were fin-

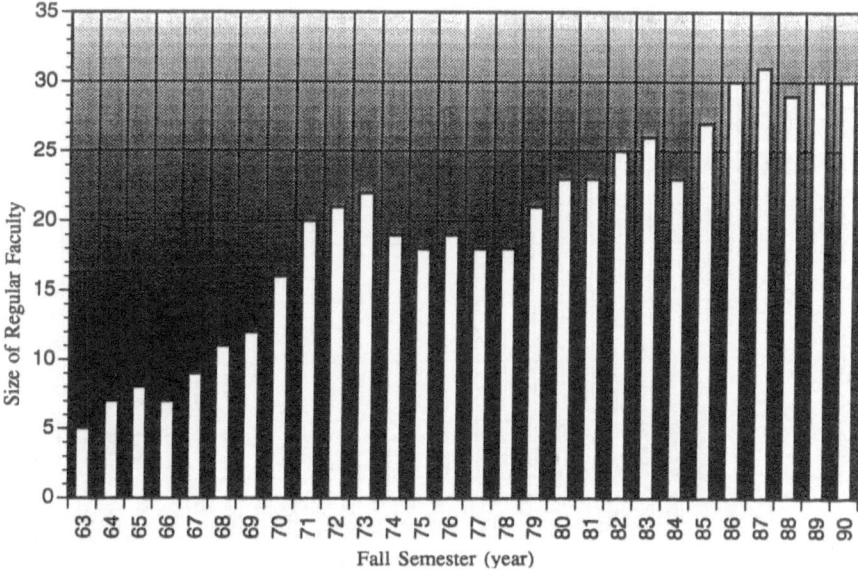

Figure 2.2. Growth of the regular faculty in the Department of Computer Sciences from 1963–1990.

ished, and bids had been sent out requesting a completion date of August 1985.

New faculty were hired in 1983 and 1984, but three associate professors (Apostolico, Marinescu, and Wagstaff) and five assistant professors (Bajaj, Dyksen, Mehrotra, Melhem, and Schnyder) did not adequately replace four professors, three associate professors, and two assistant professors. Furthermore Apostolico and Marinescu came from Europe and were not well established in the United States as typical associate professors, and Wagstaff's research area borders on mathematics.

4.5. Recovery

Recovery from these crises occurred in 1985. Moving into the newly renovated Computer Sciences building dramatically improved morale: Not only was the environment greatly improved, but there was an opportunity to start teaching and research laboratories of all kinds: The computing facilities had the type of space (if not yet all the equipment) needed to provide first-class facilities. This physical improvement was accompa-

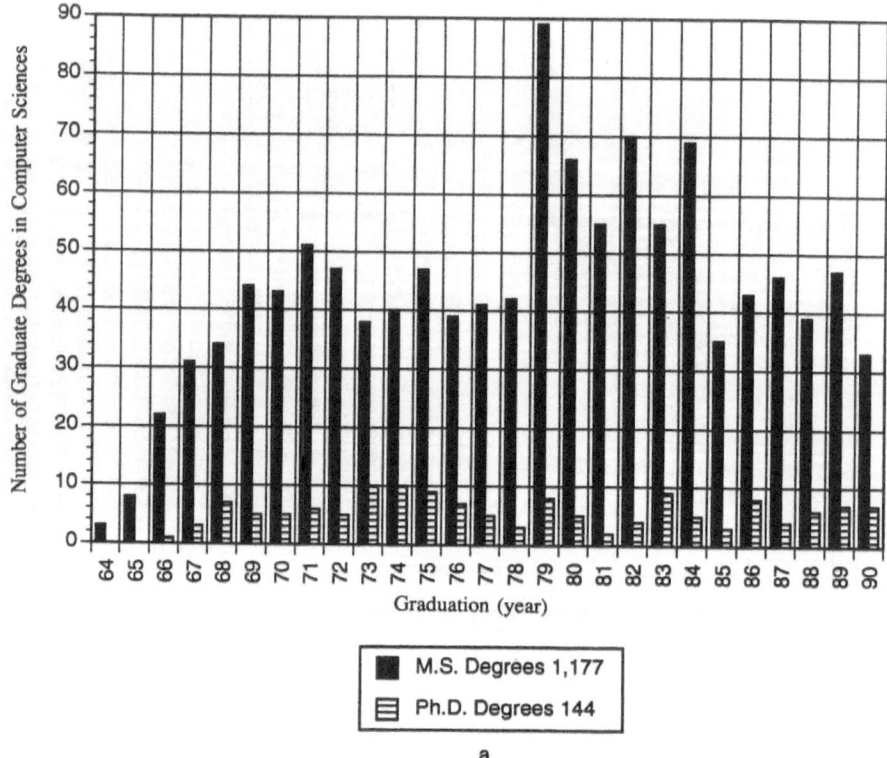

Figure 2.3. (a) Graduate degrees awarded in computer sciences from 1964–1990. **(b)** Undergraduate degrees awarded in computer sciences from 1968–1990

nied by initial solid evidence that the flood of students was receding: Only a little over 300 in the entering freshmen class had declared computer science majors.

Even though severe damage was caused by some of these crises, there had been other real success in meeting some of them. From 1980–1989 the department's budget increased from $1.1 million to $3 million, at least a million dollars more than the inflation rate. Increases in the early 1980s seemed to be instantly consumed by the crises at hand, but they were building a base for the recovery in the second half of the decade.

The first priority after the faculty exodus in 1983–1984 was to rebuild the faculty. The nationwide shortage of computer scientists made this a difficult challenge, but one that had to be met. New hiring really began in

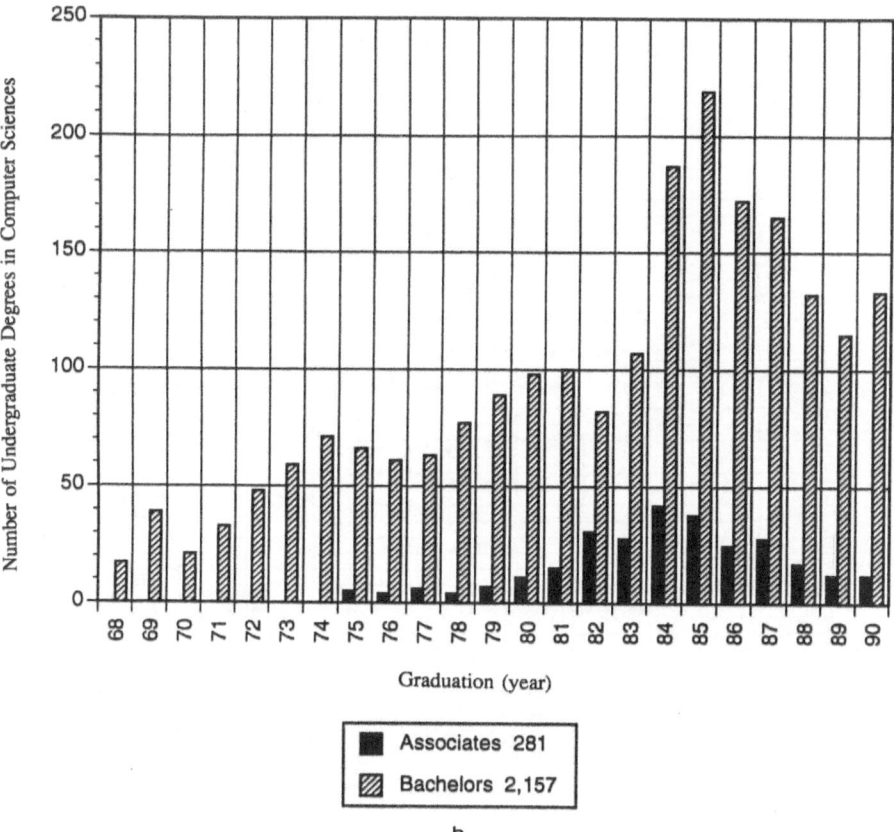

Figure 2.3. (*Continued*)

earnest in 1984 with six new regular faculty appointments. By 1989 the regular faculty had grown to 30, of which 18 were hired in 1983 or later. Not one of the 19 regular faculty hired in the 8-year period 1968–1975 remained; there were five "old timers," Conte, Gautschi, Lynch, Rice, and Rosen; and seven "middle-aged" faculty members. Most of the new faculty hired was of course young even though losses had been heaviest among the more senior faculty. Five associate professors were hired, but the majority were relatively new to the rank. Three full professors were hired. Rao Kosaraju was appointed the Loveless Distinguished Professor of Computer Sciences in 1986, and the department was thrilled to have acquired such a distinguished theoretician. Unfortunately he returned to

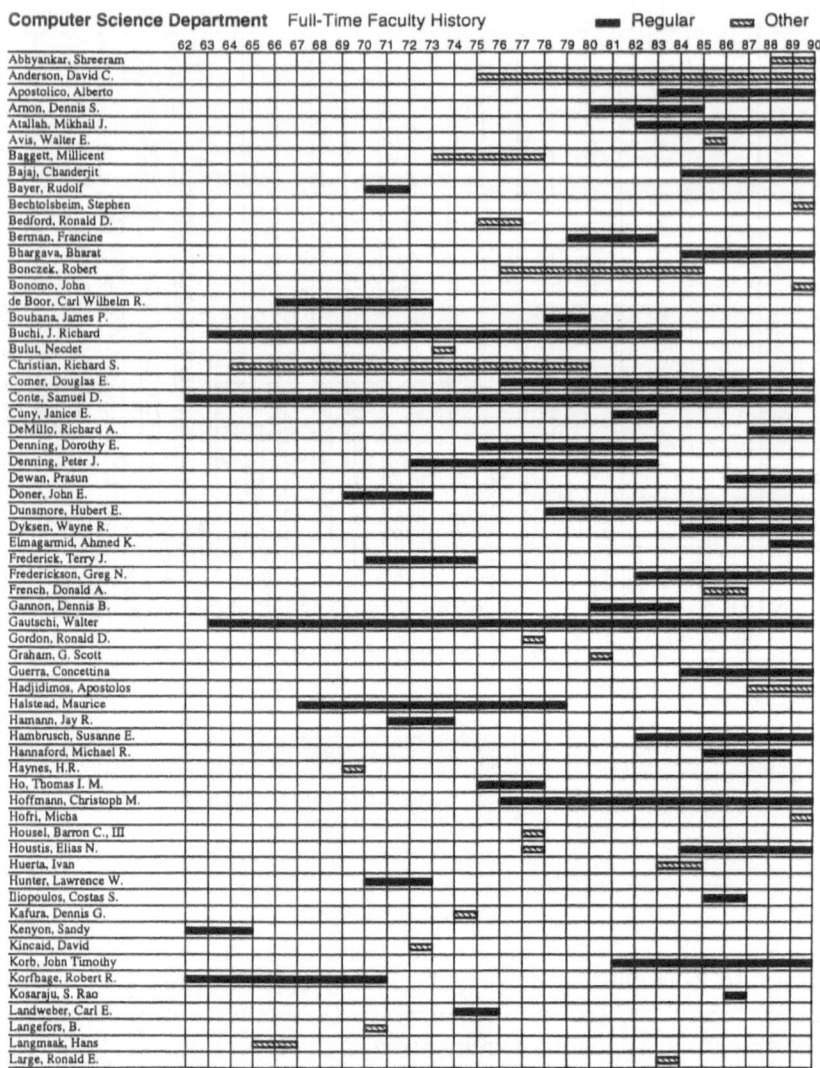

Figure 2.4. Full-time faculty in computer sciences. The year marks indicate the summer, so Bayer was on the faculty during academic years 1970–1971 and 1971–1972.

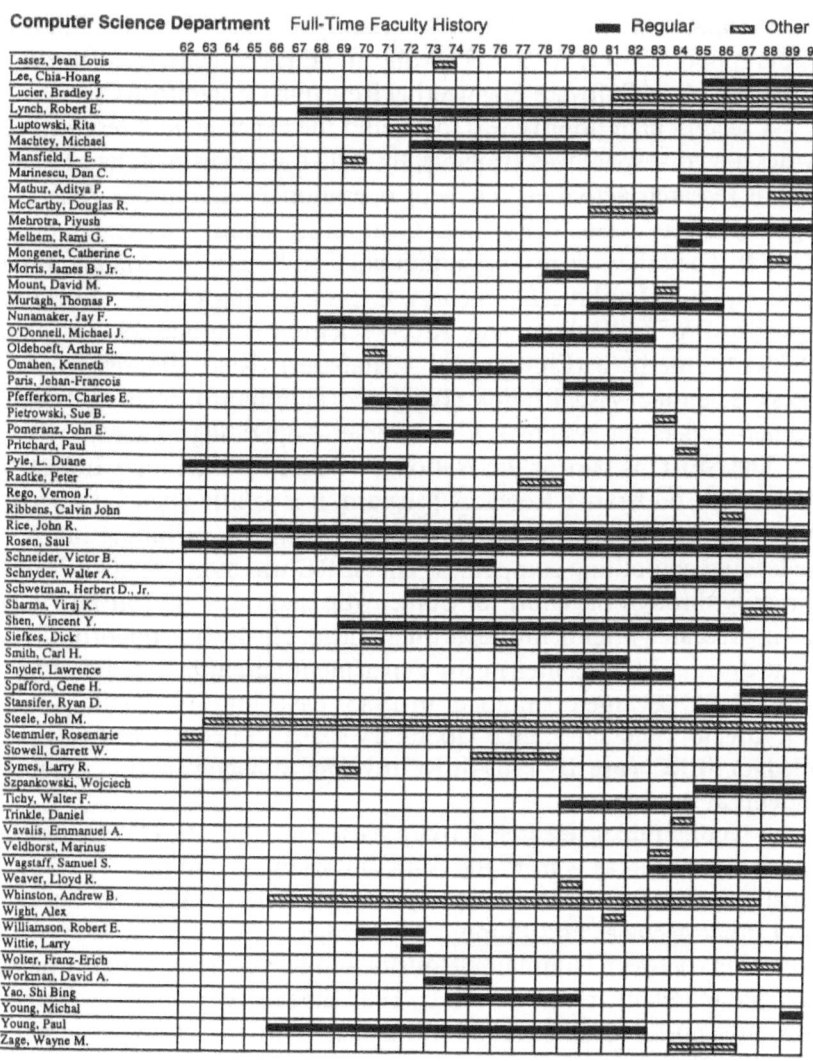

Figure 2.4. (*Continued*)

Johns Hopkins after a year because of family reasons. The other full professors appointed were Richard DeMillo and Elias Houstis. DeMillo came as director of the Software Engineering Research Center (SERC).

A second high priority was to expand the experimental research activities now that space was available. By 1989 the department had 11 substantial research activities, ten with operational laboratories. The two largest projects were SERC and Computing about Physical Objects (CAPO). The others were Computational Combinatorics (Atallah, Frederickson, and Hambrusch—theory), Cypress (Doug Comer—networking), ELLPACK (Dyksen and Rice—scientific computing), Graphics (Dyksen), Interbase (Elmagarmid—databases), Raid (Bhargava—data bases), Scientific Visualization (Bajaj and Hoffmann), Shadow Editing (Comer—operating systems), Xinu (Comer—operating systems).

The SERC is part of the National Science Foundation's Industry–University Cooperative Research program. It is jointly operated with the University of Florida and has 15 industry affiliates, including many of the leading computing companies. The SERC was established at Purdue primarily through the efforts of Conte, who had taken up software engineering research after being department head. He saw the opportunity to create an important center in the department and after 2 years of hard work, SERC became operational in 1985. DeMillo came as the permanent director, and substantial laboratory space and equipment was provided for SERC's use. By 1989 SERC involved 12 faculty and 14 graduate students at Purdue.

A second major research activity started in 1987, the CAPO project. Its principal support is from the National Science Foundation's Coordinated Experimental Research program, but it has substantial support from other agencies and Purdue. This project originated in 1986 from discussions between Hoffmann, Houstis, and Rice. The eventual proposal included many other faculty, and by 1989 the project involved seven faculty, three postdocs, and over 20 research assistants and staff personnel.

Growth in research in general, and experimental research in particular, is perhaps best illustrated by the increase in research funding from $447 thousand in 1980 to $3.6 million in 1989. Not surprisingly there was also a substantial increase in the number of Ph.D. students during this period and some decrease in the number of M.S. students.

The new space acquired on moving into the Computer Sciences building also allowed the department to establish teaching laboratories. In the first year, 1985, there were four—two for computer sciences 110 (an elementary personal-computer-based service course), one for computer

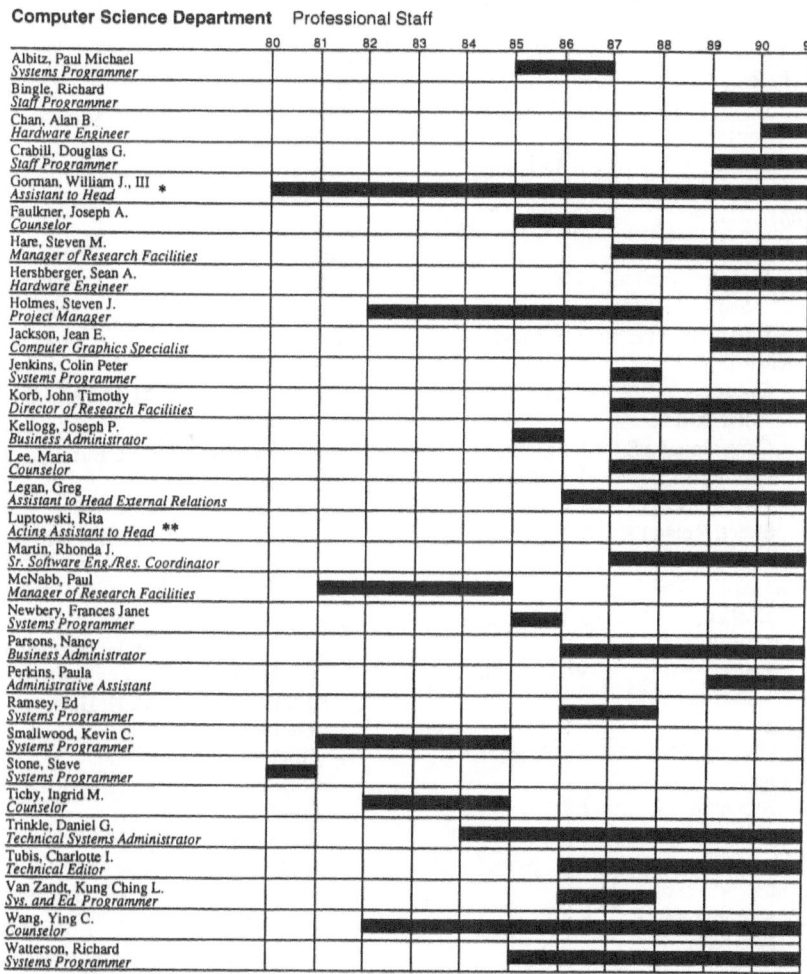

Figure 2.5. Professional staff in computer sciences from 1975–1991; the year indicates the academic year in which a staff member came, left, or was appointed from nonprofessional staff positions at Purdue. The position title is the most recent if more than one position was held.

Table 2.5.
Ph.D. Graduates in Computer Sciences Showing Time of Graduation
and Thesis Adviser

Ph.D. graduate	Major professor	Ph.D. graduate	Major professor
1966		**1970**	
June		June	
Usow, Karl H.	J. R. Rice	Oldehoeft,	S. D. Conte
August		Arthur E.	
Brown,	S. D. Conte	Pruess,	C. deBoor
Kenneth M.		Steven A.	
1967		August	
June		Bass, Leonard J.	P. R. Young
Brainerd, Walter	J. R. Buchi	Silverston,	S. D. Conte
Scott		Stefan M.	
Kalan, James E.	J. S. Maybee	**1971**	
August		January	
Evans,	S. D. Conte	Frailey,	M. H. Halstead
Bernard B.		Dennis J.	
Kerr, Douglas S.	S. D. Conte	Mei, Peng-Siu	J. R. Buchi
Landweber,	J. R. Buchi	June	
Lawrence H.		Blair, James C.	S. Rosen
Sweet, Roland A.	J. S. Maybee	Noonan,	M. H. Halstead
1968		Robert E.	
January		**1972**	
Hosken,	J. R. Buchi	June	
William H.		Boyce,	M. H. Halstead
Zahar,	W. Gautschi	Raymond F.	
Ramsay V. M.		DeLutis,	M. H. Halstead
June		Thomas	
Hoff, June C.	J. R. Rice	Gregory	
August		Hochgesang,	M. H. Halstead
Burchard,	J. R. Rice	Guy T.	
Hermann G.		Nylin, William	M. H. Halstead
1969		C., Jr.	
June		Shaprio,	M. H. Halstead
Axsom, Larry E.	S. Rosen	Michael D.	
Desautels,	S. Rosen	August	
Edouard J.		Berk, Toby S.	M. H. Halstead
Gibbs,	R. E. Korfhage	Dodson,	C. deBoor
Norman E.		David S.	
Symes,	J. R. Rice	December	
Lawrence R.		Lancaster,	V. B. Schneider
August		Ronald Leo	
Dershem,	R. E. Lynch	Pekarek, Edward	R. E. Lynch
Herbert L.		G., Jr.	
Phillips,	W. Gautschi		
James L.			
Smith,	L. D. Pyle		
Douglas K.			

Table 2.5. (*Continued*)

Ph.D. graduate	Major professor	Ph.D. graduate	Major professor
1973		**1974** (*continued*)	
May		December	
Aird, Thomas J.	J. R. Rice	Heiman,	M. F. Neuts
Arsenault,	J. F. Nunamaker,	David I.	
James R.	Jr.	Ho,	J. F. Nunamaker,
Conti,	T. J. Frederick	Thomas I. M.	Jr.
Dennis M.		Kafura,	V. Y. Shen
Lassez,	J. R. Buchi	Dennis G.	
Jean-Louis		Verbrugge,	J. F. Nunamaker,
Mickunas,	V. B. Schneider	William G.	Jr.
Marshall D.		**1975**	
Roman,	S. D. Conte	May	
Roger V.		Denning,	H. D. Schwetman
August		Dorothy E.	
Bulut, Necdet	M. H. Halstead	December	
Housel, Barron	M. H. Halstead	Cox, George W.	V. B. Schneider
C., III		Elci, Atila	M. H. Halstead
Iverson, James	J. F. Nunamaker,	MacLennan,	V. B. Schneider
A., Jr.	Jr.	Bruce J.	
Oldehoeft,	J. R. Rice	**1976**	
Rodney R.		May	
December		Blosser,	J. F. Nunamaker,
Buten,	V. Y. Shen	Patrick A.	Jr.
Richard E.		Lemme,	J. R. Rice
Krause, Kenneth	V. Y. Shen	James M.	
Leroy		Puk, Richard F.	R. Garrett
Swenson,	A. B. Whinston	Wade,	V. B. Schneider
Donald E.		Bradford W.	
1974		August	
May		Bonczek,	A. B. Whinston
Collins,	P. R. Young	Robert H.	
William J.		Fletcher,	H. D. Schwetman
Schutte,	M. H. Halstead	Sharon K.	
Lawrence J.		Kahn, Kevin C.	P. J. Denning
Zweben,	M. H. Halstead	December	
Stuart H.		Graham,	P. J. Denning
August		Gordon S.	
Anderson,	W. Gautschi	Konsynski,	J. F. Nunamaker,
Larry A.		Ben R.	Jr.
Dahl, William J.	J. F. Nunamaker,		
	Jr.		
Friedman,	V. B. Schneider		
Frank L.			
Zislis, Paul M.	M. H. Halstead		

(*continued*)

Table 2.5. (*Continued*)

Ph.D. graduate	Major professor	Ph.D. graduate	Major professor
1977		**1981**	
August		August	
Gordon, Ronald D.	M. H. Halstead	Joseph, Deborah A.	P. R. Young
Schwartz, Mayer D.	P. J. Denning	Tolopka, Stephen J.	H. D. Schwetman
Winklmann, Karl A.	P. R. Young	December	
1978		Chew, Leslie Paul	M. J. O'Donnell
August		**1982**	
Long, Timothy J.	P. R. Young	May	
Ottenstein, Karl J.	M. H. Halstead	Ward, William A., Jr.	J. R. Rice
Ottenstein, Linda M.	M. H. Halstead	August	
Poplawski, David A.	C. M. Hoffman	Waddle, Vance E.	A. B. Whinston
December		December	
Bruell, Steven C.	H. D. Schwetman	Brumfield, Jeffrey A.	P. J. Denning
Mead, Robert L., Jr.	H. D. Schwetman	Dittert, Eric R.	M. J. O'Donnell
1979		Hedlund, Kye Sherrick	L. Snyder
May		Hsiao, Ching-Chih	L. Snyder
Gehringer, Edward F.	H. D. Schwetman	**1983**	
Simon, Richard T.	P. J. Denning	May	
August		Mount, David	C. M. Hoffmann
Boisvert, Ronald F.	J. R. Rice	Reed, Danny A.	H. D. Schwetman
December		Schrader, David K.	P. J. Denning
Balbo, Gianfranco	P. J. Denning	Thebault, Stephen	V. Y. Shen
Hevner, Alan R.	S. B. Yao	August	
Miller, James R.	D. C. Anderson	Agrawal, Subhash C.	P. J. Denning
1980		Arthur, James D.	D. E. Comer
May		December	
Dennis, T. Donald	P. J. Denning	Capka, David M.	P. R. Young
August		**1984**	
Fasel, Joseph H., III	P. J. Denning	May	
December		Bishop, Matthew	D. E. Denning
Woodfield, Scott N.	V. Y. Shen	Bondi, Andre B.	P. J. Denning
		August	
		Wang, Andrew	H. E. Dunsmore
		December	H. D. Schwetman
		Li, Kuo-Cheng	

Table 2.5. (*Continued*)

Ph.D. graduate	Major professor	Ph.D. graduate	Major professor
1985		**1988**	
May		May	
Peterson, Larry Lee	D. E. Comer	Brown, Robert L.	D. E. Comer and P. J. Denning
August		Willis, Craig E.	J. T. Korb
Bechtolsheim, Stephen V.	D. B. Gannon	August	
Hwang, Yeou-Huei	D. B. Gannon	Bhasker, Parthasarathy	A. B. Whinston
Kerola, Teemu Tapani	H. D. Schwetman	Christara, Christina C.	E. N. Houstis
December		Rathi, Mahesh Kumar	S. D. Conte
Kapauan, Alejandro A.	D. B. Gannon	Shannon, Gregory E.	G. N. Frederickson
Panetta, Jairo	D. B. Gannon	December	
Yu, Tze-Jie	H. E. Dunsmore	Kim, Myung-Soo	C. Bajaj
1986		Leu, Pei-Jyun	B. Bhargava
May		Narten, Thomas	D. E. Comer
Kortekangas, Atte Juhani	A. B. Whinston	**1989**	
Pan, Shuh-Shen James	A. B. Whinston	August	
August		Bonomo, John Paul	W. R. Dyksen
Droms, Ralph E.	D. E. Comer	Guan, Dah Jyh	G. N. Frederickson
Kent, Christopher A.	D. E. Comer	Gupta, Ajay Kumar	S. E. Hambrusch
Ribbens, Calvin J.	J. R. Rice	Yavatkar, Rajendra Shivaram	D. E. Comer
Ruan, Zuwang	W. F. Tichy	December	
1987		Rodger, Susan Hatcher	G. N. Frederickson
August		**1990**	
Goodrich, Michael T.	M. J. Atallah	May	
Janardan, Ravi	G. N. Frederickson	Browne, Shirley Victoria	B. Bhargava
Ruggieri, Cristina	T. P. Murtagh	Riedl, John Thomas	B. Bhargava
December		August	
Krishnamurthy, Balachander	J. T. Korb	Chuang, Jung-Hong	C. M. Hoffmann
		Tsay, Jyh-Jong	M. J. Atallah

sciences 230 (now computer sciences 180, the first course for computer
sciences majors), and one for graduate courses in operating systems and
networking. By 1989 this number had doubled. Operating laboratories
are considerably more expensive in manpower (never mind maintaining
equipment) than ordinary lecture courses, since you must have laboratory
assistants and supervisors of various kinds. The funding for this expansion
came primarily from the reduction in computer science majors: As fewer
sections of certain courses were needed, teaching assistants were reas-
signed to help in labs.

5. HISTORICAL DATA

Some historical data were given earlier, namely, departmental milestones and events, entering freshmen in computer sciences, and the size
of regular faculty. Figures 2.3 a and b show the number of degrees awarded
at all levels in computer sciences from 1964–1990. Figure 2.4 lists full-
time faculty from 1962–1990 and their number of years in the department. Full-time refers to the appointment at Purdue, although several of
these faculty members were only part-time in computer sciences. Part-
time faculty in other departments or PUCC include Abhyankar, Anderson, Bonczek, Christian, French, Gautschi, Lucier, Lynch, Rice (until
1983), Rosen, Schwetman, Steele, and Whinston. Figure 2.5 lists all the
professional staff since the first, William Gorman, was appointed in 1975;
staff positions are also given. Table 5 lists all the Ph.D. graduates, with
their advisers, from 1966–1990.

ACKNOWLEDGMENTS. We acknowledge valuable discussion and input
from Samuel Conte, Walter Gautschi, William Gorman, Felix Haas, Robert Lynch, and L. Duane Pyle.

References

1. Rosen, Saul and Rice, John R. "The origins of computing and computer science at
   Purdue University." CSD-TR-1004. Computer Science Department, Purdue University
   (1990).
2. Denning, Peter J., Rice, John R., Snyder, Lawrence, and Young, Paul. "A plan for excellence in computer sciences." (July 15, 1981, revised August 26, 1981).
3. Atallah, Mikhail, Comer, Douglas, Dunsmore, H. E., Frederickson, Greg, and Rice,
   John. "A five year plan for excellence." CSD-TR 651. Computer Sciences Department,
   Purdue University (1986).

3

Overview: Carnegie Mellon University Master of Software Engineering Program

Norman E. Gibbs

Carnegie Mellon University (CMU) decided to offer a professional master of software engineering (MSE) degree program beginning in the fall of 1989. The program is a joint effort between the School of Computer Science and the Software Engineering Institute (SEI).

1. THE CMU MSE

The purpose of the CMU MSE program is to prepare people to assume leadership roles in software development within industry. The program focuses on engineering software products and software systems, with a heavy emphasis on design and evaluation. Apprenticeships with top designers are integrated with formal education. The program gives potential software designers an opportunity to interact with and stimulate each other. Although respecting and following a disciplined development process are important aspects of engineering, we feel our program gains strength by building on, and interacting with, the existing CMU research community. This allows us to apply state-of-the-art computer science to engineering software in addition to simulating an idealized software development process. The goals of the MSE program are consistent with

Norman E. Gibbs • Carnegie Mellon University

Studies in Computer Science, edited by John R. Rice and Richard A. DeMillo. Plenum Press, New York, 1994.

Table 3.1.
MSE Degree Curriculum

Year	Courses
Fall semester first year	Formal methods in software engineering
	Advanced system design principles
	Computer science elective
Spring semester first year	Software creation and maintenance
	Software analysis
	Software project management
	Computer science elective
Fall semester second year	Software development studio
	Software engineering seminar
	Required theory course
	Advanced computer science elective
Spring semester second year	Software development studio
	Software engineering seminar
	Required business course
	Advanced computer science elective
Summer second year	Software development studio

some of the challenges laid out by Brooks.[1] We address his challenge to industry and academia by seeking out and cultivating great designers.

The MSE degree program requires 2 years of full-time study. For admission students must have 2 years of software development experience. We also expect students to have mastered programming in the small, discrete mathematics, and material usually covered by core courses in an undergraduate computer science degree program. Although many of our students are not necessarily interested in earning a Ph.D., the plan is to work with students who have that level of potential but have chosen a career in building systems instead of research and advanced development. These are the kind of people who perhaps aspire to become the vice president of product development instead of the vice president of research. Table 1 gives an overview of the 2-year curriculum.

The first year of the program provides a foundation in the state-of-the-art and state-of-the-practice in software engineering. It is a variation of the six-core software engineering courses that were designed by the SEI as part of its work to advance software engineering education.[2] There is emphasis on formal methods and systems engineering, both of which provide a basis for making technical decisions later. In particular the course in advanced system design principles includes state-of-the-practice programming systems. First-year computer science electives are senior-undergraduate or first-year graduate-level courses; these are required to make certain that students have a broad basis of current computer science knowledge.

The second year of the program centers around a software development studio that runs for a calendar year. During the first and second semesters, teams of students plan a project and then execute it using the skills they acquired during the first year of the MSE program. We emphasize applying these skills to engineer or reengineer part of a software system. Students are expected to reexamine and evaluate their solution toward the end of the studio. Time is allocated during the last summer actually to plan some experiments, make changes, and then measure the effect on the artifact. We feel that typical student project work as currently taught does not allow time for adequate reflection on either the process used or the product developed.

During this second year opportunities are available for significant interaction with, and stimulation from, other creative people. The software engineering seminar is one such example. People who have made substantial contributions to software engineering are invited to Carnegie Mellon to interact with the studio students. Normally these visitors spend a day sharing lessons learned and their own personal philosophy, with the goal of stimulating students to change or defend their beliefs. A second day is spent on a student presentation of the studio project. The students report progress to date and defend choices they have made. Visitors react to the project and provide feedback. Since we believe technical communication is vital to being a productive software engineer, we require students to write about the visitor, the visitor's philosophy, and what effect the exchange of information had on their own views. Assignments are graded on both technical content and effectiveness of the technical writing. Students' oral presentations are also evaluated and used in determining their seminar grade.

The seminar and studio were offered for the first time in the spring and summer of 1990 to four part-time students from the SEI. The first full class of first-year students was admitted in the fall of 1990. We expect to have about 30 students in each year for a total of 60 students in the program.

POSTSCRIPT

This chapter is a summary of a talk given at the symposium to honor Samuel D. Conte on November 3, 1989. Sam was chairman of the computer science department when I entered Purdue in the fall of 1964 as a mathematics graduate student. Sam became my adviser when I switched to computer science in the summer of 1965. In 1967 when I became a doctoral candidate with Bob Korfhage as my thesis adviser, Sam served as a member of my examination committee along with Paul Young and Lou Cote. I defended my thesis in May of 1969 and became the first Purdue computer science Ph.D. to graduate without taking any numerical analysis courses!

I am grateful for the friendship and career guidance Sam has provided me for the past 20 years. It is clear why Sam was such a successful department head. In addition to his vision, taste, and high standards, he really cares about Purdue's graduates, encourages them to contribute, and applauds their successes.

ACKNOWLEDGMENTS. Much of the vision for the seminar and studio is that of A. Nico Habermann, Former dean of Carnegie Mellon's School of Computer Science. Other major contributors in defining this program were Jim Tomayko and Mark Ardis. Jim took the lead in shaping and refining the concept of the software development studio, led the faculty through a simulation of the first prototype in the spring of 1989, and taught the first set of students during the spring and summer of 1990. Mark took the lead in defining the SEI's six core courses mentioned in Reference 2, and he has made the largest contribution to defining and tailoring them for the CMU MSE. Other contributors include Roger Dannenberg, Harvey Hallman, M. Satyanarayanan, Mary Shaw, Doug Tygar, and Jeannette Wing.

References

1. Brooks, F. P. Jr. "No silver bullet." *IEEE Comput.* **20**(4), 10–19 (1987).
2. Ford, G. A., and Gibbs, N. E. "A master of software engineering curriculum: recommendations from the software engineering institute." *IEEE Comput.* **22**(9), 59–71 (1989).

4

Lessons Learned in Building a Successful Undergraduate Information Systems Academic Program

Thomas I. M. Ho

1. INTRODUCTION

Since 1978, the Department of Computer Technology (CPT), an undergraduate computer information systems (CIS) program in Purdue University's School of Technology, has successfully followed an innovative approach to meeting the critical need for competent, occupationally ready information systems professionals. The department opened its doors in the fall of 1978 to 60 students. Today its enrollment exceeds 500 students in five locations!

Of the more than 90% of its graduates who have been placed, all have been placed in positions in the information systems field. Starting annual salaries for graduates have been increasing steadily and by 1989 averaged almost $29,000.

The program's success can be attributed to the department's pursuit of a market-driven strategy for developing its curriculum, faculty, facilities, and industrial relations. This chapter discusses the principles guiding the creation and development of a successful market-driven program and identifies critical success factors and the corporate values of CPT at Purdue.

We are offering this contribution to the symposium to honor Sam Conte because he himself has had a major influence in the genesis of CPT

4

Thomas I. M. Ho • Carnegie Mellon University

Studies in Computer Science, edited by John R. Rice and Richard A. DeMillo. Plenum Press, New York, 1994.

at Purdue. He was instrumental in selecting CPT's founding head, and he is the founder of Purdue's Department of Computer Sciences, which has educated both of the heads who have led CPT during its 10-year history. Therefore the CPT department at Purdue also owes much to Sam Conte!

2. HISTORY OF INFORMATION SYSTEMS EDUCATION AT PURDUE

The history of information systems education at Purdue began in the late 1960s when the Department of Computer Sciences added the information systems option to its curriculum. Purdue's offerings in information systems education were expanded further when the Department of Computer Technology was created in 1978.

3. MARKET-DRIVEN STRATEGY

A successful CIS program is market driven. The current drive to harness information technology for competitive advantage[1] makes it imperative to produce information systems practitioners who are responsive to market needs. The drive for competitive advantage also makes the employers of information systems graduates much more sensitive to market-driven strategies.

4. CURRICULUM

A market-driven CIS curriculum has the following characteristics:

• Balance between conceptual foundations and methodology

• Prominent role for instructional development

• Consistency and continuity in course delivery

4.1. Balance between Conceptual Foundations and Methodology

Methodology describes what skills are characteristic of the curriculum's graduates. Conceptual foundations explain why progressive methods work well. A successful curriculum rests on a foundation that promotes consistency and continuity. Based on conceptual foundations that promote understanding knowledge and on methodology that promotes mastering skills, a successful curriculum strives for balance between conceptual foundations and methodology. For example in the case of software engineering, Gibbs[2] recognizes that curriculum is based on current best practice and emerging principles.

We should distinguish education from training. Gibbs[2] says

> Education is a long-term activity designed to build a foundation of knowledge and reasoning abilities; training is a short-term activity with a specific goal. Training builds upon an educational foundation to develop a skill or to teach performance of a process rather than reasoning about processes. The challenge to educators . . . is to provide the appropriate foundation so that the expected advancements in technology can be used effectively after relatively short training periods. (p. 595)

In an information systems development context, methods for information system development are supported by such conceptual foundations as systems concepts[3] and the software life cycle.[4]

The conceptual foundations for systems concepts enable us to deal with the size and complexity of relevant systems, for example computer, organization, and information systems. Furthermore systems concepts promote the development of problem-solving skills for problem identification and solution.

The conceptual foundation of the system life cycle recognizes a phased approach to information system development. A paramount concern is defining requirements before design and implementation. Other important concerns include the appropriate proportion of effort among the development phases and the iterative nature of system development activities.

These conceptual foundations enable students to understand why development methods work, when to apply development methods to appropriate situations, when a system development activity is finished, and if a system development activity has been done correctly.

Methods based on systems concepts include the systems approach to problem solving: defining the problem, identifying alternatives, evaluating alternatives, and selecting a solution from alternatives.

Significant systems development methods include data-centered design,[5] that is system modeling motivated by data structure; and process decomposition, that is decomposition motivated by function. These methods feature documentation standards that impose discipline on information system development. Another indispensable methodology for systems development includes oral and written communications skills.[6]

Among the relevant skills, defining information requirements and subsequent design of an information system are paramount. These skills must be mastered in an environment that promotes defining and enforcing standard practices. Finally a strong documentation ethic is promoted to control information system lifetime costs.

With respect to conceptual understanding, if graduates understand why a method is effective in practice, they will be able to explain why it would be advantageous to adopt that technique. In this way the level of professional practice will ultimately be raised. The necessity for this technology transfer is recognized by Redwine *et al.*, who claim that it takes 15–20 years for new software technology to be accepted in industry![7]

4.2. Prominent Role for Instructional Development

Equal concern for how we teach as well as what we teach motivates a prominent role for instructional development. This development process produces objectives, instructional activities, and evaluation.

The need to specify educational objectives in computing curriculum design has been recognized by Ford and Gibbs,[4] who use Bloom[8] to specify objectives for a software-engineering curriculum. These objectives tell students what they should be able to do after completing instruction; assist the teacher in selecting instructional activities and determining appropriate evaluation; and communicate to others, for example prospective employers, what the instruction is attempting to accomplish. Based on the objectives, instructional activities are designed to involve students in actively acquiring new knowledge and practicing new skills. A wide variety of alternatives spans a broad spectrum of instructional activities, for example team-oriented projects, and different media, for example lectures, films, or courseware.

Evaluation serves several purposes; it measures student achievement, especially to demonstrate mastery; it assesses the entire instructional process; it determines students' attitudes about instruction; and it diagnoses teaching and learning problems. Again a wide variety of alternatives spans a broad spectrum of evaluation mechanisms, for example examinations, student peer review, group discussions, and surveys.

4.3. Consistency and Continuity in Course Delivery

A prominent role for instructional development ensures consistency and continuity in course delivery. Identifying conceptual foundations and methodology contributes significantly to defining educational objectives. Aside from its obvious contribution to improving instruction, educational objectives also have considerable value in marketing a program to prospective students and employers.

5. FACULTY

This section discusses faculty qualities and practices.

5.1. Qualifications

A market-driven strategy for faculty selection ensures that all faculty have graduate degrees that are predominantly in relevant areas of study, for example computer science and business administration. Of equal importance, a market-driven strategy for faculty selection ensures that all faculty members have either industrial computing or teaching experience. The majority of the faculty must have practical industrial computing experience predominantly in the area of business applications. It is especially crucial for the practical experience to be relevant to progressive practice, for example computer-aided software engineering, and to such productivity tools as database management systems and teleprocessing monitors. Furthermore it is desirable if at least some of the faculty has had management experience, for example computing operations or network management. Another relevant faculty qualification, especially for those lacking a terminal degree, is professional certification, such as the Certificate in Data Processing (CDP) from the Institute for the Certification of Computer Professionals.

5.2. Motivation

Faculty should be engaged in an active program of professional development that includes teaching as well as computing activities. With respect to teaching, all faculty members should be active participants in an institutional program of instructional improvement, such as the College Teaching Workshop sponsored by Purdue's Center for Instructional Services. Additional opportunities include faculty colloquia and enrollment in education courses to help the faculty sharpen its teaching skills.

5.3. Professional Activities

Appropriate professional activities include participating in conferences, for example Information Systems Education Conference (ISECON), and publishing in journals devoted to improving information systems education, for example *CIS Educator Forum*. In addition to other scholarly activities, the faculty professional activities should be very evident in textbook publishing to ensure that instructional development efforts have an appropriate outlet for disseminating the results of these development efforts.

Finally the faculty should make contributions to the information systems profession through active participation and leadership activities in appropriate professional organizations, such as the Data Processing Management Association.

6. INSTRUCTIONAL COMPUTING FACILITIES

A market-driven instructional computing environment exhibits appropriate diversity, and it is representative of industrial computing environments. Its hardware includes large (mainframe) as well as small (personal) computers, and its hardware is representative of that commonly found in organizations where its graduates expect to seek employment. Its communications infrastructure is adequately robust to demonstrate the trend toward distributed computing. In the case of software, instructional computing facilities should contain industry-standard tools, and such productivity tools as a database management system and computer-aided software engineering are essential.

The information systems community has recognized the importance of defining an information technology architecture for the coherent application of information technology in an organization, for example crucial components for an information technology architecture define standards for telecommunications and data management in an organization. As a role model for students, the instructional computing facilities of an information systems program should conform to an information technology architecture; for example, the local area network providing access to shared resources for faculty office workstations and student laboratory workstations should conform to an architecture that supports industry standards. The data management software supporting data management courses should conform to an architecture that supports industry or defacto standards.

7. INDUSTRIAL RELATIONS

This section discusses the relationship between a successful CIS program and industry.

7.1. Industry Advisory Committee

A market-driven information systems program must have an industry advisory committee[9] composed of information systems professionals highly committed to the cause of information systems education. These professionals should provide appropriate breadth by representing computing consumers as well as suppliers. Among computing consumers application breadth will ensure that a wide variety of industry groups are represented. Computing suppliers should include hardware vendors, software vendors, and computing and consulting services providers.

Major activities of the Industry Advisory Committee are usually in the areas of curriculum, placement, facilities, and professional development. Curriculum balance and relevance are the product of extensive involvement by the Industry Advisory Committee.

7.2. Placement

Placement should be a significant performance measure for a market-driven information systems program. It is reasonable to expect that over 90% of the graduates of such a program will be placed in relevant positions that demonstrate the program is meeting its objectives of preparing systems analysts, database specialists, consultants, and trainers.

8. CONCLUSION

Critical success factors for an undergraduate information systems academic program are its curriculum, faculty, facilities, and industrial relations. A CIS academic program and its graduates can and must be actively marketed to an audience of prospective employers and students.

References

1. Parsons, Gregory L. "Information technology: a new competitive weapon." *Sloan Manage. Rev.* (fall 1983).
2. Gibbs, Norman E. "The SEI education program: the challenge of teaching future software engineers." *Comm. ACM* **32**(5) 594–605 (1989).
3. Davis, Gordon B., and Olson, Margrethe H. *Management Information Systems: Conceptual Foundations, Structure, and Development.* New York: McGraw-Hill, 1985.
4. Ford, Gary A., and Gibbs, Norman E. "A master of software engineering curriculum." *IEEE Comput.* **22**(9) 59–71 (1989).
5. Martin, James. *Information Engineering, Book 1, Introduction.* Englewood Cliffs, NJ: Prentice Hall, 1989.
6. Harriger, Alka R., and Ho, Thomas I. M. "A data-processing communications skills course." *Proc. 17th SIGCSE Technical Symposium on Computer Science Education* (February 1986). 97–102.
7. Redwine, S. T. Jr.; Becker, G. L.; Marmor-Squires, A. B.; Martin, R. J.; Nash, S. H.; and Riddle, W. E. "DoD-related software technology requirements, practices, and prospects for the future." IDA Paper P-1788. Institute for Defense Analyses, Alexandria, VA (June 1984).
8. Bloom, B. *Taxonomy of Educational Objectives: Handbook I: Cognitive Domain.* New York: David McKay, 1956.
9. Koleski, Mary M.; Koleski, Raymond A., and Ho, Thomas I. M. "Building the bridge between business and education: using advisory boards effectively." *Proc. DATACON '87* (March 1987).

III

RESEARCH CONTRIBUTIONS

5

Polynomial Interpolation in Several Variables

C. de Boor

I want to thank the organizers for inviting me to this meeting as it gives me the opportunity to help celebrate Sam Conte who gave me my first academic job. More than that, he provided my children with many years of summer camp in the wilds of New Hampshire and Wisconsin, and at least two of them think that those summers in New Hampshire were essential for their growing up (and I tend to agree with them).

Now I realize that Sam does not yet know what I am talking about, so I will explain. I was young and impetuous when I came to Purdue, and ready to complain about everything, including the courses I had to teach and the books I had to use. Sam's textbook was not exempted from these gratuitous comments. But, instead of becoming miffed or angry, Sam merely invited me to work with him on a revision. Now, that may have ruined the book, as far as Sam is concerned, for it made it a much harder book. But it and a later edition have continued to sell enough copies to allow me the luxury of sending my children to summer camps in faraway places, and for that my children and I will forever be grateful.

1. INTRODUCTION

One of the things I changed rather drastically in that textbook was the treatment of polynomial interpolation. I was then (and still am) much

C. de Boor • University of Wisconsin-Madison

Studies in Computer Science, edited by John R. Rice and Richard A. DeMillo. Plenum Press, New York, 1994.

impressed with the efficiency of the divided difference notion. It is a some-what tricky notion for the beginning student, and its treatment in the current edition is still not quite right. Perhaps we will get it right in the next one. In any case, polynomial interpolation occurs in the first real chapter of the book since polynomial interpolation is fundamental to much of numerical analysis.

It has therefore been something of a puzzle and disappointment to me that there is not a theory of multivariate polynomial interpolation as elegant and convincing and as basic as the univariate theory.

The trouble is easy to spot: Univariate polynomial interpolation starts with the observation that, for every set Θ of $k + 1$ points, and for every function f defined (at least) on Θ, there is exactly one polynomial p of degree $\leq k$ that matches f at Θ; that is, for which

$$p_{|\Theta} = f_{|\Theta}$$

Thus, when someone walks in with $k + 1$ points on the line, we immedi-ately reach for $\Pi_k :=$ polynomials of degree $\leq k$ as the space from which to choose the interpolant to given data at those points. But if our point set Θ is a subset of the plane or, more generally, of $\mathbb{R}^d$ for $d > 1$, then we do not know what to reach for. We would like to reach again for Π_k, but now it is not always possible to come up with a Π_k whose dimension

$$\dim\Pi_k(\mathbb{R}^d) = \binom{k + d}{d}$$

matches the cardinality of Θ; for example, with two points in the plane, we have too many points for Π_0 and too few points for Π_1. Further, even if $\#\Theta = \dim\Pi_k$, it may not be possible to interpolate from Π_k to every f on Θ. For example, if we take three points in the plane, then we can usually interpolate at those points with a linear polynomial, but if these three points happen to lie on a line, then our given f has to be linear before we can find an interpolant from Π_1, and even if we do, there are now many different interpolants.

Thus, the difficulty has been to come up, for given $\Theta \subset \mathbb{R}^d$, with a polynomial space P for which the pair $\langle \Theta, P \rangle$ is correct in the sense that any f defined (at least) on Θ matches exactly one $p \in P$ on Θ, that is, for which the restriction map

$$P \to \mathbb{R}^{\Theta} : p \mapsto p_{|\Theta}$$

is invertible. Generically, any polynomial space P with $\dim P = \#\Theta$ would do. The difficulty with multivariate polynomial interpolation has been that the point sets Θ one usually deals with are anything but generic. They may be regular meshes or lie on (other) simple algebraic surfaces.

This difficulty has been dealt with in the past in at least three ways.

2. STANDARD APPROACHES

Firstly, most past work has been spent deriving conditions on the set Θ for $\langle \Theta, \Pi_k \rangle$ to be correct. While much of this work is a variation on the eternal theme that a matrix is invertible if and only if its determinant is not zero, some of it is truly inspired. For example, Chung and Yao[1] (see also Ref. 2) start with a sequence $a_1, a_2, \ldots, a_n \in \mathbb{R}^d$ such that $0, a_1, a_2, \ldots, a_n$ are in **general position,** which means that no (proper) hyperplane can contain more than d of these $n + 1$ points. This implies that

$$\forall I \subseteq \{1, \ldots, n\} \text{ with } \#I = d \qquad \exists! x_I \qquad s.t. \ \forall i \in I \qquad 1 + a_i * x_I = 0$$
$$\forall i \notin I \qquad 1 + a_i * x_I \neq 0$$

since it implies that any d of the a_i must be linearly independent, thus providing that unique point x_I, but also implies that, in addition to the d points a_i, $i \in I$, no point a_i with $i \notin I$ can lie in the hyperplane

$$\{x \in \mathbb{R}^d : 1 + x * x_I = 0\}$$

This shows that the functions

$$l_I(x) := \prod_{i \notin I} \frac{1 + a_i * x}{1 + a_i * x_I}$$

are well-defined and, being products of $n-d$ linear factors, are elements of Π_{n-d}, and satisfy the conditions

$$l_I(x_J) = \delta_{IJ}$$

Thus, for arbitrary f,

$$\sum_I l_I f(x_I)$$

interpolates to f on

$$\Theta := \{x_I : I \subset \{1, \dots, n\}, \#I = d\}$$

Further, since

$$\#\Theta = \binom{n}{d} = \dim\Pi_{n-d}$$

this is the unique interpolant to f on Θ from Π_{n-d}.

Altogether, this is a most elegant generalization of the Lagrange form familiar from univariate polynomial interpolation. Its failing is simple: It is rarely of help in the common situation that one is given Θ.

Secondly, an entirely different effort, along the lines of the Newton form, was started by Gasca and Maeztu[3] some years ago. I follow these authors in describing the idea in the bivariate context. They start with a first instalment Θ_1 of data points all on a straight line, say $l_1(x) = 0$. The interpolating polynomial p_1 for these is chosen as the unique interpolating polynomial of appropriate degree that is constant along lines perpendicular to the data line $l_1(x) = 0$. (Actually, Gasca and Maeztu permit greater freedom in the choice of p_1, but this will suffice to get the basic idea across.) A second instalment Θ_2 of data points, all on some straight line $l_2(x) = 0$, is dealt with by constructing the unique polynomial p_2, of appropriate degree and constant along lines perpendicular to the second line, that matches the modified data

$$\frac{f - p_1}{l_1}$$

at Θ_2. This ensures that the polynomial

$$p_1 + l_1 p_2$$

matches f at $\Theta_1 \cup \Theta_2$. A set of points on a third data line leads to the interpolant

$$p_1 + l_1 p_2 + l_1 l_2 p_3$$

in which p_3 matches the modified function

$$\frac{f - p_1 - l_1 p_2}{l_1 l_2}$$

at the data points on the third line; and so forth.

This scheme has the advantage of providing an interpolant in a form that is efficient for evaluation. Further, it is not that difficult to add repeated interpolation points to achieve osculatory (that is, Hermite) interpolation. On the other hand, there may be many ways of writing Θ as a disjoint union of sets on straight lines, and there is, offhand, no reason to prefer one over any of the others. Also, compared to other possibilities, the degree of the resulting interpolating polynomial may be much higher than is necessary.

Finally, the most intriguing method for me was one I learned from the thesis of Kergin,[4] and which seems to have been inspired by Pierre Milman (see, for example, Reference 5). Here, one interpolates at the $k + 1$ points in Θ by polynomials of degree $\leq k$, exactly as in the univariate case. Of course, one must then deal with all the additional degrees of freedom available from $\Pi_k(\mathbb{R}^d)$ when $d > 1$. These are used in the Kergin scheme to make sure that various mean-value theorems hold for the interpolant Kf to given f, of the following kind:

Mean-Value Conditions. *For every subset* T *of* Θ, *and for every homogeneous polynomial q of degree j* : = #T $- 1$, *there exists some point τ in the convex hull of* T *at which* $q(D)(f - Kf)(\tau) = 0$.

Here and below, $p(D)$ is the constant-coefficient differential operator $\sum_\alpha c(\alpha) D^\alpha$ obtained by "evaluating" the polynomial $p : x \mapsto \sum_\alpha c(\alpha) x^\alpha$ at $x = D$.

Kergin proves that there is exactly one linear projector K on $C^{(k)}(\mathbb{R}^d)$ into Π_k that satisfies all the Mean-Value Conditions. This makes it possible even to let some Θ coalesce and thereby obtain Hermite interpolation in the limit. For example, if all the points coalesce at some point z, then Kf is necessarily the Taylor expansion of f, at z, to terms of order k.

Kergin interpolation is particularly close to univariate polynomial interpolation in the sense that, when applied to any "plane wave" $f : x \mapsto g(\vartheta * x)$ (with g some univariate function), then

$$(Kf)(x) = (I_{\vartheta*_\Theta}g)(\vartheta*x)$$

with $I_{\vartheta*_\Theta}g$ the *uni*variate interpolant to g, at the points

$$\vartheta*\Theta := \{\vartheta*\theta : \theta \in \Theta\}$$

I am particularly fond of Kergin interpolation since it led Micchelli[6] to the recurrence relations for simplex splines and so started the outpouring of work on multivariate B-splines of the last ten years. But, as a means of multivariate polynomial interpolation, its greatest drawback is the fact that the interpolant it provides has a much higher degree than may be required.

Of course, I am free to make all these negative comments about other people's efforts because I am about to describe a new effort, by my colleague Amos Ron and myself, that avoids all the difficulties I complained about. I leave it to you and others to complain about the flaws in our approach.

3. NEW APPROACH

The approach centers on constructing a map

$$\Theta \mapsto \Pi_\Theta$$

that assigns to each finite point set $\Theta \in \mathbb{R}^d$ a polynomial space Π_Θ for which $\langle \Theta, \Pi_\Theta \rangle$ is correct.

Since almost any polynomial space P with $\dim P = \#\Theta$ gives a correct $\langle \Theta, P \rangle$, it would be good to have some guidelines. I give now a commented list of desired properties, based on the list Amos Ron put together when he talked about our scheme a year ago at the Texas A&M Approximation Theory meeting.

P1: well-defined, that is, $\langle \Theta, \Pi_\Theta \rangle$ should be correct, regardless of the choice of Θ.

P2: continuity (if possible), that is, small changes in Θ should not change Π_Θ by much. There are limits to this. For example, if $\Theta \subset \mathbb{R}^2$ consists of three points, then one would usually choose $\Pi_\Theta = \Pi_1$. But, as one of these points approaches some point between the two other points, this choice has to change in the limit, hence it cannot change continuously. As it turns out (see Reference 7), our scheme is continuous at every Θ for which $\Pi_k \subseteq \Pi_\Theta \subseteq \Pi_{k+1}$ for some k.

P3: coalescence $\Rightarrow$ osculation (if possible), that is, as points coalesce, Lagrange interpolation should approach Hermite interpolation. This, of course, depends on just how the coalescence takes place. If, for example, a point spirals in on another, then we cannot hope for osculation. But if, for example, one point approaches another along a straight line, then we are entitled to obtain, in the limit, a match at that point also of the directional derivative in the direction of that line.

P4: translation-invariance, that is,

$$\forall \{p \in \Pi_\Theta, a \in \mathbb{R}^d\} \; p(a + \cdot) \in \Pi_\Theta$$

This means that Π_Θ is independent of the choice of origin, and it implies that Π_Θ is *D-invariant*, that is, it is closed under differentiation.

P5: coordinate-system independence, that is, a linear change of variables $x \mapsto Ax$ (for some invertible matrix A) should affect Π_Θ in a reasonable way. Precisely,

$$\forall \{\text{invertible } A\} \; \Pi_{A\Theta} = \Pi_\Theta \cdot A^T$$

This implies that Π_Θ inherits any symmetries that Θ may have. It also implies (with a line or two of argument) that each $p \in \Pi_\Theta$ is constant along any lines orthogonal to the affine hull of Θ.

P6: dilation-invariance, that is,

$$\forall \{p \in \Pi_\Theta, \alpha \in \mathbb{R}\} \; p(\alpha \cdot) \in \Pi_\Theta$$

This implies that Π_Θ is spanned by homogeneous polynomials. Note that P4 and P6 together are quite restrictive in the sense that the only spaces of smooth functions satisfying P4 and P6 are polynomial spaces.

P7: minimal degree, that is, the elements of Π_Θ should have as small a degree as is possible, since we would like the same property for the resulting interpolant. Here is the precise description:

$$\langle \Theta, P \rangle \text{ correct} \Rightarrow \forall j \; \dim P \cap \Pi_j \leq \dim \Pi_\Theta \cap \Pi_j$$

Equivalently,

$$\mathrm{deg}_{I_\Theta}p \leq \mathrm{deg}p \qquad \text{for every} \qquad p \in \Pi$$

This implies, for example, that if $\langle \Theta, \Pi_k \rangle$ is correct, then $\Pi_\Theta = \Pi_k$. In other words, in the most heavily studied case, namely of Θ for which Π_k is an acceptable choice, our assignment would also be Π_k.

P8: monotonicity, that is,

$$\Theta \subset \Theta' \Rightarrow \Pi_\Theta \subset \Pi_{\Theta'}$$

This makes it possible to develop a Newton form for the interpolant. Also, in conjunction with P2, P7, and P9, this ties our scheme closely to standard choices.

P9: Cartesian product $\Rightarrow$ tensor product, that is,

$$\Pi_{\Theta \times \Theta'} = \Pi_\Theta \otimes \Pi_{\Theta'}$$

In this way, our assignment in the case of a rectangular grid coincides with the assignment standard for that case. In fact, by P8, it coincides with the standard assignment even when Θ is a **shadow** subset of a rectangular grid

$$\underset{i=1}{\overset{d}{\times}} \{xi(1), \ldots, xi(\gamma(i))\}$$

that is, $\theta = \{\theta_\alpha : \alpha \in \Gamma\}$ for

$$\theta_\alpha := (x1(\alpha(1)), \ldots, xd(\alpha(d)))$$

with

$$\alpha \in C_\gamma := \{1, \ldots, \gamma(1)\} \times \cdots \times \{1, \ldots, \gamma(d)\}$$

and Γ an **order-closed** subset of C_γ, that is, $\alpha \in \Gamma$ and $\beta \leq \alpha$ implies $\beta \in \Gamma$. Thus,

$$\Gamma = \bigcup_{\alpha \in \Gamma} C_\alpha$$

Since, for any $\alpha \in \Gamma$, the subset

$$\Theta_\alpha := \{\theta_\beta : \beta \in C_\alpha\}$$

of Θ is a Cartesian product of sets from $\mathbb{R}$, our assignment for it is necessarily

$$\Pi_\alpha := \mathrm{span}\{(\ )^\alpha : \beta \le \alpha\}$$

by P9. By P8, each such Π_α must be contained in Π_Θ, hence

$$\mathrm{span}\{(\ )^\beta : \beta \in \Gamma\} \subset \Pi_\Theta$$

and, since

$$\dim\Pi_\Theta = \#\Theta = \#\Gamma$$

Π_Θ must coincide with that span. Here and below,

$$(\ )^\beta : x \mapsto x^\beta := x_1^{\beta(1)} \cdots x_d^{\beta(d)}$$

is a self-evident notation for the power map.

P10: constructible, that is, it should be possible to produce Π_Θ in finitely many arithmetic steps.

This list is detailed enough to determine Π_Θ uniquely in certain simple situations. For example, if $\#\Pi_\Theta = 1$, then necessarily $\Pi_\Theta = \Pi_0$ (by P7). If $\#\Theta = 2$, then, by P5 and P7, necessarily $\Pi_\Theta = \Pi_1(\mathrm{affine}(\Theta)) :=$ all linear polynomials that are constant in any direction perpendicular to the affine hull of Θ, that is, to the straight line containing Θ. If $\#\Theta = 3$, then $\Pi_\Theta = \Pi_k(\mathrm{affine}(\Theta))$, with $k := 3 - \dim \mathrm{affine}(\Theta)$. The case $\#\Theta = 4$ is the first one that is not clear-cut. In this case, we again have

$$\Pi_\Theta = \Pi_k(\mathrm{affine}(\Theta)), \qquad k := 4 - \dim \mathrm{affine}(\Theta)$$

but only for $k = 1, 3$. When $\mathrm{affine}(\Theta)$ is a plane, we can use P4–P6 to normalize to the situation that $\Theta \subset \mathbb{R}^2$ and $\Theta = \{0, (1, 0), (0, 1), \theta\}$, with θ, offhand, arbitrary. Since Π_1 is the choice for the set $\{0, (1, 0), (0, 1)\}$, this means that $\Pi_\Theta = \Pi_1 + \mathrm{span}\{q\}$ for some homogeneous quadratic polynomial q. While P4–P6 impose further restrictions, it seems possible to construct a suitable map $\mathbb{R}^2 \to \Pi_2^0 : \theta \mapsto q$ (into *homogeneous* quadratic polynomials) in many ways so that the resulting $\Theta \mapsto \Pi_\Theta$ has all the properties

P1–P10, except P8 perhaps. But neither Amos Ron nor I have so far been able to show that there is only one map $\Theta \mapsto \Pi_\Theta$ satisfying all conditions P1–P10. On the other hand, it can be shown (see Reference 8) that

$$\Pi_\Theta = \cap_{p_{|\Theta}=0} \ker p_\uparrow(D)$$

with $p_\uparrow$ the **leading term** of the polynomial p, that is, the unique homogeneous polynomial for which $\deg(p - p_\uparrow) < \deg p$.

Of course, we did not make up the above list and then set out to find the map $\Theta \mapsto \Pi_\Theta$. Rather, Amos Ron noticed that the pair $\langle \Theta, (\exp_\Theta)_\downarrow \rangle$ is always correct, and this motivated us to study the assignment

$$\Pi_\Theta := (\exp_\Theta)_\downarrow$$

To explain,

$$H := \exp_\Theta := \mathrm{span}(e_\vartheta)_{\vartheta \in \Theta}$$

with

$$e_\vartheta : x \mapsto e^{\vartheta \cdot x}$$

the **exponential** with **frequency** ϑ. Further, for any space H of smooth functions,

$$H_\downarrow := \mathrm{span}\{f_\downarrow : f \in H\}$$

with $f_\downarrow$, the **least** of f, the first nontrivial term in the power series expansion

$$f = f^{(0)} + f^{(1)} + f^{(2)} + \cdots$$

for f, in which $f^{(j)}$ is the sum of all terms of (homogeneous) degree j, all j. Thus, $f_\downarrow$ is the homogeneous polynomial of largest degree for which

$$f = f_\downarrow + \text{higher order terms}.$$

It is not difficult to verify that this assignment satisfies P4–P6, P8–P9, and I will take up P10 in a moment. But it may not be clear why this has anything to do with interpolation.

4. REPRESENTATION OF POINT EVALUATION BY AN EXPONENTIAL

To make the connection, you need to be aware of the fact that the rule

$$\langle p, f \rangle := p(D)f(0)$$

defines a pairing between polynomials p and smooth functions f and that e_ϑ represents the linear functional $p \mapsto p(\vartheta)$ with respect to this pairing, that is,

$$\langle p, e_\vartheta \rangle = p(\vartheta)$$

Further, $\langle \cdot, \cdot \rangle$ is an inner product on (real) polynomials, as can be seen from the fact that

$$\langle p, q \rangle = \sum_\alpha \frac{(D^\alpha p)(0)(D^\alpha q)(0)}{\alpha!}, \qquad p, q \in \Pi \tag{1}$$

This suggests (as detailed in Reference 7) the construction of a basis for $H_\downarrow$ of the form $g_{1\downarrow}, \ldots, g_{n\downarrow}$ so that $\langle g_{i\downarrow}, g_j \rangle = 0$ if and only if $i \neq j$, with g_1, $g_2, \ldots, g_n$ a basis for H constructed from a basis $f_1, f_2, \ldots, f_n$ for H by a variant of the Gram–Schmidt process. Specifically, with suitable g_1, g_2, $\ldots, g_{j-1}$ already available (and spanning the same space as $f_1, f_2, \ldots, f_{j-1}$), one would compute

$$g_j := f_j - \sum_{i<j} g_i \frac{\langle g_{i\downarrow}, f_j \rangle}{\langle g_{i\downarrow}, g_i \rangle}$$

thereby ensuring that

$$\langle g_{i\downarrow}, g_j \rangle = 0, \qquad i < j \tag{2}$$

while $g_j \neq 0$ (by the linear independence of the f_i), and therefore $\langle g_{j\downarrow}, g_j \rangle$ $\neq 0$. The further modification

$$g_i \leftarrow g_i - g_j \frac{\langle g_{j\downarrow}, g_i \rangle}{\langle g_{j\downarrow}, g_j \rangle}$$

does not disturb the biorthogonality in Equation 2 already achieved, and it guarantees that

$$\langle g_{j\downarrow}, g_i \rangle = 0, \qquad i < j$$

In this way, one obtains a basis $g_1, g_2, \ldots, g_n$ for H for which

$$\langle g_{j\downarrow}, g_i \rangle = 0 \Leftrightarrow i \neq j$$

But this implies that the matrix $(\langle g_{i\downarrow}, g_j \rangle)$ is invertible, hence (since $g_1, g_2, \ldots, g_n$ and $f_1, f_2, \ldots, f_n$ are bases for the same space) the matrix $(\langle g_{i\downarrow}, f_j \rangle)$ is also invertible. If we start this calculation specifically with $f_j := e_{\vartheta_j}$ for all j, then this last matrix equals

$$(g_{i\downarrow}(\vartheta_j))$$

and this proves that the pair $\langle \{\vartheta_1, \ldots, \vartheta_n\}, H_\downarrow \rangle$ is correct. Further, for given f,

$$\sum_i g_{i\downarrow} \frac{\langle f, g_i \rangle}{\langle g_{i\downarrow}, g_i \rangle}$$

is the unique interpolant to f from $H_\downarrow = \Pi_\Theta$, with

$$\langle f, g_i \rangle := \sum_j a_{ij} f(\vartheta_j)$$

in case $g_i =: \sum_j a_{ij} f_j$.

5. NUMERICS

Actual calculations depend a bit on just how one intends to represent this interpolant. While it is possible in principle to use a Newton form, it seems, as a first try, sufficient to write the interpolant in power form. One would want to shift this form, for example by the average of the ϑ_j, to avoid an obvious source of bad condition. For simplicity, I will ignore here this shift. Further, it seems advisable to use the **modified power form**

$$p = \sum_{\alpha} \frac{|\alpha|!}{\alpha!} (\ )^{\alpha} \frac{D^{\alpha}p(0)}{|\alpha|!}$$

since its evaluation by the following "nested multiplication" (or "Horner's scheme") is immediate. (I have not been able to find this technique in the literature, but I have not looked for it very hard, either.) In this scheme, one sets

$$c(\alpha) := \frac{D^{\alpha}p(0)}{|\alpha|!}, \qquad |\alpha| = \deg p$$

and generates from this

$$c(\alpha) := \frac{D^{\alpha}p(0)}{|\alpha|!} + \sum_{i=1}^{d} x_i c(\alpha + i_i), \qquad |\alpha| = k$$

for $k = \deg p - 1, \deg p - 2, \ldots, 0$, with i_i the ith unit vector. This works because one obtains

$$c(0) = \sum_{|\alpha| \le \deg p} \frac{D^{\alpha}p(0)}{|\alpha|!} n_{\alpha} x^{\alpha}$$

with n_{α} the number of different increasing paths to α from the origin through points of $\mathbb{Z}_+^d$. This number is

$$n_{\alpha} = \binom{|\alpha|}{\alpha} = \frac{|\alpha|!}{\alpha!}$$

hence $c(0) = p(x)$.

Thus the goal of the calculation are the numbers

$$\frac{D^{\alpha}p(0)}{|\alpha|!}$$

for the interpolant p, and the calculations involve the scalar product

$$\langle p, q \rangle = \sum_{\alpha} \frac{(D^{\alpha}p)(0)(D^{\alpha}q)(0)}{\alpha!}$$

with $p \in \Pi$ and q "smooth". This implies that it is sufficient in the calculations to deal with any function g entirely in terms of the (first few entries in the) corresponding vector

$$Dg := (D^\alpha g(0))$$

(except for the function f to be interpolated, for which we know, offhand, nothing other than the vector $f_{|\Theta} = (f(\vartheta) : \vartheta \in \Theta))$. Note that $D(g_\downarrow)$ is obtained from Dg by direct truncation, hence also the needed computational step of obtaining $g_\downarrow$ from g can be carried out trivially in terms of the vector Dg.

While actual calculations require the imposition of some ordering on the points $\vartheta \in \Theta$ and the integer vectors $\alpha \in \mathbb{Z}_+^d$, it is more convenient, and less messy notationally, not to stress this computational requirement. Thus, for the time being, I let the ϑ in Θ and the $\alpha \in \mathbb{Z}_+^d$ index themselves. This means that our calculations start with the matrix

$$V := (D^\alpha e_\vartheta(0) : \vartheta \in \Theta, \alpha \in \mathbb{Z}_+^d)$$

whose rows are indexed by $\vartheta \in \Theta$ and whose columns are indexed by $\alpha \in \mathbb{Z}_+^d$. Since $p(D)e_\vartheta = p(\vartheta)$ for any polynomial p, the matrix V is the **Vandermonde** matrix for Θ, that is,

$$V = (\vartheta^\alpha : \vartheta \in \Theta, \alpha \in \mathbb{Z}_+^d)$$

This suggests the following slight detour, and this detour provides some insight into the special nature of our assignment $\Theta \mapsto \Pi_\Theta$.

6. CONNECTION TO GAUSS ELIMINATION

Consider, for the moment, the possibility that we have not yet made up our minds from which polynomial subspace P to interpolate at Θ. We could then consider all possible choices for P by looking at the linear system

$$V? = f_{|\Theta} \tag{3}$$

Any solution c with all but finitely many of its entries zero provides a polynomial, namely the polynomial $p := \sum_\alpha (\ )^\alpha c(\alpha)$, that agrees with f on

Θ, and vice versa. We could now try to determine particularly "good" interpolants p. A possible criterion is that p have smallest possible degree. We could achieve this by ordering the columns of V by degree, that is, by $|\alpha|$, and then applying **elimination,** that is, Gauss elimination with partial pivoting, to V, in just the way it is taught in Linear Algebra courses. The result is a factorization

$$LW = V$$

with L unit lower triangular, and W in row echelon form. This means that there is a sequence $\beta_1, \beta_2, \ldots, \beta_n$ that is strictly increasing, in the same total ordering of $\mathbb{Z}_+^d$ that was used to order the columns of V, and so that, for some ordering $\{\vartheta_1, \vartheta_2, \ldots, \vartheta_n\}$ of Θ and for all j, the entry $W(\vartheta_j, \beta_j)$ is the first nonzero entry in the row $W(\vartheta_j, :)$ of W. This makes the square matrix

$$U := (W(\vartheta_i, \beta_j) : i, j = 1, \ldots, n)$$

upper triangular and invertible, and so provides the particular interpolant $\sum_i (\ )^{\beta_i} \alpha(i)$, whose coefficient vector

$$a := (LU)^{-1}(f(\vartheta_1), \ldots, f(\vartheta_n)) \tag{4}$$

is obtainable from the original data $f_{|\Theta}$ by permutation followed by forward- and back substitution.

There is no reason to believe that the resulting sequence $\beta_1, \beta_2, \ldots, \beta_n$ always consists of consecutive terms. It is exactly this fact that has prevented the development of a simple theory of multivariate polynomial interpolation. Rather, elimination has to face the numerical difficulty of deciding when all the pivots available for the current step in the current column are "practically zero", in which case the pivot search is extended to the entries in the next column (and in any row not yet used as pivot row). But this can also be viewed positively. Just as partial row pivoting has the "smallness" of the factors L and U as its goal, so the additional freedom of column pivoting allowed here provides further means of keeping the factors L and U "small". The smaller these factors, the better is the condition of the corresponding basis $((\ )^{\beta_j} : j = 1, \ldots, n)$ for the polynomial space P selected, when considered as a space of functions on Θ.

Surprisingly, the computational process for Π_Θ outlined earlier differs from this straightforward approach in only one detail: the entries of V are grouped by polynomial degree. In effect, V is viewed as the matrix

$$V := (D^k f_\vartheta(0)) = (\vartheta^k : \vartheta \in \Theta, \, k = 0, 1, 2, \cdots) \qquad (5)$$

with *vector* entries

$$\vartheta^k := (\vartheta^\alpha : |\alpha| = k)$$

Note that

$$D^k g := (D^\alpha g(0) : |\alpha| = k)$$

represents the nontrivial part of $D(g_\downarrow)$ in case $g_\downarrow$ has degree k. Now we cannot expect elimination to zero out all entries in the pivot column below the pivot row. We can merely expect to make these entries *orthogonal* to the pivot element. The particular scalar product relevant here is

$$\langle D^k g, D^k q \rangle := \sum_{|\alpha|=k} \frac{D^\alpha g(0) D^\alpha q(0)}{\alpha!}$$

since, with this definition and in terms of the scalar product in Equation 1 for polynomials defined earlier,

$$\langle g_\downarrow, q \rangle = \langle g_\downarrow, q^{(k)} \rangle = \langle D^k g, D^k q \rangle$$

in case $k := \deg g_\downarrow$.

It is now easy to verify (see Reference 9) that the earlier Gram–Schmidt-like algorithm, applied to $f_j := e_{\vartheta_j}, j = 1, \ldots, n$, is Gauss elimination with *column* pivoting applied to the matrix in Equation 5. Once this is understood, it is also understood that Gauss elimination with *row* pivoting (that is, with possible reordering of the points in Θ) is just as effective. In fact, row pivoting provides the mechanism for choosing a "good" order in which to introduce the interpolation points into the calculations. Note that elimination with row pivoting necessarily leads to the same polynomial space, since Π_Θ does not depend on any particular ordering of the points in Θ and, with the ordering suggested by Gauss elimination with row pivoting, the two algorithms coincide.

This last remark is but one example of the importance of the theoretical underpinnings provided by Reference 7, even though the calculations turn out to be nothing more than Gauss elimination (with a twist). For example, is it obvious from these calculations alone that $\Pi_\Theta \subset \Pi_{\Theta'}$, in case $\Theta \subset \Theta'$, or that, during Gauss elimination with partial pivoting, the next column has to contain a nontrivial pivot if the current column fails to contain one?

7. COMPUTATIONAL DETAILS

The calculations can be organized as follows. At the jth step, one looks for a pivot of the current order k among the rows not yet used as pivot rows. This means that one looks for $i \geq j$ that maximizes

$$\frac{\langle D^k g_i, D^k g_i \rangle}{\langle D^k f_i, D^k f_i \rangle}$$

Here and below, g_i denotes the function obtained from $f_i := f_{\vartheta_i}$ by the elimination process as carried out so far; specifically,

$$g_i \perp g_{j_l} \quad \text{for} \quad l < j \leq i$$

A row interchange (in all pertinent matrices) is made to bring the relatively largest pivot "element" into row j; k_j is set to the current k; and the appropriate multiple

$$\text{LU}(i, j) := \frac{\langle D^k g_j, D^k g_i \rangle'}{\langle D^k g_j, D^k g_j \rangle'} \tag{6}$$

of row j is subtracted from row i for all $i > j$. Here, the scalar product

$$\langle D^k g, D^k f \rangle' := \langle D^k g, D^k f \rangle k! = \sum_{|\alpha|=k} \frac{|\alpha|!}{\alpha!} D^\alpha g(0) D^\alpha f(0) \tag{7}$$

is used instead of $\langle D^k g, D^k f \rangle$, since this makes the requisite weights integers (the multinomial coefficients), but it does not change the ratios in Equation 6.

It seems computationally efficient to compute the entire column LU $(:, j)$ by Equation 6, for later use, but set

$$\text{LU}(j,j) := \langle D^k g_j, D^k g_j \rangle'$$

It may of course happen that

$$\frac{\langle D^k g_i, D^k g_i \rangle}{\langle D^k f_i, D^k f_i \rangle} < \text{tol}, \qquad \forall i \geq j$$

with tol some necessarily assigned tolerance. Then it is time to increase the order k by one and look again. As claimed earlier, there must now be some nonzero pivot available (though there is no guarantee that it will pass our tolerance test). Since we have no way of knowing *a priori* what the maximal degree in Π_Θ is going to be, it seems best to generate the columns of V as needed. Thus, at this stage, we must generate

$$V_k := (\vartheta^\alpha : \vartheta \in \Theta, \ |\alpha| = k)$$

for the new value of k. It seems most efficient to assume that, at this point, we still have in hand V_{k-1}, hence we can generate V_k by the appropriate multiplication of the entries of V_{k-1} by the components of the ϑ_r. The initial V_0 is the $n \times 1$-matrix $[1, 1, \ldots, 1]^T$. Further, having recorded the earlier elimination steps $1, \ldots, j-1$ in LU, we can compute the vectors $D^k g_i$ from V_k by forward substitution, that is, by applying L_j^{-1} from the left, with L_j the unit lower triangular matrix that agrees with LU in its first $j-1$ columns and below the diagonal, and has zeros otherwise.

In the end, we have available in our working array all the relevant entries of the vectors $Dg_i = (D^\alpha g_i(0) : \alpha)$; hence we can construct our interpolant p in the form $\sum_i g_i c(i)$, with

$$c := D^{-1} U^{-1} L^{-1} \left(f(\vartheta_1), \ldots, f(\vartheta_n) \right)$$

and with L, U, and D the unit lower triangular, unit upper triangular, and diagonal matrix, respectively, whose nontrivial terms we stored in the array LU. Actually, since we have used the scalar product in Equation 7, $c(i)$ is too small by a factor $(\deg g_i)!$, hence just right for the modified power form discussed earlier.

8. INTERPOLATION AT THE VERTICES OF A REGULAR HEXAGON

Figure 1 shows (part of) the polynomial interpolant to the data $f(\vartheta_j) = (-1)^j$, with

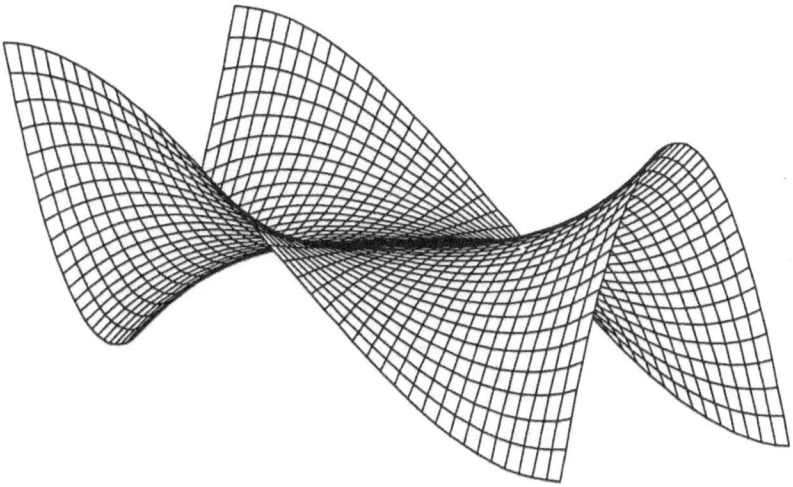

Figure 5.1. The cubic term in interpolation at the hexagon points.

$$\vartheta_j := (\cos(2\pi j/6), \sin(2\pi j/6)), \qquad j = 1, \ldots, 6$$

For six generic points in the plane, one expects to interpolate from Π_2 since its dimension is 6. but these particular six points lie on the unit circle, that is, the quadratic polynomial

$$p_2 := 1 - (\ )^{2,0} - (\ )^{0,2}$$

vanishes on Θ, so Π_2 cannot be correct for this Θ. Since any five of these points are linearly independent over Π_2, we know that Π_Θ has the form

$$\Pi_\Theta = \Pi_1 + (\Pi_2^0 \ominus \text{span}(p_2)) + \text{span}(p_3)$$

with the orthogonal complement in the space Π_2^0 of homogeneous second-degree polynomials taken in terms of the scalar product in Equation 1, and with p_3 a particular homogeneous cubic polynomial. In fact, p_3 coincides, up to a scalar multiple, with the interpolant depicted in Figure 1, for the following reason: By symmetry, there are three straight lines through the origin that do not contain any interpolation point and are such that reflection across any one of them leaves Θ invariant but changes the given function values to their negatives, hence this reflection must change the interpolant to its negative, and therefore the interpolant must vanish along these three lines. But this implies that all its derivatives of

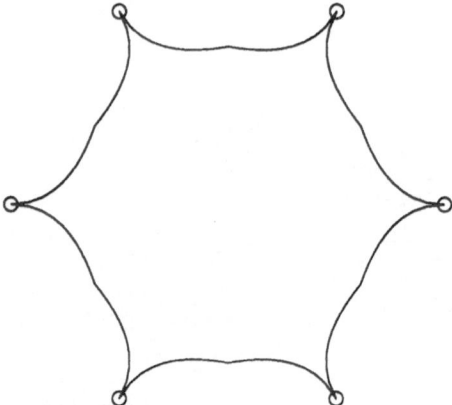

Figure 5.2. The Lebesgue function for interpolation at the hexagon points ○ equals 1 on this entire domain.

order ≤ 2 at the origin must be zero. This argument, incidentally, shows that, for this (highly symmetric) Θ, the Properties P1–P10 uniquely determine Π_Θ.

This resolves in a simple way the following puzzle: Since in this case $A\Theta = \Theta$ for $A :=$ rotation by $\pi/3$, we know from Property P5 that $\Pi_\Theta = \Pi_\Theta \cdot A$. Since, up to scalar multiples, p_3 is the unique cubic homogeneous polynomial in Π_Θ, this leads to the (careless) conclusion that p_3 must have the symmetry $p_3 = p_3 \cdot A$. But that implies that p_3 is constant on Θ, hence necessarily coincident with the appropriate multiple of the constant function $(\ )^0$ (note that Π_0 is contained in any Π_Θ, by Properties P7 and P8). The picture reminds us of the fact that, strictly speaking, we only know that $\mathrm{span}(p_3) = \mathrm{span}(p_3) \cdot A$, for, according to the picture, $p_3 \cdot A = -p_3$.

The Lagrange polynomial associated with the point $(1,0)$ is given by

$$l(x) := ((1 + 2x_1 + 2x_1^2 + x_1^3) - x_2^2(2 + 3x_1))/6$$

This makes it easy to determine its zero set, hence to see that it and its five rotates are nonnegative on a rather large portion of the hexagon. This domain is shown in Figure 2. At any point of this domain, the value of the interpolating polynomial is an average of the given function values. Equivalently, the Lebesgue function of the process (that is, the sum of the absolute values of all the Lagrange polynomials) is 1 on this entire domain. In univariate polynomial interpolation, the Lebesgue function is 1 on a set larger than just the interpolation points only for linear interpolation.

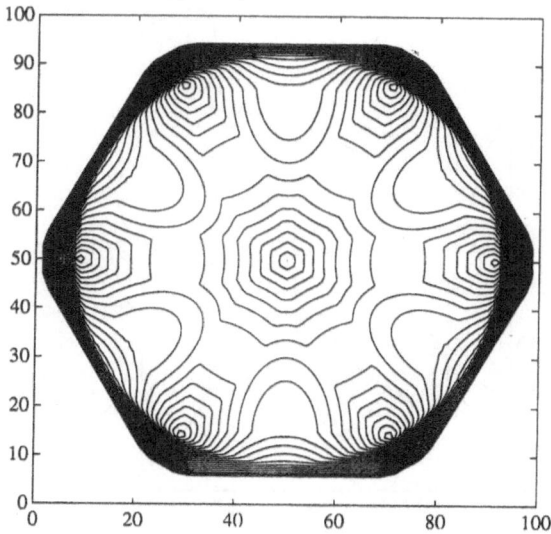

Figure 5.3. Contour lines for values 1, 1.05 . . . , 2 of Lebesgue function for interpolating at hexagon points and their center.

For the hexagon points, Π_Θ does not contain Π_2; hence the interpolant provides only a second-order approximation (as we let the diameter of the circle of points shrink). By also adding the center of the circle, Π_Θ becomes $\Pi_2 + \text{span}(p_3)$ (by P7 and P8). The additional function is the polynomial p_2 mentioned earlier; it serves as the Lagrange polynomial for the new point. The other Lagrange polynomials are $l - p_2/6$ and its five rotates. Now the Lebesgue function equals 1 only at the interpolation points. But, as Figure 3 shows, the Lebesgue function does not exceed 1.5 on the hexagon spanned by the points, and it does not exceed 1.7 on the unit disk. This says that, as a map on continuous functions on the unit disk in the max-norm, this interpolation scheme has norm less than 1.7. That is remarkable.

9. INTERPOLATION AT 40 RANDOMLY CHOSEN POINTS

Figure 4 shows contour lines (corresponding to ten equally spaced function values between maximum and minimum value) of the absolute error in the polynomial interpolant to

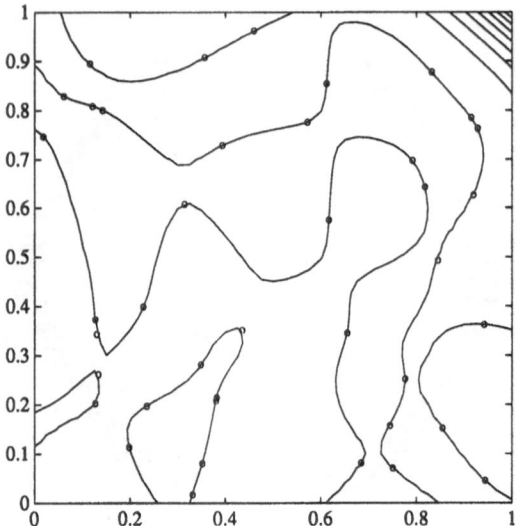

Figure 5.4. Contour lines for error in interpolating at 40 random points.

$$f: x \mapsto \exp(-x_1^2 - x_2^2)$$

at 40 points chosen at random from the square $[0 \ . \ . \ 1]^2$. These interpolation points are also marked in Figure 4. Not surprisingly, they all fall on the zero contour line and so indicate that the error is near zero in most of the square. Only near the corners of the square is the error not close to zero. In fact, the maximum error on the square $[0 \ . \ . \ 1]^2$ turned out to be $2.6e - 4$. (The calculations were done with MATLAB, hence in roughly 16-decimal-digit arithmetic. The maximum difference between the input function values and the corresponding values of the computed interpolating polynomial was $7.8e - 16$.) Examples like these are making me re-examine the standard conviction that polynomial interpolation at many points is not expected to be useful. It may well be that this is less true in several variables than in one, since, in several variables, the polynomial degree usually grows much slower than the number of data points if an interpolating polynomial of smallest possible degree is used. On the other hand, there is no reason to expect that the Lebesgue function behaves any better in several variables than in one.

ACKNOWLEDGMENTS. This research was supported by the National Science Foundation under Grant No. DMS-8701275 and by the US Army under contract no. DAAL03-87-K-0030.

References

1. Chung, K. C., and Yao, T. H. "On lattices admitting unique Lagrange interpolations." *SIAM J. Numer. Anal.* **14**, 735–741 (1977).
2. Dahmen, W., and Micchelli, C. A. "On limits of multivariate B-splines." *J. Anal. Math.* **39**, 256–278 (1981).
3. Gasca, M., and Maeztu, J. I. "On Lagrange and Hermite interpolation in $\mathbb{R}^k$." *Numer. Math.* **39**, 1–14 (1982).
4. Kergin, P. "Interpolation of C^k Functions," Ph.D. diss., Univ. of Toronto, Canada, (1978); published as: "A natural interpolation of C^k functions." *J. Approx. Theory* **29**, 278–293 (1980).
5. Micchelli, C. A., and Milman, P. "A formula for Kergin interpolation in $\mathbb{R}^k$." *J. Approx. Theory* **29**, 294–296 (1980).
6. Micchelli, C. A. "A constructive approach to Kergin interpolation in $\mathbb{R}^k$: multivariate B-splines and Lagrange interpolation." *Rocky Mt. J. Math.* **10**, 485–497 (1980).
7. de Boor, C., and Ron, A. "On multivariate polynomial interpolation." *Constr. Approx.* **6**, 287–302 (1990).
8. de Boor, C., and Ron, A. "The least solution for the polynomial interpolation problem." *Math. Z.* **210**, 347–378 (1992).
9. de Boor, C., and Ron, A. "Computational aspects of polynomial interpolation in several variables." *Math. Comp.* **58**, 705–727 (1992).

6

Exterior Point Algorithm for Linear Programming Implemented on the SX-2 Supercomputer

L. Duane Pyle† and Sang-Ha Kim

1. INTRODUCTION

In introducing three survey articles by Anstreicher, Monma and Wright,[1] the editor of the March 1989 *SIAM News* made the following comments about linear programming (LP) problems:

> According to current estimates, more than \$100 million in human and computer time is invested yearly in the formulation and solution of linear programming problems. Businesses, large and small, use linear programming models to optimize communications systems and to schedule transportation networks, to control inventories, to plan portfolios, to maximize output . . .
>
> Invented in the mid-1940s by George Dantzig and improved in various ways in the intervening four decades, the simplex method continues to be the workhorse algorithm for solving linear programming problems. It is no wonder, then, that the announcement in 1984 of a method [AT&T researcher N. Karmarkar's Projective algorithm[2]] with the potential for dramatic improvement in computational effectiveness over the simplex method made front-page news in major newspapers and magazines throughout the country.

† Deceased.

L. Duane Pyle • University of Houston   Sang-Ha Kim • Korea Institute for Science and Technology

Studies in Computer Science, edited by John R. Rice and Richard A. DeMillo. Plenum Press, New York, 1994.

The set of solutions of an LP problem can be shown to consist of points that simultaneously (1) satisfy a related linear system, (2) are non-negative, and (3) satisfy a saddle point condition given in the duality theorem of LP.[3] If bounded point sets satisfying Properties 1 and 2 form a convex polyhedron

$\wedge$: Set of all convex linear combinations of a

finite number of extreme points and vertices

Algorithms for solving LP problems can be classified by type of sequence generated relative to $\wedge$, as follows: boundary point (B), interior point (I), and exterior point (E). Most research to date has been concerned with either B or I: type algorithms—the Simplex algorithm (Type B), Karmarkar's projective algorithm (Type I). The only Type E algorithms mentioned in the three *SIAM NEWS* articles previously cited are Phase I procedures employed to generate an initial (boundary or interior) point that, in general is not a solution.

Boundary Point and Interior Point algorithms typically generate a sequence of points that satisfy Properties 1 and 2; the goal is to terminate in a point satisfying Property 3. The worst case performance of the Boundary Point and Interior Point algorithms that has been implemented in commercial LP problem-solving systems is intimately associated with the complexity of the vertex structure of $\wedge$.

Whether designed to solve LP or nonlinear programming problems, each of the following six Boundary Point and Interior Point algorithms makes essential use of a projector P that is orthogonal in an inner-product space associated with the weighted generalized inverse of a related matrix:[4]

- Simplex algorithm (B.1)[5]
- Generalized Simplex algorithm (B.2)[6]
- Gradient Projection algorithm (B.3)[7]
- Variable Metric algorithm (B.4)[8]
- Interior Gradient Projection algorithm (I.1)[9]
- Affine Scaling algorithm (I.2)[10]

This common feature suggests that new techniques for solving LP and nonlinear and integer programming problems can be found by viewing the mathematical structure of optimization problems from the perspective of the generalized inverse and its related constructs. The Static and Dynamic Proximity Map algorithms discussed here are Type E algorithms that illustrate this idea. These algorithms generate a sequence of points that satisfy Properties 1 and 3; the goal is to terminate in a point satisfying Property 2. While such sequences appear to have little connection with the complexity of the vertex structure of the polyhedron $\wedge$, this remains an open question.

It is interesting to note that although in the worst case, the Simplex algorithm is an exponential time algorithm, whereas the Projective algorithm[2] is a polynomial time algorithm, the algorithm that AT&T has implemented in its hardware and software system KORBX is the Dikin, Karmarkar et al. Affine Scaling algorithm.[10] Referring to the Affine Scaling algorithm, Anstreicher observes that at present,

> There is no polynomial complexity result for the algorithm, and indeed such a result appears to be unlikely due to the properties of its continuous extension (the limit of the algorithm as the stepsize goes to zero). In particular, with a bad starting point the affine scaling algorithm is susceptible to the same Klee–Minty examples that show the simplex method to be capable of exponential behavior in the worst case. Even showing that the algorithm is convergent turns out to be relatively difficult—at present the proof requires a nondegeneracy assumption, which in practice often fails to hold.[11]

2. DUALITY THEOREM OF LINEAR PROGRAMMING—STANDARD FORM

J. von Neumann is responsible for the supposition of this theorem, which owes its proof to Gale, Kuhn, and Tucker.[3]

> If $\tilde{x}$ is feasible for the primal problem, then $\tilde{x}$ is optimal if and only if there exists $\tilde{W}$, feasible for the dual problem, such that $(\tilde{x}, c) = (\tilde{W}, b)$.

Without loss of generality, the primal problem can be expressed as follows.

Primal.1: Maximize (x, c) where $Ax = b$, $x \geq \theta$ (θ is a vector of zeros).

Primal.1 is the special case of the primal problem obtained when M_1 and N_2 are empty.

2.1. Simplex Algorithm

It can be shown that if the set

$$\wedge = \{x \mid Ax = b \qquad x \geq \theta\}$$

is bounded, then the set V of vertices of $\wedge$ contains at least one vertex that is an optimal solution of Primal.1.[5] Thus in solving LP problems, consideration may be restricted to V.

Initiated at some vertex v, Algorithm B.1 first tests for optimality by applying the duality theorem to the problem Primal.2 whose special form is discussed in the following paragraph.

The coefficient matrix $[I, A_B^{-1}A_N]$ of Primal.2 is obtained by applying the Gauss–Jordan Reduction process to a matrix $[A_B, A_N]$ containing an appropriate permutation of the columns of A. It can be shown that if A is m by n, where $m < n$ and rank $A = m$, then (nondegenerate) vertices v of $\wedge$ correspond to partitions $[A_B, A_N]$ of the columns of A, where A_B is m by m, nonsingular, and $A_B^{-1}b > \theta$. Then except for a permutation of indices,

$$v = \begin{bmatrix} A_B^{-1}b \\ \theta \end{bmatrix}$$

If some of the elements of $A_B^{-1}b$ are zero, v is said to be degenerate.

For simplicity of exposition, assume the columns of A have been permuted so that

$$A = [A_B, A_N]$$

and consider the corresponding partition of the vector c:

$$c = \begin{bmatrix} c_B \\ c_N \end{bmatrix}$$

Letting

$$\bar{c}_N = c_N - (A_B^{-1}A_N)^T c_B$$

denote the vector of relative (also called reduced) costs,[5] it follows that

$$d = \begin{bmatrix} \theta \\ \overline{\bar{c}_N} \end{bmatrix} = c - A^T\pi$$

where

$$\pi = (A_B^T)^{-1}c_B = (A_B^{-1})^T c_B$$

Thus if

$$A\tilde{x} = b, \text{ then } (\tilde{x}, d) = (\tilde{x}, c - A^T\pi) = (\tilde{x}, c) - (\tilde{x}, A^T\pi) = (\tilde{x}, c) - (b, \pi)$$

where (b, π) is a constant.

Now defining Primal.2, maximize (x, d) where

$$[I, A_B^{-1}A_N]x = A_B^{-1}b > \theta \qquad x \geq \theta$$

it follows that Primal.1 and Primal.2 are equivalent in the sense that the respective sets of feasible and optimal solutions are identical, where

$$v = \begin{bmatrix} A_B^{-1}b \\ \theta \end{bmatrix}$$

is feasible for Primal.2.

Since the sets M_1 and N_2 corresponding to Primal.2 are empty, the associated dual is as follows.

Dual.2: Minimize $(w, A_B^{-1}b)$ where

$$\begin{bmatrix} I \\ (A_B^{-1}A_N)^T \end{bmatrix} w \geq d = \begin{bmatrix} \theta \\ \bar{c}_N \end{bmatrix} \qquad w \text{ unrestricted}$$

If $\bar{c}_N \leq \theta$, then $\tilde{w} = \theta$ is feasible for Dual.2, and since

$$(v, d) = 0 = (\tilde{w}, A_B^{-1}b)$$

it follows from the Duality theorem that the vertex v is optimal for Primal.2.

If $\bar{c}_N /\leq \theta$, at least one element $(\tilde{c}_N)_s > 0$ [typically the index s is chosen so that $(\bar{c}_N)_s = \max(\bar{c}_N)_j)$]. A vertex

$$v' = v + \alpha_{\max}E^{(s)}$$

adjacent to v can then be determined such that

$$(v', c) > (v, c)$$

where $\alpha_{\max}$ is the solution of the following (trivial) LP problem.

Line Search.1: Maximize α where $v + \alpha E^{(s)} \geq \theta$, and $E^{(s)}$ is the sth column of the n by $(n - m)$ matrix

$$\varepsilon = \begin{bmatrix} -A_B^{-1} A_N \\ I \end{bmatrix}$$

The fact that $A_B^{-1} b > \theta$ ensures that $v' \geq \theta$ for α sufficiently small, and since $A\varepsilon = 0$, $Av' = Av = b$, v' is feasible for Primal.2 (and Primal.1).

Movement along a vector $E^{(s)}$ from vertex v to an adjacent vertex v' corresponds to replacing the rth column of A_B with the sth column of A_N, where $(v)_r > 0$ and $(v')_r = 0$. This entire process, called a Algorithm B.1 iteration, is then repeated at v'. Since there is a finite number of vertices of $\wedge$, an optimal vertex is eventually obtained.

Since $\varepsilon^T c = \bar{c}_N$,

$$E^{(j)T} c = [E^{(j)}, c] = \|E^{(j)}\| \|c\| \cos\gamma j = (\bar{c}_N)_j$$

where

$$\|y\| = \sqrt{(y, y)} = (y^T y)^{1/2}$$

and γj is the angle between $E^{(j)}$ and c; thus

$$(v', c) = (v, c) + \alpha_{\max}(\bar{c}_N)_s$$

Vectors $E^{(j)}$ lie along the edges of $\wedge$ that intersect in the vertex v. There are $(n - m)$ such vectors, each in the null space of A,

$$N(A) = \{x \mid Ax = \theta\}.$$

Since the columns of ε are linearly independent, they form a basis for $N(A)$.

Letting $\eta^{(j)} = (1/\|\mathbf{E}^{(j)}\|)\mathbf{E}^{(j)}$, it follows that

$$\left(\frac{\bar{c}_j}{\|\mathbf{E}^{(j)}\|}\right)\eta^{(j)} = (\mathbf{c}, \eta^{(j)}\eta^{(j)} = \eta^{(j)}\eta^{(j)T}\mathbf{c}$$

is the orthogonal projection $[P_1(j)]\mathbf{c}$ of the gradient $\mathbf{c}$ of $(x, \mathbf{c})$ on the associated one-dimensional face of $\wedge$, where

$$\|\mathbf{E}^{(j)}\|^{-2}\mathbf{E}^{(j)}\mathbf{E}^{(j)T} = \eta^{(j)}\eta^{(j)T} = P_1(j) = [P_1(j)]^2 = [P_1(j)]^T.$$

Thus Algorithm B.1 test for optimality can be expressed in the following geometric terms: A nondegenerate vertex v is optimal if and only if the orthogonal projection of $\mathbf{c}$ on each of the $(n - m)$, one-dimensional faces of $\wedge$ that intersect in v fails to produce at least one feasible ascent path. If this test fails, then at least one (possibly many) of these projections provides a feasible ascent path leading to an adjacent vertex v' that may be similarly tested for optimality. Once the vector $\mathbf{E}^{(j)}$ is known, it is not necessary to compute the vector $\eta^{(j)}$, and/or the projector $P_1(j)$.

It has been observed however that determining the index s based on the largest $(\bar{c}_j/\|\mathbf{E}^{(j)}\|)$ value typically reduces the number of iterations required for solution. If the $\|\mathbf{E}^{(j)}\|$ computations are appropriately organized, this often results in a reduction in total execution time. This variation, which is called the Steepest Edge Simplex algorithm,[12] selects an ascent edge $\mathbf{E}^{(s)}$ at v to minimize the angle between $\mathbf{E}^{(s)}$ and $\mathbf{c}$.

2.2. Generalization of the Simplex Algorithm

Algorithm B.2,[6] extends the Algorithm B.1 by employing the following matrix form of the Gram–Schmidt orthonormalization process:

$$P_k = Z_k(Z_k^T Z_k)^{-1}Z_k^T = [P_k]^2 = [P_k]^T$$

where subsets composed of k columns chosen from ε form the n by k matrices Z_k that determine orthogonal projectors P_k and the associated orthogonal projections $P_k\mathbf{c}$ of $\mathbf{c}$ on certain k-dimensional faces P_k of $\wedge$ that intersect in the nondegenerate vertex v, where $k = 1, 2, \ldots, k_{max}$. k_{max}, which cannot exceed $(n - m)$, is determined either by the nature of the geometry of $\wedge$ at v or by imposing some upper limit suggested by computational experience. Unless an upper limit is set, k_{max} typically varies from $(n - m)$ at a minimizing vertex to 0 at a maximizing vertex.

Note that the total number of faces of $\wedge$ that intersect in a nondegenerate vertex is $2^{n-m} - 2$ and when $k_{max} = n - m$, projection is on $\wedge$.

The k linearly independent columns of ε that form Z_k are selected sequentially, determining faces $F_1, F_2, \ldots, F_k, F_{k+1}, \ldots$ of $\wedge$, so that ascent along $P_{k+1}c$ in F_{k+1} is both feasible and at a rate greater than along $P_k c$ in F_k. By construction

$$(\text{dimension } F_{k+1}) = (\text{dimension } F_k) + 1$$

and $F_k \subset P_{k+1}$. This process, called steep-face selection, uses positive generalized reduced costs $\overline{c}_j^{\{k\}}$ in selecting superbasic variables to determine a k-dimensional face F_k of $\wedge$ intersecting in v, where for $k = 1, 2, \ldots, k_{max}$.

1.

$$\overline{c}_j^{\{k\}} = [(I - P_{k-1})\mathbf{E}^{(j)}, \mathbf{c}] = [\mathbf{E}^{(j)}, (I - P_{k-1})\mathbf{c}]$$

for j values in the index set corresponding to the columns in A_N.

2. $P_0 = 0$, thus $\overline{c}_j^{\{1\}} \equiv \overline{c}_j$.

Letting

$$(I - P_{k-1})\mathbf{c} = \Psi\{k - 1\} = \begin{bmatrix} \Psi_B\{k - 1\} \\ \Psi_N\{k - 1\} \end{bmatrix}$$

it follows that

$$\overline{c}_j^{\{k\}} = (\Psi_{N\}}^{\{k-1\}})j - [(A_N)j, \pi^{\{k\}})]$$

where

$$\pi^{\{k\}} = (A_\mathbf{B}^{-1})^T \Psi^{\{k-1\}} = (A_\mathbf{B}^T)^{-1}\Psi_B^{\{k-1\}} \quad \text{for} \quad k = 1, 2, \ldots, (n - m)$$

Due to computational implementation, the special case $k = 1$ in Relation (1), which reduces to

$$\overline{c}_j = c_j - [(A_N)j, \pi]$$

where $\pi = (A_B^T)^{-1}c_B$ is called the vector of simplex multipliers, is more commonly found in the LP literature than is the vector form

$$\bar{c}_N = c_N - (A_B^{-1}A_N)^T c_B$$

Note that the steep-face selection procedure employs the same basis A_B to determine all of the generalized reduced costs associated with the corresponding vertex and F_k is determined by considering the kth-order generalized reduced costs, F_{k+1} by considering the $k + 1$st-order generalized reduced costs, and so on. Simple examples can be constructed where $\bar{c}_{j_1}^{\{k\}} < 0$ although $\bar{c}_{j_1}^{\{k+1\}} > 0$, and where $\bar{c}_{j_2}^{\{k\}} > 0$ although $\bar{c}_{2_1}^{\{k+1\}} < 0$.

If the columns of a particular ε matrix are quite sparse, thus approximately mutually pairwise orthogonal, then the higher order reduced costs are approximately equal to the first-order reduced costs, in which case the technique called multiple pricing (selecting a k-dimensional face corresponding to the k-most positive first-order reduced cost values) seems likely to be effective. Unfortunately for a particular LP problem, it is impossible to determine *a priori* the sparsity of the relevant ε matrices, which varies from vertex to vertex. Steep-face selection can be described as a generalization of multiple pricing wherein interactions between variables are removed during the sequential selection process.

It appears that subproblems whose variable sets are determined using steep-face selection often possess optimal solutions that are near optimal for the problem involving all of the original variables.

It may be shown[13] that there is an intimate connection between the generalized reduced costs and the Kuhn–Tucker–Rosen conditions that characterize optimality for the general, nonlinear programming problem.

3. PERSPECTIVE OF THE GENERALIZED INVERSE AND RELATED CONSTRUCTS

While the orthogonal projectors exhibited in Sections 1 and 2 were obtained directly, the perspectives provided by a related algebraic entity called the generalized inverse A^I of a matrix A,[4] leads to an enhanced understanding of both the mathematical structure of optimization problems and the key role played by the associated orthogonal projectors in various algorithms devised to solve such problems numerically.

The theory relating to generalized inverses has grown quite explosively during the past 35 years, and many variations of the basic concept have been developed. Since search directions employed by the six algorithms listed in the "Introduction" are determined by the projector

$$P = I - A^{I(J,K)}A$$

for certain choices of J, K, and A, where $A^{I(J,K)}$ is the associated weighted generalized inverse of A,[4] Chapter 6 focuses on that particular generalized inverse.

It can be shown that for arbitrary A (real), there exists a unique matrix, $A^I \equiv A^{I(J,K)}$, corresponding to the pair of symmetric, positive, definite (SPD) matrices (J, K) that simultaneously satisfies the four following relations: (1) $AA^IA = A$, (2) $A^IAA^I = A^I$, (3) $(JAA^I)^T = JAA^I$, and (4) $(KA^IA)^T = KA^IA$.

The following are relevant properties of the weighted generalized inverse:

1. Of all vectors that minimize

$$\|Ax - b\|_J$$

   $x = A^Ib$ is the (unique) vector that minimizes $\|x\|_K = \sqrt{(x, Kx)}$.

2. If $A = FR^T$, where F and R have linearly independent columns, then

$$A^I = K^{-1}R(R^TK^{-1}R)^{-1}(F^TJF)^{-1}F^TJ$$

3.

$$(I - A^IA)^2 = I - A^IA \text{ (idempotent property)}$$

$$(K(I - A^IA))^T = K(I - A^IA) \text{ (self-adjoint property)}$$

   Thus $(I - A^IA)$ is a projection, orthogonal in the inner product space & (K), where $(x, y)_K \equiv (x, Ky)$.

4. The range of $(I - A^IA) = N(A)$, the null space of A. Thus if $\tilde{x} \neq \tilde{x}'$ are two solutions of $Ax = b$

$$A(\tilde{x} - \tilde{x}') = b - b = \theta$$

   and therefore $\tilde{x} = \tilde{x}' + y$, where $y \in N(A)$.

5. If $Ax = b$ is solvable, then all solutions are of the form

$$x = A^\mathbf{I}b + (I - A^\mathbf{I}A)z \qquad \text{for some} \qquad z$$

6. If $J = K = I$, then $A^\mathbf{I} = A^+$, the Moore–Penrose generalized inverse of A.

7. If $J = I$, K arbitrary SPD, and A has full row rank, then[14]

$$(I - A^\mathbf{I}A) = I - K^{-1}A^\mathrm{T}(AK^{-1}A^\mathrm{T})^{-1}A \text{ (a special case of property 2)}$$

$$= E(E^\mathrm{T}KE)^{-1}E^\mathrm{T}K \text{ (a matrix form of the Gram–Schmidt process)}$$

where the colum of E form a basis for N(A).

8. $Ax = b$ is solvabl. and only if $A(A^\mathbf{I}b) = b$.

The projectors $(I - A^\mathbf{I}A)$ employed by Algorithms B.1 and B.2, discussed in Section 2, are associated with the Moore–Penrose inverse A^+, where the matrix A corresponds to the appropriate permutation of columns of the partitioned matrix

$$\left[\begin{array}{c} A \\ \hline I \quad O \end{array}\right]$$

in which A is the m by n coefficient matrix of Primal.1; I is an $(n - m - k)$ by $(n - m - k)$ identity matrix; and $k = 1, 2, \ldots, (n - m)$ is the dimension of the related face of $\wedge$. For example Algorithm, B.1, I is $(n - m - 1)$ by $(n - m - 1)$ and the form used to represent $(I - A^\mathbf{I}A)$ corresponds to the second relationship given in Property 7.

The form of $(I - A^\mathbf{I}A)$ employed in Algorithm B.3,[7] as applied to the linearly constrained, nonlinear problem (formulated as Nonlinear.1: Maximize f(x) where Ax = b, x ≤ θ) is identical to that used by algorithm B.2 in Section 2, with the following qualifications:

1. The projection of the gradient of f(x) is involved at a feasible point $\tilde{x}$ rather than the projection of the constant vector **c**.
2. There is no provision for selecting steep k-dimensional faces of $\wedge$.
3. The computational form used in Reference 7 corresponds to the first relation given in Restriction 7

As a consequence of Qualification 2, if Algorithm B.3 is applied to Primal.1, initiated at an interior point of $\wedge$ after at most (n − m) steps, each involving a line search on a face having a dimension at least one less than that of the preceding face, a vertex is reached. When initiated at a vertex, Algorithms B.3 and B.1 are identical.

The form of $(I - A^{I}A)$ employed by Algorithm B.4,[15] as applied to Nonlinear.1, corresponds to taking $J = I$ and K equal to the Hessian matrix of $f(x)$,[14] where A is identical to that used in Algorithm B.2. Qualifications (1) and (2) again apply; the computational form used in Reference 15 corresponds to the second relation given in Restriction 7.

C. Pan has performed a number of computational experiments in which a combination of Algorithm B.4 and steep-face selection was observed to reduce both the number of iterations and the execution time required to solve a suite of linearly constrained, nonlinear programming problems.[16]

The extension of Rosen's approach employed by Algorithm B.4 uses an appropriate, locally defined inner-product space, thereby taking local curvature of the nonlinear function $f(x)$ into account in determining ascent (or descent) directions. If the function $f(x)$ is the sum of a linear and a quadratic function and x is unrestricted, then Algorithm B.4 can be shown to solve the related problem in one step.

4. INTERIOR POINT ALGORITHMS

This section discusses the Interior Gradient Projection algorithm (I.1),[9] which essentially reverses Algorithm B.3 in Section 3. Starting at a point on a face of $\wedge$ of dimension k, a feasible point is constructed that lies on a face of dimension $k + 1$. This process is repeated until a point in the interior of $\wedge$ has been obtained. The projector used in Reference 9 corresponds to the Moore–Penrose inverse. Initiated at a vertex v, a sequence of projectors is determined. The range of the initial projector,

$$(I - A^{+}A) - \overline{e}^{(1)}\overline{e}^{(1)T}$$

where

$$\overline{e}^{(1)} = \left(\frac{1}{\|(I - A^{+}A)c\|}\right)(I - A^{+}A)c$$

consists of the intersection of $N(A)$ and the manifold of points orthogonal to the projection $(I - A^{+}A)c$ of the gradient c on $N(A)$. A construction in

Reference 9 uses the preceding projector to obtain a point in the interior of $\wedge$ that has function value (v, c). From such a point, ascent along the projected gradient $(I - A^+A)c$ is possible. Using this procedure repeatedly, a sequence of interior points converging to an optimal solution can be generated. The process can be initiated at any boundary point of $\wedge$; it encounters certain combinatorial problems if initiated at a degenerate point.

The Affine Scaling algorithm (I.2.),[17,10] employs an approach that combines methods used by Algorithms I.1 and B.4. The related projector P on N(A) is dynamically determined by elements in the current iterate $x^{(j)}$ so that it moves more or less parallel to nearby boundary faces of $\wedge$.

Assuming A has full row rank and $x^{(j)}$ is a point in the interior of $\wedge$ (thus $x^{(j)} > \theta$), the Primal Affine Scaling algorithm (I.2.1)[18] employs the line search

$$x^{(j+1)} = x^{(j)} + \alpha D_j P_{AD_j} D_j c$$

where

$$P_{AD_j} = I - (AD_j)^+ AD_j$$

and

$$D_j = \text{diagonal } \{x_1^{(j)} \cdots x_n^{(j)}\}$$

As an exercise show that for any diagonal SPD matrix D

$$D(I - (AD)^+AD)D = (I - A^IA)D^2$$

where

$$A^I = D^2 A^T (AD^2 A^T)^{-1}$$

is the weighted generalized inverse of A corresponding to $J = I$, $K = D^{-2}$.

Similarly the Dual Affine Scaling Algorithm I.2.2[17] employs the search direction given by

$$D^2(A^IA)A^Ib = A^T(AD^{-2}A^T)^{-1}b$$

where

$$A^I = D^{-2}A^T(AD^{-2}A^T)^{-1}$$

is the weighted generalized inverse of A corresponding to $J = I$, $K = D^2$. Note that both AD^2A^T and $AD^{-2}A^T$ are SPD.

Using the power $\mu = 2$, where A^I corresponds to $J = I$, $K = D^{-\mu}$, in defining the related inner-product space does not appear to be particularly significant. Not only does any real number suffice, but it appears that the value $\mu = 2$ is seldom (locally) optimal in the sense that the related projection provides the greatest absolute change in (x, c) at $x^{(j)}$.[19]

To emphasize the preceding comment, we observe that for the particular Primal.1 problem where $A = [1 \quad 1 \quad 1]$, $b = [1]$, and $c = [1 \quad 1 \quad 0]^T$, starting from an arbitrary interior point, Algorithm I.2.1 corresponding to the power $\mu = 1$ requires one step to reach the (unique) optimal solution exactly, which is not the case for the algorithm corresponding to the value $\mu = 2$.

In summary both the Primal and Dual Affine Scaling algorithms can be viewed as variable metric methods where the local inner-product space is defined to take into account the distance from the current iterate $x^{(j)}$ to the nearby coordinate hyperplanes. It would seem reasonable to combine these two approaches in treating the problem Nonlinear.1 either by alternating between them or designing an algorithm to accommodate both approaches in a more fundamental way.

5. DUALITY THEOREM (ORTHOGONALITY FORM)

Since

$$(A^IAx, K^{-1}c)_K = (A^IA(A^Ib + (I - A^IA)z), K^{-1}c)_K$$
$$= (A^Ib, K^{-1}c)_K = (A^Ib, c)$$

thus

$$(x, c) = (x, (I - A^IA)K^{-1}c)_K + (x, A^IAK^{-1}c)_K$$
$$= (x, (I - A^IA)K^{-1}c)_K + (A^IAx, K^{-1}c)_K$$
$$= (x, (I - A^IA)K^{-1}c)_K + (A^Ib, c)$$

Furthermore if $Ax = b$ is solvable, the two systems

$$Ax = b \quad \text{and} \quad A^I Ax = A^I b$$

have identical sets of solutions, and then the two problems Primal.1 and Primal.3: Maximize $(x, (I - A^I A)K^{-1}c)_K$ where

$$KA^I Ax = KA^I b \quad x \geq \theta$$

have identical sets of feasible and optimal solutions.

Assuming that A^I is the weighted generalized inverse of A corresponding to $J = I$, K diagonal SPD, consider the following two LP problems.

Primal.4: Minimize $(x, - (I - A^I A)_K^{-1} c)_K$ where

$$A^I A_x = A^I b \quad x \geq \theta$$

and Dual Equivalent.4: Minimize $(y, KA^I b) = (y, A^I b)_K$ where

$$(I - A^I A)y = -(I - A^I A)K^{-1}c \quad y \geq \theta$$

If $Ax = b$ is solvable, Primal.4 is equivalent to Primal.1. It can be shown that Dual Equivalent.4 is essentially equivalent to the dual of Primal.4. The following theorem relating Primal.4 and Dual Equivalent.4 can be established.

Duality Theorem of Linear Programming—Orthogonality Form: If $\tilde{x}$ and $\tilde{y}$ are feasible for Primal.4 and Dual Equivalent.4, respectively, then $(\tilde{x}, \tilde{y})_K = 0$ if and only if $\tilde{x}$ and $\tilde{y}$ are optimal for Primal.4 and Dual Equivalent.4, respectively.

We note the following:

- The proof by Pyle and Kim,[20] follows steps similar to those used in,[21] where the generalized inverse involved is the Moore–Penrose inverse. The proof depends in an essential way on the fact that since K is diagonal SPD, $Kv \geq \theta$ if and only if $v \geq \theta$.
- When the equality constraints of Primal.4 and Dual Equivalent.4 are combined, treating the orthogonality and nonnegativity conditions separately,[23] the resulting formulation is a special case of a class of problems called Complementarity problems.[23]

The Algorithms B.1, B.2, B.3, B.4, I.1, and I.2 generate a sequence of points, each of which is nonnegative and satisfies the linear system of the associated LP problem, where the goal is to terminate in a point satisfying the test for optimality characterized by the Duality theorem. It seems reasonable to formulate algorithms that generate a sequence of points, each of which satisfies the optimality condition and the linear system, where the goal is to terminate in a nonnegative point. Such algorithms arise naturally in connection with the following equivalent fixed-point formulation of the LP problem, which is obtained by combining equality constraints in Primal.4 and Dual Equivalent.4, respectively, and the orthogonality form of the duality condition $(x, y)_K = 0$, treating the nonnegativity conditions separately. The algebra involved, although tedious, is straightforward and follows essentially the same steps as in Reference 21, modified as in Reference 24.

Fixed Point.1: Determine $z \neq \theta$ such that $P(K)z = z \geq \theta$ where

$$P(K) = \begin{bmatrix} I - A^I A - G & H \\ -H & A^I A + G \end{bmatrix}$$

$$G = (1/2)(uu^T - vv^T)K$$

$$H = (1/2)(uv^T - vu^T)K$$

$$u = \left(\frac{1}{\|(I - A^I A)K^{-1}c\|} \right)(I - A^I A)K^{-1}c$$

$$v = \left(\frac{1}{\|A^I b\|} \right)A^I b$$

$$A^I = A^{I(J,K)}$$

where $J = I$ and K is diagonal, SPD.

Suppose $\tilde{z}$ is a solution of Fixed Point.1, partitioned as follows:

$$\tilde{z} = \begin{bmatrix} \tilde{x} \\ \tilde{y} \end{bmatrix}$$

where $\tilde{x}$ and $\tilde{y}$ are each vectors of n elements.
Let

$$h = \begin{bmatrix} v \\ -u \end{bmatrix}$$

where u and v are defined above.

Assuming that $(\tilde{z}, h)_{\mathcal{H}} \neq 0$ (the case where $(\tilde{z}, h)_{\mathcal{H}} = 0$ is treated in Reference 25), form

$$\bar{z} = \left(\frac{(h, h)_{\mathcal{H}}}{(\tilde{z}, h)_{\mathcal{H}}}\right)\tilde{z} = \begin{bmatrix} \bar{x} \\ \bar{y} \end{bmatrix}$$

where $\bar{x}$ and $\bar{y}$ are each vectors of n elements and $\mathcal{H}$ = block diagonal $\{K, K\}$. Then, it may be shown[20] that

1. $(\|A^t b\|_K)\bar{x}$ is an optimal solution for Primal.1.
2. $(\bar{x}, \bar{y})_K = 0$
3. P(K) is a projector, orthogonal in the inner-product space L(K) of dimension 2n, where

$$[z^{(1)}, z^{(2)}]_{\mathcal{H}} = [z^{(1)}, \mathcal{H}z^{(2)}]$$

6. PROXIMITY MAP ALGORITHMS

This section discusses constructive realizations of the duality theorem of linear programming (orthogonality form). We begin with a definition: Given a closed convex set Γ in an inner-product space $\mathcal{L}(\mathcal{H})$, let $\mathcal{G}$ be a map that associates with each point $z \in \mathcal{L}(\mathcal{H})$ a point $\mathcal{G}(z) \in \Gamma$ such that

$$\|z = \mathcal{G}(z)\|_{\mathcal{H}} \leq \|z - r\|_{\mathcal{H}}$$

for all $r \in \Gamma$: Then $\mathcal{G}$ is called a proximity map of $\mathcal{L}(\mathcal{H})$ onto Γ.

This definition leads to the following theorems:

- Let P be a projector, orthogonal in $\mathcal{L}(\mathcal{H})$; then, P is a proximity map of $\mathcal{L}(\mathcal{H})$ onto the range of P.
- Let $\mathcal{H}$ be diagonal and SPD; then the map

$$M(w) = (1/2)(|w| + w)$$

is a proximity map of $\mathcal{L}(\mathcal{H})$ onto the nonnegative orthant $\{w' \in \mathcal{L}(\mathcal{H}) | w' \geq \theta\}$, where

$$|w| = [|w_1|, \ldots, |w_{2n}|]^T$$

6.1. Static Proximity Map Algorithm (E.1)

Define the sequence $\{z^{(j)}\}$, where for arbitrary $z^{(0)} > \theta$,

$$z^{(j+1)} = M([P(K)]z^{(j)}) \qquad j = 0, 1, 2, \ldots$$

$P(K)$ is defined as in Fixed Point.1, and $M(w) = (1/2)(|w| + w)$.[25,26]

Then we have the following theorem: The sequence $\{z^{(j)}\}$ converges to a solution of Fixed Point.1. The proof, by Pyle and Kim,[20] follows steps similar to those used in the proof of a theorem given in Reference 25 with inner products in $\mathcal{L}[\mathcal{H}(K)]$, where $\mathcal{H}$ is block diagonal $\{K, K\}$, and K is diagonal SPD.

6.2. Dynamic Proximity Map Algorithm (E.2)

The dynamic version of the proximity map algorithm is obtained by replacing the constant matrix K employed in each iteration of the static version (Algorithm E.1) by using a sequence of matrices $\{K_j\}$, where K_j changes from iteration to iteration.[20] Typically K_j is taken equal to $D_j^{-\mu}$ for some fixed value of μ including, but not restricted to $\mu = 2$, where

$$D_j = \text{diagonal} \{ |x_1^{(j-1)}| \cdots |x_n^{(j-1)}| \} \qquad j = 1, 2, \ldots$$

$$D_0 = I$$

$$\begin{bmatrix} x^{(j)} \\ y^{(j)} \end{bmatrix} = [P(Kj)]z^{(j)}$$

where

$$z^{(j+1)} = M([P(K_j)]z^{(j)})$$

for $j = 0, 1, 2, \ldots$; and $z^{(0)} > \theta$ is arbitrary.

Since the relative magnitudes of the diagonals of D_j appear to provide the essential mechanism involved when $x_i^{(j)} <$ tolerance, $(D_j)_{ii}$ is set to unity.

While convergence of Algorithm E.2 remains an open question judging from computational experience (see Section 7.) and considering the continuity of the processes involved in the static version (Algorithm E.1), a proof based on restricting changes made in K_j at each stage seems a reasonable goal.

The most fascinating aspect of Algorithm (E.2) has been the empirical discovery of the limiting form of $P(K_j)$ as $\{K_j\}$ approaches K_{opt}, a diagonal, positive, semidefinite matrix corresponding to an optimal solution of the related LP problem in Reference 20. The authors' efforts have been focused more on attempts to analyze this aspect of the algorithm than on convergence questions. A conjecture summarizing this discovery is given in Section 8. Some parts of the conjecture have been established formally; others seem to be less tractable, which would seem to be consistent with Anstreicher's observation, "Even showing that the [Affine Scaling] algorithm is convergent turns out to be relatively difficult . . ."[11]

The sequence $\{Pz^{(j)}\}$ generated by either Proximity Map algorithm lies in 2n-space. If $P\tilde{z} = \tilde{z} \neq \theta$, then $\tilde{z} > \theta$ implies $(\tilde{x}, \tilde{y})_K > 0$, which contradicts $(\tilde{x}, \tilde{y})_K = 0$. Thus the set of points

$$\Omega = \{z \mid (I - P)z = \theta, z \geq \theta\}$$

has an empty (relative) interior; that is there exists no $z > \theta$ in Ω. Unless $Pz^{(j)} \geq \theta$ for some j [in which case $\tilde{z} = Pz^{(j)} = P\tilde{z} \geq \theta$], $Pz^{(j)}$ is a (relative) exterior point for Ω. Appropriately scaled the first n elements of $Pz^{(j)}$ satisfy the equality constraints of Primal.4, and the second n elements satisfy the equality constraints of Dual Equivalent.4. One or the other subvector, possibly both, typically contains at least one negative element. Thus the corresponding subvector is a (relative) exterior point for the associated feasible set of solutions.

7. COMPUTATIONAL EXPERIMENTS

The XMP library (which has no connection *per se* with the Cray X-MP computer) is an integrated collection of Fortran subroutines commonly used to solve optimization problems. Written by R. E. Marsten,[27,28] this well-documented, widely used, Algorithm B.1-based suite of computer programs is typically employed to input problem data in standard mathematical programming format, solve the related LP problem(s), then output results for large, sparse problems.

The XMP's hidden data structure approach was used to experiment with the generalization of Algorithm B.1 discussed in Section 2. and the Proximity Map algorithms discussed in Section 6., drawing subroutines from the XMP library, augmented by appropriate extensions and modifications, and all programs running on the SX-2 supercomputer (roughly the equivalent of a single CPU Cray Y-MP). Data sets treated were either large transportation problems[5] or NETLIB problems.[29] The more than 50 problems contained in the Netlib data sets were found to be highly degenerate.

Results for a subset containing 30 NETLIB problems have been published, both by Monma and Morton[30] and by Adler *et al.*[17] where solution times for the Dual Affine Scaling algorithm are compared with those of the LP subsystem of MINOS,[15] another Algorithm B.1-based code. The greatest relative speedup was by a factor of 8 for the Netlib problem designated Scsd8. This problem, together with Scsd6 and Scsd1 (with speedups of 4 and 2.5, respectively reported in Reference 17), was solved using the Dynamic Proximity Map algorithm. The results, stated in terms of iterations required, follow.

    i As the solution sequence approaches an optimal solution, the Dynamic Proximity Map algorithm apparently speeds up (see Section 8).

    ii Application of the steep-face selection technique discussed in Section 2 appears to yield subproblems whose optimal solutions are near optimal for the original problem.

    iii Recovery of an optimal vertex, starting from an optimal, nonvertex boundary point (both the Affine Scaling and Proximity Map algorithms typically fail to converge to a vertex) seems to be a process for which the approach discussed in Section 2 is well suited.

    iv Rapid solution of systems with SPD coefficient matrix AD^2A^T, where A is large and sparse, is the key element in reducing overall computation time required by all of the algorithms discussed in Chapter 6, except for Algorithm B.1.

To use a polyalgorithm approach:

1. Initially apply Algorithm B.1 to determine a feasible vertex, eliminate redundant equations, and obtain the factored form of the initial basis.
2 Apply the Algorithm B.2 discussed in Section 2 to select a subproblem and generate an initial interior point of $\wedge$.
3. Solve that subproblem using Algorithm I.2 initially; after a few iterations, switch to the Dynamic Proximity Map algorithm.
4. Recover a vertex solution using Algorithm B.2.
5. Repeat from Step 2 as required.

8. APPARENT STRUCTURE OF $P(K_j)$ AS $\{K_j\} \to K_{opt}$

This section describes the current state of our understanding about the projectors $P(K_j)$ that are determined by a sequence of diagonal SPD matrices converging to a diagonal, positive semidefinite matrix corresponding to an optimal solution of the related LP problem. The composition of these projectors is both interesting and intricate. For example when the related boundary point $\tilde{x}$ is a (nondegenerate) vertex of $\wedge$, the projectors exhibit large scalar multiples of $\tilde{x}$ as columns of a certain submatrix. When convergence is to a degenerate vertex or a boundary point of $\wedge$ that is not a vertex, the situation is more complex. Additional research is required to achieve a deeper understanding of the underlying structures involved.

Suppose that $\{x^{(j)}\} \to \tilde{x}$, where $\tilde{x}$ is an optimal (nondegenerate) vertex, $x_i^{(j)} \neq 0$ for all (i, j), and each $x^{(j)}$ satisfies the linear system in Primal.1. Let

$$\bar{c}_N = c_N - (A_B^{-1} A_N)^T c_B, \text{ where } \pi = (A_B^T)^{-1} c_B,$$

be the vector of reduced costs associated with $\tilde{x}$ and define a sequence of projectors $\{P(K_j)\}$, as in Fixed Point.1, where $J = I$, $K_j = D_j^{-\mu}$, $\mu = 2$ and

$$D_j = \text{diagonal} \{ |x_1^{(j)}| \cdots |x_n^{(j)}| \}$$

Denoting the columns of H_j in

$$P(K_j) = \begin{bmatrix} I - A_j^I A - G_j & H_j \\ -H_j & A_j^I A + G_j \end{bmatrix}$$

as

$$H_j = [h_j^{(1)}, \ldots, h_j^{(n)}]$$

consider the following.

Conjecture.1[20] encompasses the following relationships
1. If $\tilde{x}_i = 0$, $h_j^{(i)} = \alpha_j^{(i)}$, where $\lim_{j \to \infty} \alpha_j^{(i)} = 0$ if $\bar{c}_i = 0$
   If $\bar{c}_0 \neq 0$, then $\lim_{j \to \infty} (\alpha_j^{(i)})^{-1} = 0$.
2. If $\tilde{x}_i > 0$, then $\lim_{j \to \infty} h_j^{(i)} = \theta$.
3. $\lim_{j \to \infty} A_j^I b = \tilde{x}$.

4. $\lim_{j \to \infty} \|A_j^I b\|_{K_j} = \sqrt{m}$.

5. $\lim_{j \to \infty} (I - A_j^I A) D_j^2 c = \theta$.

6. $\lim_{j \to \infty} u_j = \theta$

Formal proofs have been constructed for relationships 3 and 4;[20] the remaining relationships are supported by numerical experiments.

ACKNOWLEDGMENTS. Support for this research has been provided in part by HNSX Supercomputers, Inc. Research and development following directions implied by the structure of the polyalgorithm is on-going, supported, in part, by HNSX Supercomputers, Inc., the joint venture between Honeywell and Nippon Electric Company (NEC), which markets NEC's line of SX Supercomputers in the United States.

The authors gratefully acknowledge word processing assistance provided by Nancy Tran; technical assistance in connection with the SX-2 Supercomputer provided by T. Sasakura, HNSX Supercomputers, Inc.; supported provided by Dr. Bjorn Mossberg, HNSX Supercomputers, Inc.; access to the SX-2 Supercomputers provided by HNSX Supercomputers, Inc.; and inspiration provided by Dr. A. Charnes, University of Texas at Austin, and Dr. G. B. Dantzig, Stanford University.

References

1. *SIAM News* 22 (1989).
2. Karmarkar, N. "A new polynomial time algorithm for linear-programming." *Combinatorica* 4 (1984).
3. Goldman, A. J., and Tucker, A. W. "Theory of linear programming." In *Linear Inequalities and Related Systems,* H. W. Kuhn and A. W. Tucker, eds., Princeton Univ. Press, Princeton, NJ, 1956.
4. Ben-Israel, A., and Greville, T. N. E. *Generalized Inverses: Theory and Applications.* New York: Wiley, 1974.
5. Dantzig, G. B. *Linear Programming and Extensions.* Princeton Univ. Press, Princeton, NJ: 1963.
6. Pyle, L. D. "Generalizations of the simplex algorithm." Dept. of Comp. Sc. Tech. Rept. UH-CS-88-07 (1988).
7. Rosen, J. B. "The gradient projection method for nonlinear programming, part I. linear constraints." J. SIAM 8 (1960).
8. Sargent, R. W. H. "Reduced gradient and projection methods for nonlinear programming." In *Nonlinear Methods for Constrained Optimization,* P. E. Gill and W. Murray, eds. Academic Press, New York, 1974.

9. Pyle, L. D., and Cline, R. E. "The generalized inverse in linear programming—interior gradient projection methods." *SIAM J. Appl. Math.* **24** (1973).

10. Dikin, I. I. "Iterative solution of problems of linear and quadratic programming." *Sov. Math.* Doklady **8** (1967).

11. Anstreicher, K. M. "Progress in interior point algorithms since 1984." SIAM-News **22** (1989).

12. Goldfarb, D., and Reid, J. K. "A practical steepest edge simplex algorithm." *Math. Prog.* **12** (1977).

13. Pyle, L. D. "The generalized inverse in nonlinear programming—equivalence of the Kuhn-Tucker, Rosen and generalized simplex algorithm necessary conditions." *Proc. 1976 Bicentennial Conf. of Math. Prog.* Nat. Bur. of Standards, Washington, DC (1978).

14. Pyle, L. D. "The weighted generalized inverse in nonlinear programming—active set selection using a variable metric generalization of the simplex algorithm." *Proc. International Symposium on External Methods and Systems Analysis.* Lect. Notes in Econ. and Math. Systems 174, Springer–Verlag, New York, 1980.

15. Murtach, B. A., and Saunders, M. A. "Large-scale linearly constrained optimization." *Math. Prog.* **14** (1978).

16. Pan, C. "A computational study of steep-facet selection for linearly constrained nonlinear programming, implemented in MINOS." Ph.D. diss., Univ. of Houston, 1986.

17. Adler, I., Karmarkar, N., Resende, M. G. C., and Veiga, G. "An implementation of Karmarkar's algorithm for linear programming." Technical Report 86-8. Operations Research Center, Univ. of California, Berkeley (1986).

18. Gay, D. M. "Pictures of Karmarkar's linear-programming algorithm." Comp. Sc. Tech. Rpt. no. 136, A.T.&T. Bell Laboratories (January 1987).

19. Shum, C. S. "A computational study of a one-parameter family of affine interior-point algorithms." M.S. thesis, Univ. of Houston, 1988.

20. Kim, S. "Mathematical projectors in optimization problems." Ph.D. diss., Univ. of Houston, 1989.

21. Pyle, L. D. "The generalized inverse in linear programming—basic structure." *SIAM J. Appl. Math.* **22** (1972).

22. Pyle, L. D. "The generalized inverse in quadratic programming and complementarity problems; basic structure." Internal Technical Report. A.T.&T. Bell Laboratories, Holmel, NJ (1970).

23. Cottle, R. W., and Dantzig, G. B. "Complementary pivot theory of mathematical programming." *Lin. Alg. App.* **1** (1968).

24. Shih, C. T. "A computational study of a nonnegative fixed-point formulation of the linear programming problem. M.S. thesis, Univ. of Houston, 1986.

25. Cline, R. E., and Pyle, L. D. "The generalized inverse in linear programming—an intersection projection method and the solution of a class of structured linear programming problems." *SIAM J. Appl. Math.* **24** (1973).

26. Nguyen, T. M. "Applications of generalized inverse to circulant matrices, intersection projections, and linear programming." Ph.D. diss. Univ. of Houston, 1982.

27. Marsten, R. E. "The design of the XMP linear-programming library." *ACM Trans. Math. Softw.* **7** (1981).

28. Marsten, R. E. *XMP Technical Reference Manual.* Dept. of M.I.S., Univ. of Arizona (1987).

29. Gay, D. M. "Electronic mail distribution of linear-programming test problems." *Math. Prog. Soc. Committee on Alg. Newsletter* **13** (1985).

30. Monma, C. L., and Morton, A. J. "Computational experience with a dual affine variant of Karmarkar's method for linear programming." Bell Comm. Res. Tech. Rpt.

APPENDIX: Numerical Illustrations

The following linear programming problem illustrates Primal.1: Maximize $(x, -c)$ {that is, minimize (x, c)} where

$$Ax \cong Tx = b, \qquad x \geq \theta$$

$$T = \begin{bmatrix} 1 & 0 & 0 & 0 & 1 & 0 & 0 & 0 \\ 0 & 1 & 0 & 0 & 0 & 1 & 0 & 0 \\ 0 & 0 & 1 & 0 & 0 & 0 & 1 & 0 \\ 0 & 0 & 0 & 1 & 0 & 0 & 0 & 1 \\ 1 & 1 & 1 & 1 & 0 & 0 & 0 & 0 \\ 0 & 0 & 0 & 0 & 1 & 1 & 1 & 1 \end{bmatrix}$$

$$b = \begin{bmatrix} 50 \\ 60 \\ 40 \\ 10 \\ 90 \\ 70 \end{bmatrix} \qquad c = \begin{bmatrix} 7 \\ 5 \\ 8 \\ 0 \\ 2 \\ 3 \\ 4 \\ 0 \end{bmatrix}$$

This particular type of linear programming problem, called a Transportation problem,[5] can be represented by the following rectangular cell structure, where the goal is to assign nonnegative values x_i to each cell so that the resulting cell entries in each row and column sum to the nonnegative numbers that appear to the right and below the structure (thus giving a feasible solution), where $c_1 x_1 + \cdots + c_8 x_8$ is as small as possible (thus giving an optimal solution).

7	5	8	0	
x_1	x_2	x_3	x_4	90
2	3	4	0	
x_5	x_6	x_7	x_8	70
50	60	40	10	

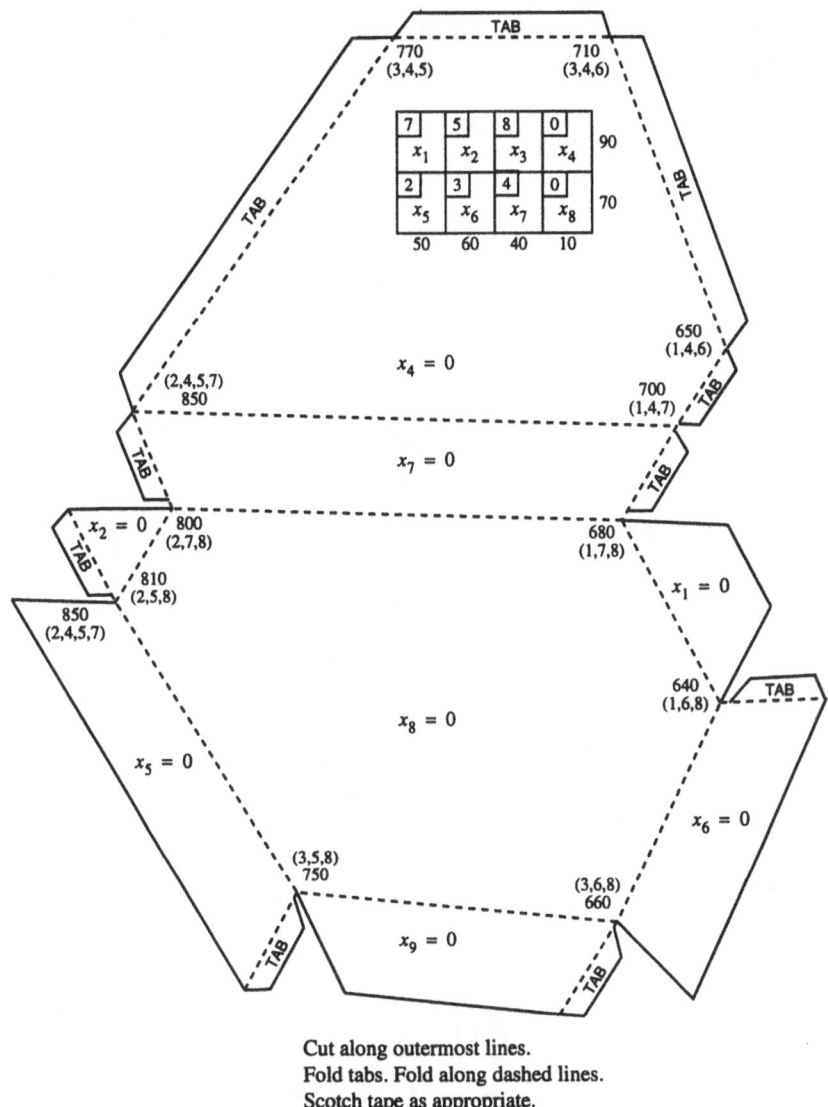

Figure 6.1. Pattern to construct a three-dimensional model for the sample LP problem.

It is easy to show that the rank of T is 5 (any one of the equations can be ignored), and since $n = 9$ (dimension of $\wedge$) = $n -$ rank $T = 8 - 5 = 3$; thus $\wedge$, a three-dimensional subset of three-space, can be constructed (see Figure 6.1.).

Nongenerate vertices, such as $v =$ [50 40 0 0 0 20 40 10]^T, contain precisely five positive elements. One of the vertices of this problem, $[50 \quad 0 \quad 40 \quad 0 \quad 0 \quad 60 \quad 0 \quad 10]^T$, is degenerate. The optimal solution is

$$v_{opt} = [0 \quad 60 \quad 20 \quad 10 \quad 50 \quad 0 \quad 20 \quad 0]^T$$

The projector $P(K)$, where $k = I$ (corresponding to the More–Penrose inverse) is exhibited in Table 1.

Figures 6.2 and 6.3 are taken from Reference 1, where they were used

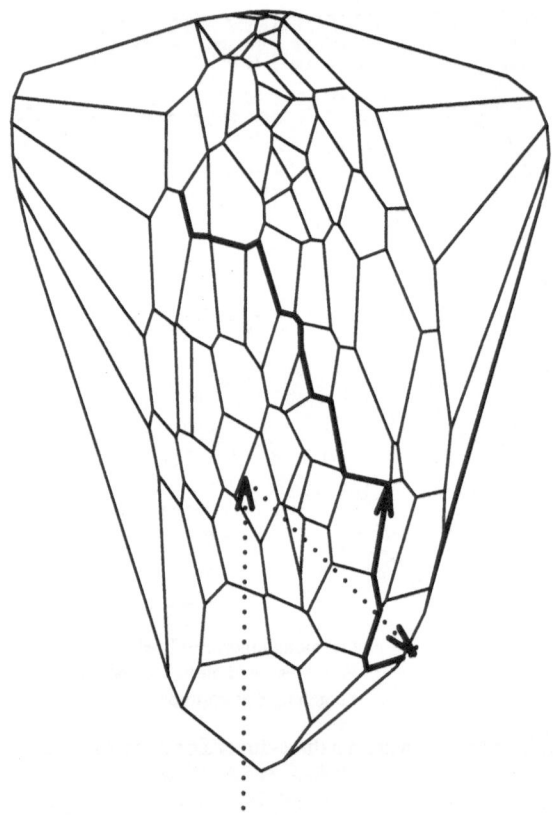

Figure 6.2. Solution path followed by Algorithms B.1 and the generalized simplex B.2 for a three-dimensional LP problem. The dotted lines show the initial phase I steps taken by Algorithm B.1 to locate the feasible region. The Algorithm then moves from vertex to vertex on the edge of the feasible region (solid line). The generalized simplex Algorithm B.2 follows the very heavy solid line. (Courtesy of David Gay, AT&T Bell Laboratories.)

Table 6.1.
The Projector $P(k)$ for $k = I$ for a Degenerate Vertex

0.38492	0.01673	-.09435	0.00598	-.21087	0.19213	0.23359	0.02883	0.00000	-.13732	-.02380	-.13549	-.16478	-.06042	-.10802	0.10253
0.01673	0.49917	-.01655	-.12910	0.18096	-.25233	0.18110	0.17024	0.13732	0.00000	0.08422	-.12267	-.08239	0.06591	-.04028	0.13366
-.09435	-.01655	0.41260	-.04538	0.23675	0.18743	-.29868	0.07386	0.02380	-.08422	0.00000	-.10436	-.11535	-.02563	-.07324	0.08605
0.00598	-.12910	-.04538	0.25394	0.041497	0.18607	0.08335	-.24445	0.13549	0.12267	0.10436	0.00000	0.06591	0.11901	0.05676	0.04028
-.21087	0.18096	0.23675	0.041497	0.25328	-.01808	-.12283	-.01301	0.16478	0.08239	0.115357	-.06591	0.00000	0.11535	0.01648	0.09887
0.19213	-.25233	0.18743	0.18607	-.01808	0.46119	-.04819	-.15126	0.06042	-.06591	0.02563	-.11901	-.11535	0.00000	-.06957	0.10802
0.23359	0.18110	-.29868	0.08335	-.12283	-.04819	0.38738	-.06120	0.10802	0.04028	0.07324	-.05676	-.01648	0.06957	0.00000	0.07507
0.02883	0.17024	0.07386	-.24445	-.01301	-.15126	-.06120	0.24761	-.10253	-.13366	-.08605	-.04028	-.09887	-.10802	-.07507	0.00000
0.00000	0.13732	0.02380	0.13549	0.16478	0.06042	0.10802	-.10253	0.61508	0.50083	0.09435	-.00598	0.21087	0.06957	-.23359	-.02883
-.13732	0.00000	-.08422	0.12267	0.08239	-.06591	0.04028	-.13366	0.50083	0.50083	0.01655	0.12910	-.18896	-.19213	0.18110	-.17024
-.02380	0.08422	0.00000	0.10436	0.115357	0.02563	0.07324	-.08605	0.09435	0.01655	0.58740	0.04538	-.23675	-.18743	0.29868	-.07396
-.13549	-.12267	-.10436	0.00000	-.06591	-.11901	-.05676	-.04028	-.00598	0.12910	0.04538	0.74606	-.04149	-.18607	-.08335	0.24445
-.16478	-.08239	-.11535	0.06591	0.00000	-.11535	-.01648	-.09887	0.21087	-.18896	-.23675	-.04149	0.64672	0.01808	0.12283	0.01301
-.06042	0.06591	-.02563	0.11901	0.11535	0.00000	0.06957	-.10802	0.06957	-.19213	-.18743	-.18607	0.01808	0.53881	0.04819	0.15126
-.10802	-.04028	-.07324	0.05676	0.01648	-.06957	0.00000	-.07507	-.23359	0.18110	0.29868	-.08335	0.12283	0.04819	0.61272	0.06120
0.10253	0.13366	0.08605	0.04028	0.09887	0.10802	0.07507	0.00000	-.02883	-.17024	-.07396	0.24445	0.01301	0.15126	0.06120	0.75239

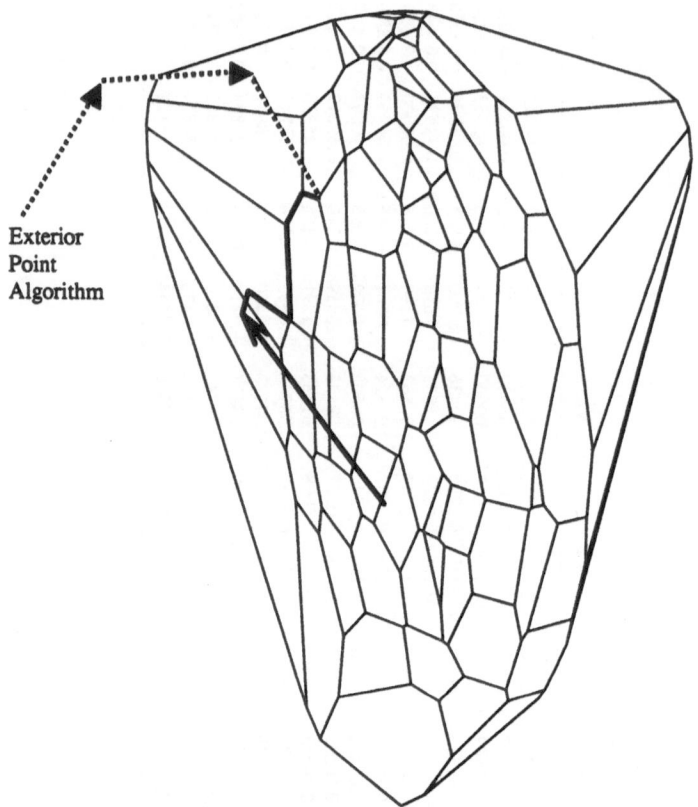

Exterior
Point
Algorithm

Figure 6.3. Solution path followed by interior point (solid) and exterior point (dotted) Algorithms for the three-dimensional LP problem. (Courtesy of David Gay, AT&T Bell Laboratories.)

courtesy of Dr. David Gay, AT&T Bell Laboratories. These graphics have been modified to show solution paths typically followed by boundary point, interior point and exterior point algorithms for solving LP problems.

Parallel Multilevel Methods

David M. Young, Jr. and Bi Roubolo Vona

1. INTRODUCTION

Chapter 7 is concerned with iterative methods for solving the linear system

$$Au = b \qquad (1)$$

where A is a given square nonsingular $N \times N$ matrix and b is a given vector. A frequently used procedure for solving Equation 1 involves choosing a standard basic iterative method of the form

$$u^{(n+1)} = G_s u^{(n)} + k_s \qquad (2)$$

where for some nonsingular (splitting) matrix Q_s we have

$$\begin{cases} G_s = I - Q_s^{-1}A \\ k_s = Q_s^{-1}b \end{cases} \qquad (3)$$

Examples of such iterative procedures are Richardson's method, where $Q_s = I$, and the Jacobi method, where $Q_s = D$. (Here D is the diagonal matrix whose diagonal elements are the same as those of A.) We refer to the method in Equation 2 as a smoothing iteration, and we use the subscript s to distinguish these methods from other types of iterative methods that

David M. Young • University of Texas at Austin   Bi Roubolo Vona • University of Texas at Austin

Studies in Computer Science, edited by John R. Rice and Richard A. DeMillo. Plenum Press, New York, 1994.

we will consider later. If the matrices A and Q_s are symmetric and positive definite (SPD) then the iterative method in Equation 2 is *symmetrizable* in the sense of Hageman and Young,[1] and hence the eigenvalues of G_s are real and less than one. The convergence of a symmetrizable method can be speeded up by using a polynomial acceleration procedure, such as Chebyshev acceleration or conjugate gradient acceleration. Such a procedure can be defined by a family of polynomials $P_0(x)$, $P_1(x)$, $P_2(x)$, . . . of degrees 0, 1, 2, . . . such that $P_k(1) = 1$ for all k. It can be shown for example see Hageman and Young,[1] that for any polynomial acceleration procedure we have*

$$u^{(n)} - \bar{u} = P_n(G_s)(u^{(0)} - \bar{u}) \qquad (4)$$

where $\bar{u} = A^{-1}b$ is the true solution of Equation 1. If v is an eigenvector of G_s associated with the eigenvalue μ, then v is also an eigenvector of $P_n(G_s)$ associated with the eigenvalue $P_n(\mu)$. Moreover since G_s is similar to a diagonal matrix, G_s has N linearly independent eigenvectors $v^{(1)}$, $v^{(2)}$, . . . $v^{(N)}$, and we can represent the initial error $\epsilon^{(0)} = u^{(0)} - \bar{u}$ in terms of these eigenvectors. Thus for some c_1, c_2, . . . , c_N, we have

$$\epsilon^{(0)} = u^{(0)} - \bar{u} = \sum_{i=1}^{N} c_i v^{(i)} \qquad (5)$$

Evidently the nth-error vector $\epsilon^{(n)}$, is given by

$$\epsilon^{(n)} = u^{(n)} - \bar{u} = \sum_{i=1}^{N} c_i P_n(\mu_i) v^{(i)} = \sum_{i=1}^{N} c_i' v^{(i)} \qquad (6)$$

where

$$c_i' = c_i P_n(\mu_i) \qquad (7)$$

The idea of polynomial acceleration is to choose the $\{P_n(\mu)\}$ so that all of the coefficients $c_i' = c_i P_n(\mu_i)$ of $\epsilon^{(n)}$ become as small as possible. Let us write $P_n(\mu)$ in the form

---

* The formula in Equation 4 can be rewritten in the computable form

$$u^{(n)} = P_n(G_s)u^{(0)} + Q_{n-1}(G_s)k_s$$

where $Q_{n-1}(G_s) = (I - P_n(G_s))(I - G_s)^{-1}$ is a polynomial of degree $n - 1$ in G_s.

$$P_n(\mu) = \prod_{i=1}^{n} \frac{\mu - a_i}{1 - a_i} \tag{8}$$

where $a_1, a_2, \ldots, a_n$ are the zeros of $P_n(\mu)$. To make c_i' small for a given i, we could choose $P_n(\mu)$ so that there is a root a_k near μ_i. However if μ_i is close to one, this means choosing some a_k near one, and this introduces a large factor $(1 - a_k)^{-1}$. Thus it is much more difficult to reduce a component c_i' associated with a large eigenvalue μ_i than to reduce a c_i' associated with a small eigenvalue.

It would be helpful if we could construct an iteration procedure that could be used occasionally to reduce substantially the components c_i of the initial error vector $\epsilon^{(0)}$ of Equation 5 corresponding to large values of μ_i. We would refer to such an iteration as a macroiteration. Following a macroiteration with several iterations of an acceleration procedure of the type in Equation 4, we would expect to obtain a substantial error reduction for relatively little computational effort. To construct a macroiteration procedure, we seek a splitting matrix Q_M very close to A. Given such a Q_M, the macroiteration procedure is defined by

$$u^{(n+1)} = G_M u^{(n)} + k_M \tag{9}$$

where

$$\begin{cases} G_M = I - Q_M^{-1}A \\ k_M = Q_M^{-1}b \end{cases} \tag{10}$$

If Q_M is extremely close to A, then $G_M = Q_M^{-1}(Q_M - A)$ is very small and has very small eigenvalues. (In fact in the extreme case where $Q_M = A$, the eigenvalues are of course all zero.) In Chapter 7 we give some examples where splitting matrices Q_M can be constructed in a systematic manner that are close to A. We refer to methods involving macroiterations where the splitting matrix Q_M is very close to A as multilevel methods.

Because of the potentially large increase in the speed of convergence that can result from using macroiterations, we are prepared to expend a relatively large amount of effort to carry out such iterations as compared to the work required for one iteration of a standard iterative method, such as the Jacobi method. On the other hand, the effort required for the macroiteration should not be so great that the total computational effort, including necessary applications of the macroiterations and repeated use of the polynomial acceleration procedure, is as great, or nearly as great, as that required by using the polynomial acceleration procedure alone.

In Chapter 7 we consider several examples of multilevel methods. First we consider the solution of a model problem using a nine-point difference equation. We use a macroiteration procedure based on the standard five-point difference equation. Next we consider the solution of a model problem using the standard five-point difference equation where the macroiteration procedure is based on a skewed five-point difference equation. In each case for the model problem defined in Section 2, the given matrix A, the matrix G_s for the basic iterative method in Equation 2, and the matrix G_M of the macroiteration procedure have the same eigenvectors. Moreover in each case, the eigenvalues of G_M corresponding to the large eigenvalues of G_s are very small. On the other hand, for the skewed five-point and for the five-point case, the eigenvalues of G_M corresponding to small eigenvalues of G_s are very large. In such cases using macroiterations alone would not yield convergence. This difficulty can be easily overcome in either of two ways. First for each macroiteration, we could apply several smoothing iterations based on Equation 2. Alternatively we could use an inner-smoothing procedure, which involves choosing a suitable matrix H and replacing G_M and k_M in Equation 1.10 by

$$\begin{cases} G'_M = I - HQ_M^{-1}A \\ k'_M = HQ_M^{-1}b \end{cases} \tag{11}$$

We could also choose a suitable matrix K and replace G_M and k_M by

$$\begin{cases} G'_M = I - Q_M^{-1}KA \\ k'_M = Q_M^{-1}Kb \end{cases} \tag{12}$$

For other examples of multilevel methods, we consider two-level multigrid methods applied to model problems in one and two dimensions. We consider totally parallel multigrid methods, introduced by Frederickson and McBryan,[2] wherein we consider more than one coarse grid. Thus there are two coarse grids in one dimension and four coarse grids in two dimensions. In the two dimensional case, we assume that A corresponds to the standard five-point finite difference equation with grid size h. The matrix Q_M corresponds to a five-point difference equation for each of the four grids associated with the grid size $2h$. To restrict residuals from the fine grid to the coarse grid, we can use either injection or a smoothing procedure. Similarly we can transfer corrections from coarse grids to the fine grid without interpolation, or we can use interpolation. If a smoothing process is used for residual restriction and interpolation is used to transfer corrections, the macroiteration matrix can be written in the form

$$G'_M = I - HQ_M^{-1}KA \qquad (13)$$

where H corresponds to interpolating corrections and K corresponds to restricting residuals. We refer to the use of H and K as an inner-smoothing process in contrast to the outer smoothing based on the smoothing iteration procedure in Equation 2. Following Frederickson and McBryan,[2] we use an inner-smoothing process primarily to eliminate singularities in the macroiteration process.

In each of the examples considered, the smoothing iteration is the Jacobi method. Moreover matrices A, H, K, Q_M, and G_s have the same eigenvectors; hence the eigenvalues λ of G_M can be determined in terms of the eigenvalues of those matrices. In each case we obtain a factor $\hat{\lambda}(\mu)$ that is a bound on $|\lambda|$ for all eigenvalues λ of G_M associated with eigenvectors v of G_s corresponding to the eigenvalue μ. By using the function $\hat{\lambda}(\mu)$, we can as shown in Section 7 choose a good polynomial acceleration procedure based on the smoothing iteration method to reduce the error further.

We remark that the macroiteration procedure followed by a single application of the smoothing iteration procedure in Equation 2 is equivalent to using a suitable inner smoothing of the macroiteration. Thus we have

$$\begin{cases} G_s G_M = (I - Q_s^{-1}A)(I - Q_M^{-1}A) \\ \qquad = I - KQ_M^{-1}A \end{cases} \qquad (14)$$

where

$$K = Q_s^{-1}(Q_M + Q_s - A) \qquad (15)$$

In Section 7 we discuss the choice of smoothing procedures based on using macroiterations with smoothing iterations to reduce the error to a desired tolerance. Normally the rate of convergence of the smoothing iteration process is very large immediately following application of a macroiteration; convergence then slows down. At that point another macroiteration is performed, followed by another set of smoothing iterations. The process is repeated until convergence is obtained. The number of smoothing iterations performed following each macroiteration depends on the amount of work required for each macroiteration compared to the work required for each smoothing iteration.

We hope that Chapter 7 contributes to a better understanding of multilevel methods, especially multigrid methods, in terms of the standard theory of iterative methods. Even though analysis is applicable to only a very special class of problems*, it is expected to provide a guide for applying the procedures to more general problems. To this end a number of numerical experiments have been carried out based on the techniques described in Chapter 7, and additional experiments are planned. The results obtained so far are encouraging.

Dedication. The authors wish to dedicate this paper to Dr. Samuel D. Conte. One of us (Young) has known Dr. Conte for over 35 years. Their association includes 3 years as colleagues at the Ramo-Wooldridge Corporation and several years as fellow members of the Computer Science Curriculum Committee of the Association for Computing Machinery.

2. MODEL PROBLEM

In this section we consider linear systems corresponding to certain finite-difference representations of the following model problem:

$$\begin{cases} -u_{xx} - u_{yy} = f(x, y) \text{ in the unit square } \Omega = (0, 1) \times (0, 1) \\ u(x, y) = 0 \text{ on the boundary } \partial\Omega \end{cases} \quad (16)$$

We consider several finite-difference representations of this problem, and in each case we choose an integer M and represent the differential equation by a difference equation involving points on the grid $\{(ih, jh), i, j = 0, 1, 2, \ldots, M\}$, where $h = M^{-1}$ is the grid size.

For the standard five-point difference equation, we have

$$4u(x, y) - \{u(x + h, y) + u(x - h, y) + u(x, y + h) + u(x, y - h)\}$$
$$= h^2 f(x, y) \quad (17)$$

---

* For an analysis of a multigrid method as an iterative method for more general classes of problems, see Greenbaum.[10]

We also consider the nine-point difference equation (see for example Reference 3, Chap. 15)

$$20u(x, y) - 4[u(x + h, y) + u(x - h, y) + u(x, y + h) + u(x, y - h)]$$
$$- [u(x + h, y + h) + u(x + h, y - h)$$
$$+ u(x - h, y + h) + u(x - h, y - h)]$$
$$= 6h^2 \left\{ f(x, y) + \frac{h^2}{12} [f_{xx}(x, y) + f_{xx}(x, y)] \right.$$
$$\left. + \frac{h^4}{360} [f_{xxxx}(x, y) + 4f_{xxyy}(x, y) + f_{yyyy}(x, y)] \right\} \quad (18)$$

Finally we consider the skewed five-point equation

$$4u(x, y) - [u(x + h, y + h) + u(x + h, y - h)$$
$$+ u(x - h, y + h) + u(x - h, y - h)] = 2h^2 f(x, y) \quad (19)$$

Each of these systems can be represented in the form of Equation 1, where Au corresponds to the left-hand member of Equations 17, 18, or 19 as appropriate. We denoted the matrices by A_5, A_9, and A_D, respectively. The right-hand sides are denoted by $b^{(5)}$, $b^{(9)}$, and $b^{(D)}$. We can verify directly (see for example Reference 4, p. 129)[*] that the eigenvectors of A are

$$v_{p,q} = \sin p\pi x \sin q\pi y \qquad p, q = 1, 2, \ldots, M - 1 \quad (20)$$

The corresponding eigenvalues $v_{p,q}$ are for A_5

$$v_{p,q} = 4 - 2\cos p\pi h - 2\cos q\pi h = 4 - 2(a + b) \quad (21)$$

for A_9

$$v_{p,q} = 20 - 8(\cos p\pi h + \cos q\pi h) - 4\cos p\pi h \cos q\pi h$$
$$= 20 - 8(a + b) - 4ab \quad (22)$$

[*] There the relations are verified for the Jacobi iteration matrix B. However since $A = 4(I + B)$, the eigenvectors of A are the same as those of B.

for A_D

$$v_{p,q} = 4 - 4\cos p\pi h \cos q\pi h = 4 - 4ab \qquad (23)$$

Here we let $a = \cos p\pi h$ and $b = \cos q\pi h$. We frequently consider the values of $v_{p,q}$ as a and b range over the interval $[-1, 1]$.

3. FIVE-POINT/NINE-POINT MULTILEVEL METHOD

In this section we consider a multilevel method for solving the nine-point equation (Equation 18). The macroiteration is based on the five-point equation difference equation (Equation 17). The five-point difference equation is very well suited for vector and parallel computation. Thus the five-point equation can be solved using a red–black ordering (see for example Reference 1). Each of the two groups of equations, those corresponding to the red points and those corresponding to the black points, can be treated in parallel. The amount of work required to solve the five-point equation is substantially less than that required to solve the nine-point equation.*

The matrix G_M for the corresponding macroiterations is given by

$$G_M = I - \gamma A_5^{-1} A_9 \qquad (24)$$

The value of $1/6$ is suggested for γ by observing that $h^{-2}A_5$ and $(6h^2)^{-1}A_9$ both correspond to the operator $-u_{xx} - u_{yy}$. Evidently by Equations 21 and 22, the eigenvalues λ of G_M are given by

$$\lambda = \lambda(a, b) = 1 - \gamma \frac{20 - 8(a + b) - 4ab}{4 - 2(a + b)} \qquad (25)$$

where $a = \cos p\pi h$, $b = \cos q\pi h$, and $p, q = 1, 2, \ldots, M - 1$. (Here and subsequently we treat a and b as variables each ranging over the interval $[-1, 1]$.) Following Reference 2 we choose γ so that $\lim_{a \to 1 b \to 1} \lambda(a, b) = 0$. Since as can easily be shown,

---

* However multicolor orderings can be used for the nine-point equation; see for example Reference 1.

$$\lim_{\substack{a\to 1 \\ b\to 1}} \frac{20 - 8(a + b) - 4ab}{4 - 2(a + b)} = 6 \tag{26}$$

the choice $\gamma = 1/6$ is verified, and we have

$$G_M = I - \frac{1}{6} A_5^{-1} A_9 \tag{27}$$

and

$$\lambda(a, b) = 1 - \frac{1}{6}\left[\frac{20 - 8(a + b) - 4ab}{4 - 2(a + b)}\right] = \frac{1}{3}\frac{(1 - a)(1 - b)}{(2 - a - b)} \tag{28}$$

Let us now consider the Jacobi method for solving the nine-point equation. The matrix for the Jacobi method is

$$B_9 = I - \frac{1}{20} A_9 \tag{29}$$

which has eigenvalues

$$\mu = \frac{2}{5}(a + b) + \frac{1}{5} ab \tag{30}$$

Evidently μ ranges from $-3/5$ when $a = b = -1$ to 1 when $a = b = 1$. For each μ in $[-3/5,1]$, let $\Omega(\mu)$ denote the set of all (a, b) such that

$$\left(\frac{2}{5}\right)(a + b) + \left(\frac{1}{5}\right)ab = \mu$$

We seek to determine $\hat{\lambda}(\mu)$ defined by

$$\hat{\lambda}(\mu) = \underset{(a,b)\in\Omega(\mu)}{\text{Max}} |\lambda(a, b)| \tag{31}$$

For any μ in $[-3/5, 1]$, we consider the contour defined by

$$ab + 2(a + b) = 5\mu \tag{32}$$

From Equation 3.5

$$3\lambda(a, b) = \frac{1 + 5\mu - 3(a + b)}{2 - (a + b)} = \frac{1 + 5\mu - 3\alpha}{2 - \alpha} \qquad (33)$$

where $\alpha = a + b$. Evidently the last expression is a decreasing function of α, since

$$3\frac{d\lambda(a, b)}{d\alpha} = \frac{5\mu - 5}{(2 - \alpha)^2} = -\frac{5(1 - \mu)}{(2 - \alpha)^2} < 0 \qquad (34)$$

and $\mu < 1$. We now show that as we move along the contour in Equation 32 in the direction of increasing a (from $a = b$), α increases. Thus on the contour we have

$$b = \frac{(5\mu - 2a)}{(2 + a)} \qquad \text{and} \qquad \alpha = a + b = \frac{(a^2 + 5\mu)}{(2 + \alpha)}$$

Hence by Equation 32 we have

$$\frac{d\alpha}{da} = \frac{a^2 + 4a - 5\mu}{(2 + a)^2} = \frac{a^2 + 4a - 2(a + b) - ab}{(2 + a)^2} = \frac{a - b}{a + 2} > 0 \qquad (35)$$

since $a > b$. Thus the largest value of $\lambda(a, b)$ on the contour is given by $\lambda(a^*, b^*)$ where by Equation 32

$$(a^*)^2 = 5\mu - 4a^* \qquad (36)$$

or

$$a^* = -2 + [4 + 5\mu]^{1/2} \qquad (37)$$

(We reject the negative root $-2 - [4 + 5\mu]^{1/2}$, since $-1 < a^* < 1$.) Since $\mu \geq -3/5$, from Equation 31,

$$\hat{\lambda}(\mu) = \lambda(a^*, b^*) = \frac{1}{6}(1 - a^*) = \frac{5}{6}\left[\frac{1 - \mu}{3 + [4 + 5\mu]^{1/2}}\right] \leq \frac{5}{24}(1 - \mu) \quad (38)$$

Evidently since $(5/24)(1 - \mu) \leq 1/3$ for μ in $[-3/5, 1]$, we have

$$S(G_M) = \underset{-3/5 \leq \mu \leq 1}{\text{Max}} \hat{\lambda}(\mu) = \frac{1}{3} \qquad (39)$$

This bound is independent of h. More important however is the fact that as described in Section 7, we can apply a polynomial acceleration procedure based on the Jacobi method to obtain faster convergence.

4. THE SKEWED FIVE-POINT/FIVE-POINT MULTILEVEL METHOD

In this section we consider a multilevel method for solving the five-point difference equation Equation 17 where the macroiteration procedure is based on the skewed five-point difference equation Equation 19.

While the standard five-point equation is well suited for vector and parallel computation, the skewed five-point equation has the potential for even greater parallelism. Thus we can consider using a line symmetric successive overrelaxation (SSOR) procedure combined with conjugate gradient acceleration to solve the skewed five-point equation. With this procedure all of the points on a given line are uncoupled, and they can be treated simultaneously. With the standard five-point equation, on the other hand, using line iteration involves solving a number of tridiagonal linear systems for which parallelism may be difficult. We remark that the line SSOR method with Chebyshev or conjugate gradient acceleration is an order-of-magnitude faster, at least for the model problem, than the accelerated Jacobi method. However the SSOR method is not effective for the red–black ordering. Using the line SSOR method with the natural ordering of the rows makes it possible to achieve a level of parallelism equal to the number of points on a row without sacrificing the convergence rate.

We remark that as pointed out by Hackbusch,[5] using the skewed five-point formula can be regarded as a multigrid procedure where the grid size is increased by a factor of 2.5. We also note that the skewed five-point formula can be used independently on the red points and the black points. We assume in this discussion that at each step, the skewed five-point equation is solved on both sets of points.

The matrix G_M for the macroiteration for the skewed five-point or five-point procedure is given by

$$G_M = I - \gamma A_D^{-1} A_s \tag{40}$$

Here the factor $\gamma = 2$ is suggested by Equations 17 and 19, since $h^{-2}A_s$

and $(2h^2)^{-1}A_D$ both correspond to the operator $-u_{xx} - u_{yy}$. Evidently by Equations 21 and 23, the eigenvalues λ of G_M are given by

$$\lambda = \lambda(a, b) = 1 - \gamma \frac{4 - 4(a + b)}{4 - 4ab} \tag{41}$$

It is simple to show that

$$\lim_{\substack{a \to 1 \\ b \to 1}} \frac{4 - 4(a + b)}{4 - 4ab} = \frac{1}{2} \tag{42}$$

The choice of $\gamma = 2$ is verified, since $\lambda(1, 1) = 0$ if $\gamma = 2$. We have also,

$$G_M = I - 2A_D^{-1}A_S \tag{43}$$

Moreover the eigenvalues of G_M are

$$\lambda(a, b) = - \frac{(1 - a)(1 - b)}{1 - ab} \tag{44}$$

We note that the eigenvalues of G_M are nonpositive and vanish when $a = b = 1$. However there is a pole at $a = b = -1$ in the sense that

$$\lim_{\substack{a \to -1 \\ b \to -1}} \lambda(a, b) = \infty$$

As we see later, this difficulty can be remedied by using an inner smoothing. On the other hand, it can also be remedied by using an outer smoothing iteration based on the Jacobi method.

Let us now consider the Jacobi method for solving the standard five-point equation. The matrix for the Jacobi method is

$$B_S = I - \frac{1}{4}A_S \tag{45}$$

which has eigenvalues

$$\mu = \frac{1}{2}(a + b) \tag{46}$$

Evidently μ ranges from -1 when $a = b = -1$ to 1 when $a = b = 1$. We show that on a contour $a + b = 2\mu$ where μ is constant, $|\lambda(a, b)|$ is maximized when $a = b = \mu/2$. Let $\alpha = a + b$ and $\beta = a - b$. Since $ab = (\alpha^2 - \beta^2)/4$, we have

$$-\lambda(a, b) = \frac{1 - (a + b) + ab}{1 - ab} = \frac{1 - \alpha + (\alpha^2 - \beta^2)/4}{1 - (\alpha^2 - \beta^2)/4}$$

$$= \frac{[1 - (\alpha/2)]^2 - (\beta^2/4)}{[1 - (\alpha^2/4)] + (\beta^2/4)} \tag{47}$$

Evidently for fixed α, the value of $-\lambda(a, b)$ is maximized when $\beta = 0$ and $a = b = \mu$. Then we have

$$-\lambda(a, b) \leq \frac{(1 - a)^2}{1 - a^2} = \frac{1 - a}{1 + a} = \frac{1 - \mu}{1 + \mu} \tag{48}$$

and hence

$$\hat{\lambda}(\mu) = \frac{1 - \mu}{1 + \mu} \tag{49}$$

The singularity at $\mu = -1$ can be removed by inner smoothing, as shown later, or by one iteration of the damped Jacobi method (the Jacobi method with extrapolation factor $\gamma = 1/2$) whose matrix is

$$B_{[1/2]} = \frac{1}{2}(I + B_s) \tag{50}$$

Thus for $B_{[1/2]}G_M$ the eigenvalues are $\lambda' = \frac{1}{2}(1 - \mu)$. Now for $\mu = -1$, we have an eigenvalue with modulus 1. This can be improved by using another damped Jacobi method.

We now consider using two inner smoothings. First we consider an inner smoothing based on the nine-point operator defined by

$$Kv(x, y) = v(x, y)$$

$$+ \frac{1}{2}[v(x + h, y) + v(x - h, y) + v(x, y + h) + v(x, y - h)]$$

$$+ \frac{1}{4} [v(x + h, y + h) + v(x + h, y - h)$$

$$+ v(x - h, y + h) + v(x - h, y - h)] \quad (51)$$

Evidently the eigenvectors of K are $v_{p,q}(x, y) = \sin p\pi x \sin q\pi y$, and the eigenvalues are

$$v_{p,q}^{(K)} = 1 + ab + a + b = (1 + a)(1 + b) \quad (52)$$

where $a = \cos p\pi h$ and $b = \cos q\pi h$. Since $(1 + a)(1 + b) = 4$ when $a = b = 1$, we consider the modified iteration matrix

$$G'_M = I - \frac{1}{2} K A_D^{-1} A_S \quad (53)$$

whose eigenvalues are

$$\lambda' = \lambda'(a, b) = 1 - \frac{1}{2}(1 + a)(1 + b) \frac{4 - 2(a + b)}{4 - 4ab}$$

$$= \frac{2 - (a + b)}{4} + \frac{(a - b)^2}{4 - 4ab} \geq 0 \quad (54)$$

If we let $\alpha = a + b$ and $\beta = a - b$, we have

$$\lambda' = \frac{2 - \alpha}{4} + \frac{\beta^2}{4 - \alpha^2 + \beta^2} \quad (55)$$

which is an increasing function of β. Thus the maximum value of $\lambda'(a, b)$ for $a + b = \alpha = 2\mu$ corresponds to $a = 1, b = \alpha - 1 = 2\mu - 1$ if $\mu > 0$ and to $a = -1, b = \alpha + 1 = 2\mu + 1$ if $\mu < 0$.
Thus for $\mu > 0$ we have

$$\lambda'(1, 2\mu - 1) = \frac{2 - 2\mu}{4} + \frac{(2 - 2\mu)^2}{8(1 - \mu)} = 1 - \mu \quad (56)$$

For $\mu < 0$ we have

$$\lambda'(-1, 2\mu + 1) = \frac{2 - 2\mu}{4} + \frac{4(1 + \mu)^2}{4 + 4(2\mu + 1)}$$

$$= \frac{(1 - \mu)}{2} + \frac{4(1 + \mu)^2}{8 + 8\mu} = \frac{1 - \mu}{2} + \frac{1 + \mu}{2} = 1 \quad (57)$$

Thus we have

$$\hat{\lambda}(\mu) = \begin{cases} 1 - \mu & \text{if } \mu > 0 \\ 1 & \text{if } \mu < 0 \end{cases} \quad (58)$$

We have removed the singularity, but the method is still not convergent. Some inner or outer smoothing is necessary to achieve convergence.

We now consider a second inner smoothing, designed to yield a smaller value of $\hat{\lambda}(\mu)$ than that given by Equation 58, for the previously described inner smoothing. Here we let the matrix K be defined by

$$K = 4(I + B_5) = 8I - A_5 \quad (59)$$

This corresponds to the operator defined by

$$Kv(x, y) = 4v(x, y) + v(x + h, y) + v(x - h, y)$$
$$+ v(x, y + h) + v(x, y - h) \quad (60)$$

The eigenvectors of K are again $v_{p,q}(x, y) = \sin p\pi x \sin q\pi y$, and the eigenvalues are

$$v_{p,q}^{(K)} = 4 + 2(a + b)$$

where as before $\alpha = \cos p\pi h$ and $b = \cos q\pi h$. Since $4 + 2(a + b) = 8$ when $a = b = 1$, we let the modified macroiteration matrix G_M'' be defined by

$$G_M'' = I - \frac{1}{4} [4(I + B_5)A_D^{-1}A_5]$$

$$= I - (I + B_5)A_D^{-1}A_5 \quad (61)$$

The eigenvalues of G_M'' are

$$\lambda(a, b) = 1 - \left[1 + \frac{1}{2}(a + b)\right]\frac{4 - 2(a + b)}{4 - 4ab}$$

$$= \frac{(a - b)^2}{4 - 4ab} \tag{62}$$

Now let $\alpha = a + b$ and $\beta = a - b$. We have

$$\lambda(a, b) = \frac{\beta^2}{4 - \alpha^2 + \beta^2} = \frac{1}{(4 - \alpha^2)/(\beta^2) + 1} \tag{63}$$

which increases as β increases. Thus for given $\mu = \frac{1}{2}\alpha$, the largest value of $\lambda(a, b)$ is obtained when $\alpha = 1$ and $b = 2\mu - 1$ for $\mu > 0$, and when $a = -1$ and $b = 2\mu + 1$ for $\mu < 0$.
Thus we have

$$\hat{\lambda}(\mu) = \begin{cases} \lambda(1, 2\mu - 1) = \dfrac{1 - \mu}{2} & \text{for } \mu > 0 \\[4mm] \lambda(-1, 2\mu + 1) = \dfrac{1 + \mu}{2} & \text{for } \mu < 0 \end{cases} \tag{64}$$

Combining the preceding results, we have

$$\hat{\lambda}(\mu) = \frac{1 - |\mu|}{2} \tag{65}$$

Therefore we have

$$S(G_M'') \le \frac{1}{2} \tag{66}$$

This bound is independent of h. As in the case of the five-point or nine-point multilevel method, however, of greater importance is the fact that, as shown in Section 7, we can apply a polynomial acceleration procedure based on the Jacobi method to obtain faster convergence.

5. PARALLEL MULTIGRID FOR A PROBLEM IN ONE DIMENSION

We now consider a multilevel method based on a two-level multigrid method applied to the following problem in one dimension (see Reference 6):

$$\begin{cases} -u'' = f(x) & 0 < x < 1 \\ u(0) = u(1) = 0 \end{cases} \tag{67}$$

We first consider the standard three-point finite difference operator with grid size $h = M^{-1}$ defined by

$$\begin{cases} 2u(x) - u(x + h) - u(x - h) = h^2 f(x) \\ u(0) = u(1) = 0 \end{cases} \tag{68}$$

for $x = x_i = ih$, $i = 1, 2, \ldots, (M - 1)$. In the case of $M = 8$ with the grid points labeled as in Figure 7.1, the difference equation problem can be represented in the matrix form by

$$\begin{bmatrix} 2 & -1 & & & & & \\ -1 & 2 & -1 & & & & \\ & -1 & 2 & -1 & & & \\ & & -1 & 2 & -1 & & \\ & & & -1 & 2 & -1 & \\ & & & & -1 & 2 & -1 \\ & & & & & -1 & 2 \end{bmatrix} \begin{bmatrix} u_1 \\ u_2 \\ u_3 \\ u_4 \\ u_5 \\ u_6 \\ u_7 \end{bmatrix} = h^2 \begin{bmatrix} f_1 \\ f_2 \\ f_3 \\ f_4 \\ f_5 \\ f_6 \\ f_7 \end{bmatrix} \tag{69}$$

or

$$A_h u^{(h)} = b^{(h)} \tag{70}$$

We now show that the eigenvectors of A_h are given by $v^{(1)}, v^{(2)}, \ldots, v^{(M-1)}$ where

$$v^{(p)}(x) = \sin p\pi x \qquad p = 1, 2, \ldots, M - 1 = 7 \tag{71}$$

The corresponding eigenvalues are

```
         B    A    B    A    B    A    B
├──┬──┬──┬──●──┬──┬──┬──┬──┬──┬──┬──●──┬──┬──┬──┤
(-3) (-2) (-1)  0              4              8  (9) (10) (11)
            (x=0)                             (x=1)
```

Figure 7.1. Types of coarse grid points in a two-dimensional problem: h = 1/8.

$$v_p^{(h)} = 2 - 2\cos p\pi h \qquad p = 1, 2, \ldots, M - 1 = 7 \qquad (72)$$

Thus for $i = 2, \ldots, 6$ we have

$$2\sin p\pi x - \sin p\pi(x + h) - \sin p\pi(x - h) = (2 - 2\cos p\pi h)\sin p\pi x \quad (73)$$

If $i = 1$, then

$$2\sin p\pi h - \sin p\pi(2h) = 2\sin p\pi h - \sin p\pi(2h) - \sin p\pi(0)$$

$$= (2 - 2\cos p\pi h)\sin p\pi h \qquad (74)$$

A similar result holds for $i = 7$.

We now consider using a coarse grid with grid size $2h$ and with interior points x_2, x_4, and x_6. The standard three-point difference equation leads to the system

$$\begin{bmatrix} 2 & -1 & 0 \\ -1 & 2 & -1 \\ 0 & -1 & 2 \end{bmatrix} \begin{bmatrix} u_2 \\ u_4 \\ u_6 \end{bmatrix} = \begin{bmatrix} (2h)^2 f_2 \\ (2h)^2 f_4 \\ (2h)^2 f_6 \end{bmatrix} \qquad (75)$$

or

$$A_{2h} u^{(2h)} = b^{(2h)} \qquad (76)$$

A standard multigrid procedure for solving Equation 68 can be described as follows:

1. Carry out several smoothing iterations on the fine grid based on the Jacobi method or perhaps a polynomial acceleration procedure based on the Jacobi method.
2. When the convergence rate appears to be slow, compute the residual $r^{(h)} = b^{(h)} - A_h u^*$ on the fine grid. Here u^* is the most recent approximation to $\bar{u}$ obtained by iterating on the fine grid.
3. Restrict residuals from the fine grid to the coarse grid. Thus assign a residual for each point on the coarse grid as either the value at

the same point on the fine grid (injection) or as a weighted average of the neighboring points. Thus for the averaging procedure, if x is a point of the coarse grid, we may take

$$r^{(2h)}(x) = \frac{1}{2} r^{(h)}(x) + \frac{1}{4} r^{(h)}(x - h) \frac{1}{4} r^{(h)}(x + h) \qquad (77)$$

as the residual for the coarse grid at the point x. This process can be called a smoothing restriction.

4. Solve the following system for $\delta^{(2h)}$

$$A_{2h}\delta^{(2h)} = \gamma r^{(2h)} \qquad (78)$$

Here γ is a factor chosen to take account of the fact that $(2h)^{-2}A_{2h}$ and $h^{-2}A_h$ each represents the operator $-u_{xx}$. Normally we would choose $\gamma = 4$. In the case of more than two levels, we may transfer to even coarser grids to solve Equation 78.

5. Interpolate $\delta^{(2h)}$ onto the fine grid to obtain $\delta^{(h)}$. One possibility would be to let $\delta^{(h)}(x) = \delta^{(2h)}(x)$ if x is on the coarse grid and to let

$$\delta^{(h)}(x) = \frac{1}{2} \delta^{(2h)}(x - h) + \frac{1}{2} \delta^{(2h)}(x + h)$$

if x is not on the coarse grid.

6. Let $u^{(new)} = u^* + \delta^{(h)}$.
7. Go to step 1.

Frederickson and McBryan[2] considered using parallel multigrid methods. This scheme is motivated by the fact that when the (classical) standard multigrid procedure is used with a parallel machine, many of the processors are idle as we work on the coarse grid. The idle processors could be used to work on both coarse grids at the same time. (In the two-dimensional case, this could be done for all four coarse grids.) An advantage of the such a procedure is that the matrices involved as we go from one grid size to another are all the same size. The analysis is greatly simplified, and it becomes easier to study the convergence properties of the multigrid methods in terms of the standard theory of iterative methods.

Let us now consider the other coarse grid for the problem defined by Equation 67. The interior points are $x_1, x_3, x_5,$ and x_7. The points x_1 and x_7 are in some sense irregular. Thus in the case of x_1, neighboring points are x_0 and x_3, which are not equidistant from x_1. Using standard finite difference representations for $-u_{xx}$, we obtain

$$\begin{cases} \dfrac{-2u_0 + 3u_1 - u_3}{(3/2)(2h)^2} = f_1 \\[2mm] \dfrac{-u_1 + 2u_3 - u_5}{(2h)^2} = f_3 \\[2mm] \dfrac{-u_3 + 2u_5 - u_7}{(2h)^2} = f_5 \\[2mm] \dfrac{-u_5 + 3u_7 - 2u_8}{(3/2)(2h)^2} = f_7 \end{cases} \tag{79}$$

If we combine this with Equation 75 and note that $u_0 = u_8 = 0$, we obtain

$$\begin{bmatrix} 2 & 0 & -2/3 & 0 & 0 & 0 & 0 \\ 0 & 2 & 0 & -1 & 0 & 0 & 0 \\ -1 & 0 & 2 & 0 & -1 & 0 & 0 \\ 0 & -1 & 0 & 2 & 0 & -1 & 0 \\ 0 & 0 & -1 & 0 & 2 & 0 & -1 \\ 0 & 0 & 0 & -1 & 0 & 2 & 0 \\ 0 & 0 & 0 & 0 & -2/3 & 0 & 2 \end{bmatrix} \begin{bmatrix} u_1 \\ u_2 \\ u_3 \\ u_4 \\ u_5 \\ u_6 \\ u_7 \end{bmatrix} = (2h)^2 \begin{bmatrix} f_1 \\ f_2 \\ f_3 \\ f_4 \\ f_5 \\ f_6 \\ f_7 \end{bmatrix} \tag{80}$$

This can be written as

$$\hat{A}_{2h}\hat{u}^{(2h)} = \hat{b}^{(2h)} \tag{81}$$

We could apply the multigrid procedure previously described for both coarse grids. All of the operations involved (including restricting residuals and interpolating corrections) can be represented by square matrices, which, as stated earlier, greatly simplifies the analysis. Interpolating corrections can also be done by injection if desired. Before proceding with our analysis however, we replace the system in Equation 81 with the system

$$\hat{A}'_{2h}\hat{u}^{(2h)} = \hat{b}^{(2h)} \tag{82}$$

where

$$\hat{A}'_{2h} = \begin{bmatrix} 3 & 0 & -1 & 0 & 0 & 0 & 0 \\ 0 & 2 & 0 & -1 & 0 & 0 & 0 \\ -1 & 0 & 2 & 0 & -1 & 0 & 0 \\ 0 & -1 & 0 & 2 & 0 & -1 & 0 \\ 0 & 0 & -1 & 0 & 2 & 0 & -1 \\ 0 & 0 & 0 & -1 & 0 & 2 & 0 \\ 0 & 0 & 0 & 0 & -1 & 0 & 3 \end{bmatrix} \tag{83}$$

This is equivalent to the following subsystem for the points x_1, x_3, x_5, and x_7:

$$\begin{bmatrix} 3 & -1 & 0 & 0 \\ -1 & 2 & -1 & 0 \\ 0 & -1 & 2 & -1 \\ 0 & 0 & -1 & 3 \end{bmatrix} \begin{bmatrix} u_1 \\ u_3 \\ u_5 \\ u_7 \end{bmatrix} = (2h)^2 \begin{bmatrix} f_1 \\ f_3 \\ f_5 \\ f_7 \end{bmatrix} \tag{84}$$

The subsystem corresponding to Equation 79 is

$$\begin{bmatrix} 3 & -1 & 0 & 0 \\ -1 & 2 & -1 & 0 \\ 0 & -1 & 2 & -1 \\ 0 & 0 & -1 & 3 \end{bmatrix} \begin{bmatrix} u_1 \\ u_3 \\ u_5 \\ u_7 \end{bmatrix} = (2h)^2 \begin{bmatrix} 3/2f_1 \\ f_3 \\ f_5 \\ 3/2f_7 \end{bmatrix} \tag{85}$$

As a partial justification for the modification, we note that by eliminating u_2, u_4, and u_4 from Equation 68, we obtain

$$\begin{bmatrix} 3 & -1 & 0 & 0 \\ -1 & 2 & -1 & 0 \\ 0 & -1 & 2 & -1 \\ 0 & 0 & -1 & 3 \end{bmatrix} \begin{bmatrix} u_1 \\ u_3 \\ u_5 \\ u_7 \end{bmatrix} = (2h)^2 \begin{bmatrix} 1/2f_1 + 1/4f_2 \\ 1/4f_2 + 1/2f_3 + 1/4f_4 \\ 1/4f_4 + 1/2f_5 + 1/4f_6 \\ 1/4f_6 + 1/2f_7 \end{bmatrix} \tag{86}$$

If $f(x)$ were a constant, say, F, then for the original system, the first component of the right-hand side of Equation 84 would be $4h^2F$, that of Equation 85 would be $6h^2F$; and that of Equation 86 would be $3h^2F$. Thus the value for the modified system in Equation 84 is closer to that of Equation 86 than that of Equation 85.

Our real motivation for using $\hat{A}'_{2h}$ instead of $\hat{A}_{2h}$ is however that the eigenvectors of $\hat{A}'_{2h}$ are the same as those of A_h. It should be noted that the macroiterative method based on using $\hat{A}'_{2h}$ is completely consistent with

Equation 70 in the sense of Young.[4] Moreover for the model problem, as we will see, the macroiteration procedure is effective especially when certain inner smoothings are used.

Let us show that for the eigenvectors $v^{(p)}(x)$ of $\hat{A}'_{2h}$ we have $v_i^{(p)} = v^{(p)}(x_i) = \sin p\pi x_i$, $x_i = ih$, $i = 1, 2, \ldots, M - 1 = 7$ and $p = 1, 2, \ldots, M - 1 = 7$. Thus for $i = 2, \ldots, 6$, we have

$$2v_i^{(p)} - v_{i+2}^{(p)} - v_{i-2}^{(p)} = (2 - 2\cos 2p\pi h)\sin p\pi x_i = (2 - 2\cos 2p\pi h)v_i^{(p)} \quad (87)$$

For $i = 1$ we have

$$\begin{aligned}
3v_1^{(p)} - v_3^{(p)} &= 3\sin p\pi h - \sin p\pi(3h) \\
&= 2\sin p\pi h + \sin p\pi h - \sin p\pi(3h) \\
&= -\sin(-p\pi h) + 2\sin p\pi h - \sin p\pi(3h) \\
&= (2 - 2\cos 2p\pi h)\sin p\pi h
\end{aligned} \quad (88)$$

A similar expression holds for $i = 7$. Thus $v^{(p)}$ is an eigenvector of $\hat{A}'_{2h}$ with eigenvalue

$$v_p^{(2h)} = 2 - 2\cos 2p\pi h \quad (89)$$

Let us now consider the procedure that would be used with grid size $4h$. For $\hat{A}'_{4h}$ we would use

$$\hat{A}'_{4h} = \begin{bmatrix}
2 & 0 & 1 & 0 & -1 & 0 & 0 \\
0 & 3 & 0 & 0 & 0 & -1 & 0 \\
1 & 0 & 2 & 0 & 0 & 0 & -1 \\
0 & 0 & 0 & 2 & 0 & 0 & 0 \\
-1 & 0 & 0 & 0 & 2 & 0 & 1 \\
0 & -1 & 0 & 0 & 0 & 3 & 0 \\
0 & 0 & -1 & 0 & 1 & 0 & 2
\end{bmatrix} \quad (90)$$

We can easily verify that the eigenvectors of $\hat{A}'_{4h}$ are the same as those of $\hat{A}'_{2h}$ and corresponding eigenvalues are

$$v_p^{(4h)} = 2 - 2\cos 4p\pi h \qquad p = 1, 2, \ldots, 7 \quad (91)$$

Let us consider a two-level parallel multigrid procedure based on using two sets of coarse grid points. If we assume residuals are injected from the fine grid into the coarse grid, then the matrix G_M of the macroiteration is given by

$$G_M = I - \gamma(\hat{A}'_{2h})^{-1}A_h \qquad (92)$$

The extrapolation factor $\gamma = 4$ is suggested, since $(2h)^{-2}\hat{A}'_{2h}$ and $h^{-2} A_h$ are both representations of $-u_{xx}$. With $a = \cos p\pi h$, eigenvalues of A_h and $\hat{A}'_{2h}$ are $2 - 2a$ and $2 - 2(2a^2 - 1) = 4 - 4a^2$, respectively. Thus the eigenvalues λ of G_M are given by

$$\lambda = \lambda(a) = 1 - 4\frac{2 - 2a}{4 - 4a^2} = -\frac{1 - a}{1 + a} \qquad (93)$$

As expected $\lambda(1) = 0$, and this confirms the choice $\gamma = 4$. However there is a pole at $a = -1$. This can easily be eliminated by using the damped Jacobi method with iteration matrix $G_s = \frac{1}{2}(I + B_h)$ as a smoothing iteration. The eigenvalues of G_s are $\frac{1}{2}(1 + a)$, and the eigenvalues λ' of G_sG_M are

$$\lambda' = -\frac{1}{2}(1 - a) \qquad (94)$$

The pole has been eliminated, but the method does not converge, since $\lambda'(-1) = 1$. However eigenvalues λ'' of $G_s^2G_M$ are

$$\lambda'' = -\frac{1}{4}(1 - a^2) \qquad (95)$$

and

$$S(G_s^2G_M) \leq \frac{1}{4} \qquad (96)$$

Evidently

$$\lambda'' = -\frac{1}{4}(1 - \mu^2) \qquad (97)$$

where $\mu = a$ is an eigenvalue of the Jacobi method whose matrix is $B_h = I$

$-\frac{1}{2}A_h$. Thus we could use the analysis in Section 7 to study the effect of smoothing iterations on the overall process.

Let us now consider using an inner smoothing to eliminate the singularity in the multigrid process. We consider the modified macroiteration procedure defined by

$$G'_M = I - 4\left[\frac{1}{2}(I + B_h)\right](\hat{A}'_{2h})^{-1}A_h \qquad (98)$$

This macroiteration corresponds to restricting residuals $r^{(h)}(x)$ on the fine grid to obtain residuals $r^{(2h)}(x)$ on the coarse grid, where

$$r^{(2h)}(x) = \frac{1}{4}r^{(2h)}(x - h) + \frac{1}{2}r^{(h)}(x) + \frac{1}{4}r^{(h)}(x + h) \qquad (99)$$

Evidently eigenvalues $\tilde{\lambda}$ of G'_M are given by

$$\hat{\lambda} = 1 - 4\left[\frac{1}{2}(1 + a)\right]\frac{2 - 2a}{4 - 4a^2} = 0 \qquad (100)$$

Thus the process converges exactly in one macroiteration. We note that this result is not surprising, since it can be shown directly that

$$2(I + B)A_h = \hat{A}'_{2h} \qquad (101)$$

6. PARALLEL MULTIGRID FOR A PROBLEM IN TWO DIMENSIONS

We now consider a two-level parallel multigrid procedure for the model problem in Equation (16). We consider four coarse grids; see the points labeled A, B, C, and D in Figure 7.2. As in the one-dimensional case, special formulas are needed for points adjacent to the boundary. We choose those formulas so that eigenvectors of the resulting matrix A_{2h} are the same as those of A_h. It can be shown that the eigenvalues of A_h are

$$v_{p,q}^{(h)} = 4 - 2(\cos p\pi h + \cos q\pi h) \qquad (102)$$

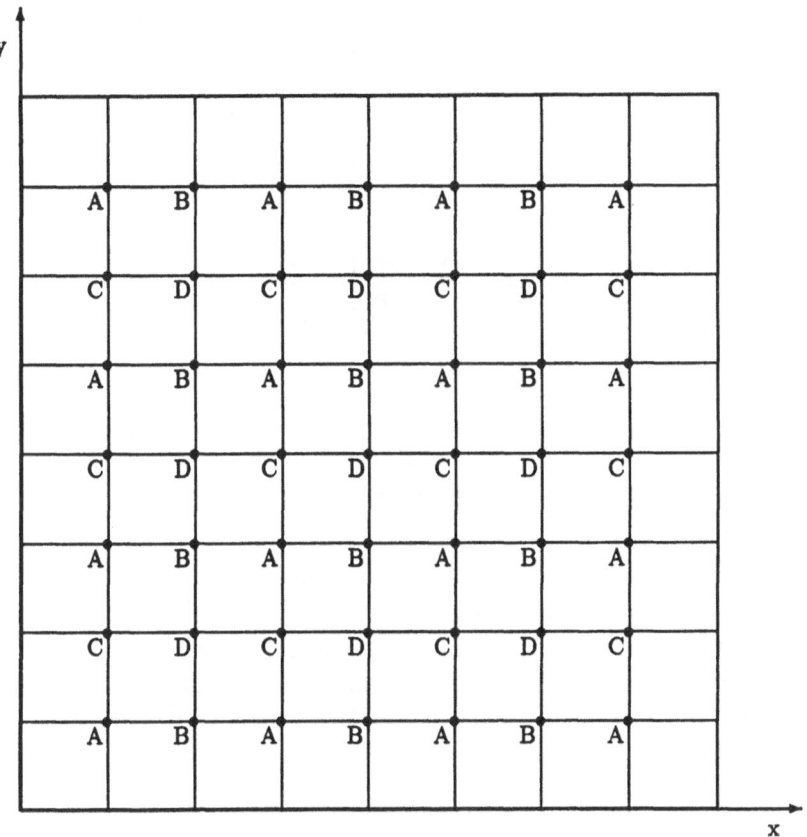

Figure 7.2. Grid points for a one-dimensional problem: $h = 1/8$.

whereas those of A_{2h} are

$$v_{p,q}^{(2h)} = 4 - 2(\cos 2p\pi h + \cos 2q\pi h) \qquad (103)$$

see Equations (20) and (21). Letting $a = \cos p\pi h$ and $b = \cos q\pi h$, we have

$$\begin{cases} v^{(h)} = 4 - 2(a + b) \\ v^{(2h)} = 8 - 4(a^2 + b^2) \end{cases} \qquad (104)$$

Let us first consider a two-level multigrid procedure involving no inner smoothings. The matrix for the macroiteration is given by

$$G_M = I - \gamma A_{2h}^{-1} A_h \qquad (105)$$

Here the value of 4 is suggested for γ, since $(2h)^{-2}A_{2h}$ and $h^{-2}A_h$ each corresponds to $-u_{xx} - u_{yy}$. With $\gamma = 4$ the eigenvalues $\lambda(a, b)$ of G_M are given by

$$\lambda(a, b) = 1 - 4\left[\frac{4 - 2(a + b)}{8 - 4(a^2 + b^2)}\right]$$

$$= -\frac{(1 - a)^2 + (1 - b)^2}{(1 - a^2) + (1 - b^2)} \leq 0 \qquad (106)$$

Since

$$\lim_{\substack{a \to 1 \\ b \to 1}} \lambda(a, b) = 0$$

the choice of $\gamma = 4$ is confirmed.

We now determine $\hat{\lambda}(\mu)$, which is the maximum value of $|\lambda(a, b)|$ on the line $2\mu = a + b$. [Here μ is an eigenvalue of the Jacobi iteration matrix and $\mu = \frac{1}{2}(a + b)$.] If we let $\alpha = a + b$ and $\beta = a - b$, we have

$$-\lambda = \frac{[1 - (\alpha/2)]^2 + (\beta^2/4)}{[1 - (\alpha^2/4)] - (\beta^2/4)} \qquad (107)$$

For fixed α, $-\lambda$ is maximized when β is as large as possible. Thus $-\lambda$ is maximized for $a = 1$ and $b = 2\mu - 1$ if $\mu > 0$ and for $a = -1$ and $b = 2\mu + 1$ if $\mu < 0$. In the case when $\mu > 0$, we have

$$-\lambda(1, 2\mu - 1) = \frac{1 - \mu}{\mu} \qquad (108)$$

In the case when $\mu < 0$, we have

$$-\lambda(-1, 2\mu + 1) = \frac{1 - \mu^2}{(-\mu)(1 + \mu)} \qquad (109)$$

Thus we have

$$
\hat{\lambda}(\mu) =
\begin{cases}
\dfrac{1-\mu}{\mu} & \text{if } \mu > 0 \\[2mm]
\dfrac{1-\mu^2}{(-\mu)(1+\mu)} & \text{if } \mu < 0
\end{cases}
\tag{110}
$$

We note that there are singularities for $\mu = 0$ and $\mu = -1$. [Actually they occur at the points $(-1, -1)$, $(1, -1)$, and $(-1, 1)$.] In any case they can be removed by using a pair of external iterations involving B and $\frac{1}{2}(I + B)$ whose eigenvalues are μ and $\frac{1}{2}(1 + \mu)$, respectively. Thus for the eigenvalues λ^* of $\frac{1}{2}(I + B)BG_M$, we have

$$
|\lambda^*| \le
\begin{cases}
\dfrac{1}{2}(1 - \mu^2) & \text{if } \mu \ge 0 \\[2mm]
\dfrac{1}{2}(1 + \mu^2) & \text{if } \mu \le 0
\end{cases}
\tag{111}
$$

Here the singularities have been removed, but the process still does not converge. However further (damped Jacobi) smoothing iterations result in convergence.

We now consider two inner-smoothing procedures. The first, suggested by Frederickson and McBryan,[2] involves using the nine-point operator K defined by Equation 51. The eigenvalues $\lambda'(a, b)$ of the resulting macroiteration matrix

$$
G'_M = I - \gamma K A_{2h}^{-1} A_h
\tag{112}
$$

are given by

$$
\lambda'(a, b) = 1 - \gamma(1 + a)(1 + b)\frac{4 - 2(a + b)}{8 - 4(a^2 + b^2)}
\tag{113}
$$

The choice of $\gamma = 1$ is suggested by the fact that $\gamma = 4$ was used for G_M since

$$
(1 + a)(1 + b) = 4 \qquad \text{for } a = b = 1
$$

With $\gamma = 1$ we obtain

$$\lambda' = \frac{(1-a)(1-b)(2+a+b)}{2[2-(a^2+b^2)]} \qquad (114)$$

It can be shown that

$$\lim_{\substack{a \to 1 \\ b \to 1}} \lambda'(a, b) = 0 \qquad (115)$$

which confirms the choice $\gamma = 1$.

We now determine $\hat{\lambda}(\mu)$ for a given eigenvalue μ of B, where $\hat{\lambda}(\mu)$ is the largest value of $|\lambda'(a, b)|$ for $a + b = 2\mu$. Let $\alpha = a + b$ and $\beta = a - b$. Then

$$\lambda'(a, b) = \frac{[1 - \alpha + (\alpha^2 - \beta^2)/4](2 + \alpha)}{2[2 - (\alpha^2 + \beta^2)/2]}$$

$$= \left[\frac{2+\alpha}{4}\right]\left\{\frac{[1-(\alpha/2)]^2-(\beta^2/4)}{1-(\alpha^2+\beta^2)/4}\right\} \qquad (116)$$

For $\alpha > 0$ the derivative of $\lambda'(a, b)$ with respect to β^2 is negative, since

$$\left(1 - \frac{\alpha}{2}\right)^2 - \left(1 - \frac{\alpha^2}{4}\right) = \alpha\left(\frac{\alpha}{2} - 1\right) < 0 \qquad (117)$$

Thus if $\mu > 0$, the largest value of $\lambda'(a, b)$ for given μ occurs when $a = b = \mu$. Then we have

$$\hat{\lambda}(\mu) = |\lambda'(\mu, \mu)| = \frac{1-\mu}{2} \qquad (118)$$

On the other hand, if $\alpha < 0$, the derivative of $\lambda'(a, b)$ with respect to β^2 is positive, since

$$\left(1 - \frac{\alpha}{2}\right)^2 - \left(1 - \frac{\alpha^2}{4}\right) = \alpha\left(\frac{\alpha}{2} - 1\right) > 0 \qquad (119)$$

Thus if $\mu < 0$, the largest value of λ' for given μ occurs when $a = -1$ and $b = 2\mu + 1$. Then we have

$$\hat{\lambda}(\mu) = \lambda'(-1, 2\mu + 1) = 1 \tag{120}$$

Therefore we have

$$\hat{\lambda}(\mu) = \begin{cases} \dfrac{1-\mu}{2} & \text{if } \mu \geq 0 \\ 1 & \text{if } \mu < 0 \end{cases} \tag{121}$$

We see that singularities have been removed, but the macroiteration procedure still does not converge. However convergence can be easily obtained by using outer smoothings.

We now consider another inner smoothing that leads to a convergent macroiteration process. Actually we use two inner-smoothing matrices K and L, where K corresponds to the five-point operator $B_{[1/2]} = \frac{1}{2}(I + B)$ used in Section 4. The (five-point) operator L is defined by

$$Lv(x, y) = v(x, y) + \frac{1}{4} [v(x + h, y + h) + v(x - h, y + h)$$

$$+ v(x - h, y - h) + v(x + h, y - h)] \tag{122}$$

The eigenvalues of the corresponding matrix are $1 + ab$. We consider the macroiteration defined by

$$G''_M = I - \gamma L \left[\frac{1}{2} (I + B) \right] A_{2h}^{-1} A_h \tag{123}$$

The eigenvalues $\lambda''(a, b)$ of G''_M are

$$\lambda''(a, b) = 1 - \gamma \frac{(1 + ab)[(1/2) + (1/4)(a + b)][4 - 2(a + b)]}{8 - 4(a^2 + b^2)} \tag{124}$$

The choice of $\gamma = 2$ is suggested. With this choice we obtain

$$\lambda''(a, b) = \frac{(1 - a^2)(1 - b^2)}{2(2 - a^2 - b^2)} + \frac{1 - ab}{4} \geq 0 \tag{125}$$

The choice of $\gamma = 2$ is confirmed, since

$$\lim_{\substack{a \to 1 \\ b \to 1}} \lambda''(a, b) = 0 \tag{126}$$

We now show that for fixed α, $\lambda''(a, b)$ is maximized if $a = b = \mu$. To do this we write $\lambda''(a, b)$ in the form

$$\lambda''(a, b) = 1 - \gamma\Gamma = 1 - 2\Gamma \tag{127}$$

where

$$
\begin{aligned}
\Gamma = \Gamma(a, b) &= \frac{(1 + ab)[(1/2) + (1/4)(a + b)][4 - 2(a + b)]}{8 - 4(a^2 - b^2)} \\
&= \frac{(1 + ab)[4 - (a + b)^2]}{8[2 - (a^2 + b^2)]} \\
&= \frac{[1 + (\alpha^2 - \beta^2)/4](4 - \alpha^2)}{8[2 - (\alpha^2 + \beta^2)/2]} \\
&= \left(\frac{4 - \alpha^2}{16}\right)\left[\frac{1 + (\alpha^2 - \beta^2)/4}{1 - (\alpha^2 + \beta^2)/4}\right]
\end{aligned}
\tag{128}
$$

Since

$$1 + \frac{\alpha^2}{4} - \left(1 - \frac{\alpha^2}{4}\right) = \frac{\alpha^2}{2} > 0$$

it follows that $\Gamma(a, b)$ increases as β increases. Therefore the largest value of $\lambda'(a, b)' = 1 - 2\Gamma(a, b)$ occurs when $\beta = 0$, that is when $a = b = \mu$. Then we have

$$\hat{\lambda}(\mu) = |\lambda''(\mu, \mu)| = \frac{1 - \mu^2}{2} \tag{129}$$

Thus with these inner smoothings, the macroiteration is convergent. We discuss the use of outer smoothings in Section 7.

7. EXTERNAL SMOOTHING

In Sections 2–5 we are concerned with determining bounds for the eigenvalues of macroiterations for several multilevel procedures. A summary of the results obtained is given in Tables 7.1–7.4.

We now consider using smoothing iterations that are performed

Table 7.1.

Summary of Bounds for the Five-Point/Nine-Point Multilevel Method

Method	Γ	γ	$\lambda = 1 - \gamma\Gamma$	μ	$\hat{\lambda}(\mu) = \text{Max } |\lambda(a, b)|$ μ fixed
Five-point/ nine-point: Basic Five-point/ nine-point	$\dfrac{20 - 8(a + b) - 4ab}{4 - 2(a + b)}$	$\dfrac{1}{6}$	$\left(\dfrac{1}{3}\right)\dfrac{(1 - a)(1 - b)}{2 - a - b} \geq 0$	$\dfrac{2(a + b) + ab}{5}$	$\left(\dfrac{5}{6}\right)\dfrac{1 - \mu}{3 + (4 + 5\mu)^{1/2}} \leq \dfrac{5}{24}(1 - \mu)$

Table 7.2.
Summary of Bounds for the Skewed Five-Point/Five-Point Procedure

Method	Γ	γ	$\lambda = 1 - \gamma\Gamma$	μ	$\hat{\lambda}(\mu) = \text{Max } \|\lambda(a,b)\|$ μ fixed
Skewed five-point/ five-point Basic	$\dfrac{4 - 2(a+b)}{4 - 4ab}$	2	$-\dfrac{(1-a)(1-b)}{1-ab} \le 0$	$\dfrac{a+b}{2}$	$\dfrac{1-\mu}{1+\mu}$
Skewed five-point/ five-point: $(1+a)(1+b)$ Inner smoothing	$(1+a)(1+b)\,\dfrac{4 - 2(a+b)}{4 - 4ab}$	$\dfrac{1}{2}$	$\dfrac{2 - (a+b)}{4} + \dfrac{(a-b)^2}{4(1-ab)} \ge 0$	$\dfrac{a+b}{2}$	$\begin{cases} 1-\mu & \text{if } \mu \ge 0 \\ 1 & \text{if } \mu \le 0 \end{cases}$
Skewed five-point/ five-point: $4 + 2(a+b)$ Inner smoothing	$\dfrac{[4 + 2(a+b)][4 - 2(a+b)]}{4 - 4ab}$	$\dfrac{1}{4}$	$\dfrac{(a-b)^2}{4(1-ab)} \ge 0$	$\dfrac{a+b}{2}$	$\dfrac{1-\|\mu\|}{2}$

Table 7.3.
Summary of Bounds for the Parallel Superconvergent Multigrid Method
in One Dimension

Method	Γ	γ	$\lambda = 1 - \gamma\Gamma$	μ	$\hat{\lambda}(\mu) = \text{Max} \|\lambda(a, b)\|$ μ fixed
One-dimension PSCMG: Basic	$\dfrac{2 - 2a}{4 - 4a^2}$	4	$-\dfrac{1-a}{1+a} \le 0$	a	$\dfrac{1-\mu}{1+\mu}$

along with macroiterations to obtain a prescribed level of error reduction. The smoothing iterations that we consider involve using a variable extrapolation procedure based on the Jacobi method. We show how the resulting composite procedure can be analyzed for certain model problems using results given in Tables 7.1–7.4.

As we see later, immediately after a macroiteration is performed, the amount of error reduction per smoothing iteration is relatively large. However as the number of smoothing iterations increases, the amount of error reduction per smoothing iteration decreases. The number of smoothing iterations to be used after each macroiteration depends to some extent on the amount of work required for a single macroiteration as compared to that required for a smoothing iteration. If the ratio r of the work per macroiteration to the work per smoothing iteration is very large, then we normally use a relatively large number of smoothing iterations (per macro.) On the other hand, if r is small, then we use fewer smoothing iterations.

In actual practice after each macroiteration, we may actually use the basic smoothing iterative method with conjugate gradient acceleration. However in our analysis here, we consider using m iterations of the following variable extrapolation procedure based on the smoothing iteration method. This procedure is defined by

$$u^{(n+1)} = \gamma_{n+1}[G_s u^{(n)} + k_s] + (1 - \gamma_{n+1})u^{(n)} \quad n = 0, 1, \ldots, m - 1 \quad (130)$$

Here $\gamma_1, \gamma_2, \ldots, \gamma_m$ are extrapolation factors. Actually instead of choosing the $\{\gamma_i\}$ we choose real numbers $a_1, a_2, \ldots, a_m$ in $[-1, 1]$ and let

$$\gamma_i = \frac{1}{1 - a_i} \qquad a_i = 1 - \frac{1}{\gamma_i} \quad (131)$$

Table 7.4.
Summary of Bounds for the Parallel Superconvergent Multigrid Method in Two Dimensions

Method	Γ	γ	$\lambda = 1 - \gamma\Gamma$	μ	$\hat{\lambda}(\mu) = \underset{\mu \text{ fixed}}{\text{Max }} \lvert\lambda(a,b)\rvert$
Two-dimension PSCMG: Basic	$\dfrac{4 - 2(a+b)}{8 - 4(a^2+b^2)}$	4	$-\dfrac{(1-a)^2 + (1-b)^2}{(1-a^2) + (1-b^2)} \leq 0$	$\dfrac{a+b}{2}$	$\begin{cases} \dfrac{1-\mu}{\mu} & \text{if } \mu \leq 0 \\[2mm] \dfrac{1+\mu^2}{(-\mu)(1+\mu)} & \text{if } \mu < 0 \end{cases}$
Two-dimension PSCMG: $(1+a)(1+b)$ Inner smoothing	$\dfrac{(1+a)(1+b)[4 - 2(a+b)]}{8 - 4(a^2+b^2)}$	1	$\dfrac{(1-a)(1-b)(2+a+b)}{2(2-a^2+b^2)} \geq 0$	$\dfrac{a+b}{2}$	$\begin{cases} \dfrac{1-\mu}{2} & \text{if } \mu \geq 0 \\[2mm] 1 & \text{if } \mu < 0 \end{cases}$
Two dimension PSCMG: $(1+ab)\dfrac{2+a+b}{4}$ Inner smoothing	$\dfrac{(1+ab)[4 - (a+b)^2]}{[2 - (a^2+b^2)]}$	2	$\dfrac{(1-a^2)(1-b^2)}{2(2-a^2-b^2)} + \dfrac{1-ab}{4} \geq 0$	$\dfrac{a+b}{2}$	$\dfrac{1}{2}(1-\mu^2)$

We discuss the choice of the $\{a_i\}$ later. We remark that conjugate gradient acceleration is in some sense the best of all polynomial acceleration procedures. Hence if we were to use conjugate gradient acceleration instead of variable extrapolation we would expect to obtain an equally good or a better convergence rate.

In our analysis we assume that

$$\hat{\lambda}(\mu) = \frac{1}{2}(1 - \mu^2) \tag{132}$$

This is true for the case of the parallel multigrid procedure in two dimensions. It is also true for the skewed five-point/five-point multilevel method if we consider as a macroiteration the actual macroiteration followed by two iterations of the damped Jacobi method with $\gamma = \frac{1}{2}$. Actually we would have $\hat{\lambda}(\mu) = \frac{1}{4}(1 - \mu^2)$. Also if we used one iteration of the damped Jacobi method, for the five-point or nine-point multilevel method, we would have $\hat{\lambda}(\mu) \leq \frac{5}{48}(1 - \mu^2)$. (Of course in this case, μ varies in the interval $[-3/5, 1]$ instead of in the interval $[-1, 1]$ as in the other cases.)

To analyze the convergence properties of the variable extrapolation procedure, we observe that we can write

$$u^{(m)} - \bar{u} = P_m(G_s)[u^{(0)} - \bar{u}] \tag{133}$$

$$P_m(\mu) = \prod_{i=1}^{m} \frac{\mu - a_i}{1 - a_i} \tag{134}$$

For any eigenvalue μ of G_s, let λ be any eigenvalue of $G_M P_m(G_s)$ associated with an eigenvector v of G_s corresponding to the eigenvalue μ. Evidently by Equations 132 and 134 we have

$$|\lambda| \leq \left| \frac{1}{2}(1 - \mu^2) \prod_{i=1}^{m} \frac{\mu - a_i}{1 - a_i} \right| \tag{135}$$

For each m we seek to determine $a_1, a_2, \ldots, a_m$ such that

$$\underset{[-1,1]}{\text{Max}} \left| \frac{1}{2}(1 - \mu^2) \prod_{i=1}^{m} \frac{\mu - a_i}{1 - a_i} \right| \tag{136}$$

is minimized. We let

$$\sigma_m = \underset{a \in R}{\text{Min}} \underset{[-1,1]}{\text{Max}} \left| \frac{1}{2}(1 - \mu^2) \prod_{i=1}^{m} \frac{\mu - a_i}{1 - a_i} \right| \tag{137}$$

For the case $m = 1$, by symmetry we have $a_1 = 0$. To determine σ_1 we observe that the maximum absolute value of the function $\phi_1(\mu) = \frac{1}{2}\mu(1 - \mu^2)$ in $[-1, 1]$ occurs when $\mu = \pm 3^{-1/2}$. Thus we have

$$\sigma_1 = \phi_1(3^{-1/2}) = 3^{-3/2} = 0.19245 \tag{138}$$

For the case $m = 2$, by symmetry we can let $a_1 = a$ and $a_2 = -a$. We seek to minimize $\underset{[-1, 1]}{\text{Max}} |\phi_2(\mu)|$ where

$$\phi_2(\mu) = \frac{1}{2(1 - a^2)} (1 - \mu^2)(\mu^2 - a^2) \tag{139}$$

The extreme values of $\phi_2(\mu)$ in $[-1, 1]$ occur when $\mu = 0$ and $\mu = \pm(1 + a^2)/2$. Moreover we have

$$\phi_2(0) = -\frac{a^2}{2(1 - a^2)} \tag{140}$$

and

$$\phi_2\left(\pm \frac{1 + a^2}{2}\right) = \frac{1 - a^2}{8} \tag{141}$$

Since $|\phi_2(0)|$ increases as a^2 increases and $|\phi_2(\pm(1 + a^2)/2)|$ decreases as a^2 increases, the optimum value of a occurs when

$$|\phi_2(0)| = \left| \phi_2\left(\pm \frac{(1+a^2)}{2}\right) \right|$$

Thus we have

$$\frac{1 - a^2}{8} = \frac{a^2}{2(1 - a^2)} \tag{142}$$

This leads to the condition

$$a^4 \pm 2a^2 + 1 = 0 \tag{143}$$

Since $a^2 < 1$, from this we obtain

$$\begin{cases} a^2 = 3 - 8^{1/2} \\ a = 2^{1/2} - 1 = 0.414214 \end{cases} \tag{144}$$

Moreover

$$\sigma_2 = \frac{1 - a^2}{8} = 0.103553 \tag{145}$$

To determine $\{a_i\}$ and σ_m for larger values of m, we used the optimization routine UMINF from the International Mathematical and Statistics (IMSL) library.[7] UMINF is designed to "minimize" a function of N variables using a quasi-Newton method and a finite difference gradient. Estimated values of the $\{a_i\}$ distributed symmetrically in $[-1, 1]$ were

Table 7.5.
Extrapolation Parameters and Error Reduction

m	σ_m	$-\log_{10}\sigma_m$	$\{a_i\}$
0	0.5	0.30103	—
1	0.19245	0.715682	0
2	0.103553	0.984837	±0.414213
3	0.064983	1.187200	$0, \pm0.618034$
4	0.044657	1.350110	$\pm0.267948, \pm0.732049$
5	0.032607	1.486689	$0, \pm0.445048, \pm0.801933$
6	0.024864	1.604429	$\pm0.198885, \pm0.566446, \pm0.847759$
7	0.019592	1.707921	$0, \pm0.347295, \pm0.652703, \pm0.879386$
8	0.015856	1.799806	$\pm0.153997, \pm0.458446, \pm0.715424$ ±0.901955
9	0.013068	1.883791	$0, \pm0.284628, \pm0.546196, \pm0.763515$ ±0.918976
10	0.010973	1.959675	$\pm0.131281, \pm0.385642, \pm0.613870$ $\pm0.800136, \pm0.931833$
11	0.009341	2.029607	$0, \pm0.241089, \pm0.468183, \pm0.667955$ $\pm0.829028, \pm0.941876$
12	0.008126	2.090123	$\pm0.112405, \pm0.326125, \pm0.532828$ $\pm0.705178, \pm0.850091, \pm0.939255$

obtained by a direct search procedure. These estimated values were then used as starting values for the minimization routine. The values of $\{a_i\}$ and corresponding values of σ_m and $-\log_{10}\sigma_m$ are given in Table 7.5. Figure 7.3 gives the behavior of $-\log_{10}\sigma_m$.

We remark that as pointed out by E. B. Saff,[8] the problem of determining $\{a_i\}$ and σ_m can be solved analytically for certain special cases including the cases

$$\hat{\lambda}(\mu) = 1 - \mu^2 \qquad \hat{\lambda}(\mu) = 1 - \mu \qquad \hat{\lambda}(\mu) = (1 - \mu)[1 + \mu]^{1/2}$$

$$\hat{\lambda}(\mu) = (1 + \mu)[1 + \mu]^{1/2}$$

Details of determining analytical solutions are given elsewhere. Chapter 7 also describes a procedure based on the use of a Remes-type

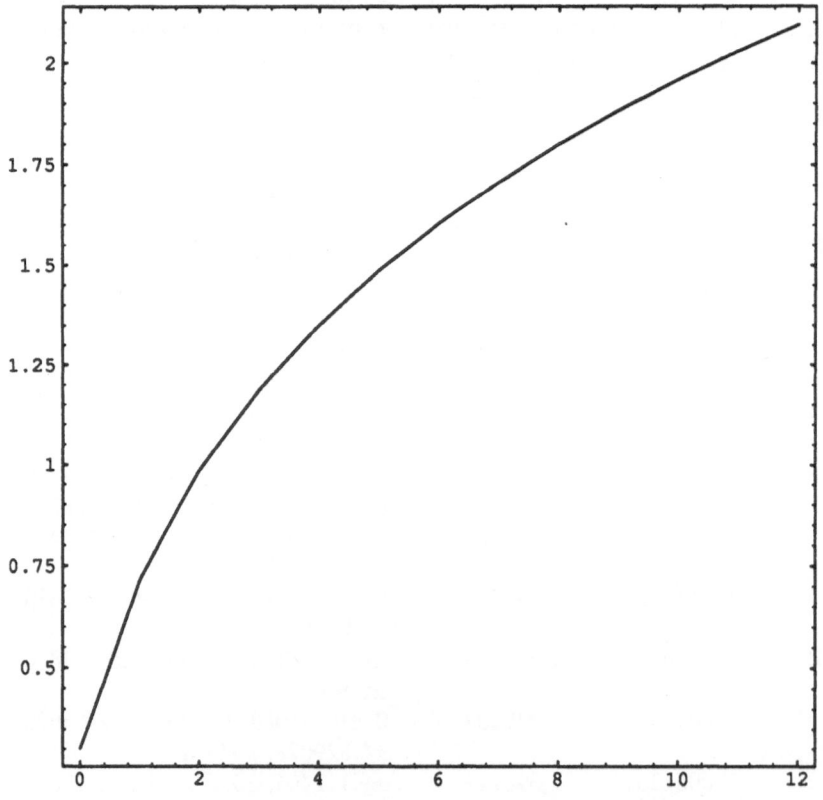

Figure 7.3. Graph of $-\log_{10}\sigma_m$ versus m.

algorithm for determining optimum polynomials in cases where an analytic solution is not available.

The optimum choice of m, the number of smoothing iterations to be carried out per macroiteration, depends on the ratio

$$r = \frac{W_M}{W_s} \tag{146}$$

where W_M is the work per macroiteration and W_s is the work per smoothing iteration. The average error reduction per smoothing iteration is given by

$$\psi(r, m) = \frac{-\log_{10}\sigma_m}{r + m} \tag{147}$$

Values of $\psi(r, m)$ for $r = 1, 2, 3(5)20$ and for $m = 0(1)12$ are given in Table 7.6. For each r the largest value of $\psi(r, m)$ is indicated by an asterisk. As expected the optimum value of m is small for small r and increases as r increases.

Table 7.6.
Average Error Reduction per Smoothing Iteration for Macroiteration
with m Smoothing Extrapolations

			$-\log_{10}\sigma_m/(r^a + m)$					
m	σ_m	$-\log_{10}\sigma_m$	$r^a = 1$	$r^a = 2$	$r^a = 5$	$r^a = 10$	$r^a = 15$	$r^a = 20$
0	0.5	0.301	0.32	0.150	0.060	0.030	0.0201	0.0150
1	0.19245	0.716	0.358[b]	0.238	0.119	0.072	0.0447	0.0341
2	0.103553	0.985	0.328	0.246[b]	0.141	0.082	0.0579	0.0448
3	0.064983	1.187	0.297	0.237	0.148	0.091	0.0660	0.0516
4	0.044657	1.350	0.270	0.225	0.150[b]	0.096	0.0711	0.0562
5	0.032607	1.487	0.248	0.212	0.149	0.099	0.0743	0.0595
6	0.024864	1.604	0.229	0.200	0.146	0.100[b]	0.0764	0.0617
7	0.019592	1.708	0.213	0.190	0.142	0.100	0.0776	0.0632
8	0.015856	1.800	0.200	0.180	0.138	0.100	0.0782	0.0643
9	0.013068	1.884	0.188	0.171	0.134	0.099	0.0785[b]	0.0650
10	0.010973	1.960	0.178	0.163	0.131	0.098	0.0784	0.0653
11	0.009341	2.030	0.169	0.156	0.127	0.096	0.0781	0.0655[b]
12	0.008126	2.090	0.161	0.149	0.123	0.095	0.0774	0.0653

[a] $r = W_M/W_s$; W_M = work required per macroiteration; W_s = work required per smoothing iteration.
[b] Maximum value.

As an example consider the case where $r = 5$. The largest value of $\psi(r, m)$ is 0.150 and occurs when $m = 4$. Error is reduced by a factor of 0.044657 (approximately a factor of 1/20) in each cycle. Four complete cycles reduce the error to 4×10^{-6}, while five complete cycles reduce it to 2×10^{-7}.

In the case of the five-point/nine-point multilevel method, we could argue that a relatively small error reduction is required. Thus the accuracy of the solution of the nine-point equation as an approximation of the true solution is of order $O(h^6)$ for small h. There would seem to be little point in requiring the error reduction to be smaller than the truncation error of the nine-point formula. We may expect to obtain a sufficiently accurate solution with a very small number of multilevel cycles and a modest number of smoothing iterations per cycle. A similar argument can be given for the skewed five-point or five-point multilevel procedure.

ACKNOWLEDGMENTS. The authors would like to acknowledge helpful discussions with a number of researchers including Paul Frederickson, Ray Tuminaro, Tony Chan, Anne Greenbaum, William Briggs, and Naomi Decker.

The research was supported in part by the National Science Foundation under Grant DCR-8518722, by the Department of Energy under Grant DE-FG05-87ER25048, and by the Cray Research Corporation under Grant LTR-DTD with The University of Texas at Austin. Support was also provided by a grant from the Texas State Higher Education Coordinating Board under the Advanced Research Projects (ARP) Program.

References

1. Hageman, Louis A., and Young, David M. *Applied Iterative Methods*. New York: Academic Press, 1981.
2. Frederickson, Paul O., and McBryan, Oliver A. "Parallel superconvergent multigrid." In *Multigrid Methods*, S. F. McCormick, ed., New York: Marcel Dekker, 1988. 195–210.
3. Young, David M., and Gregory, Robert T. *A Survey of Numerical Mathematics*, vol. 2. New York: Dover Publications, 1988.
4. Young, David M. *Iterative Solution of Large Linear Systems*. New York: Academic Press, 1971.
5. Hackbusch, Wolfgang. *Multigrid Methods and Applications*. Springer Series in Computational Mathematics. New York: Springer-Verlag, 1985.
6. Briggs, William L. *A Multigrid Tutorial*. Philadelphia: Society for Industrial and Applied Mathematics, 1987.
7. International Mathematical and Statistical Libraries. *Math/Library User's Manual*, version 1.0 of 10th ed. Houston: IMSL, 1987.

8. Private communication, February 1990.

9. Adams, Loyce M., LeVeque, Randall J., and Young, David M. "Analysis of the SOR iteration for the nine-point Laplacian." *SIAM J. Numer. Anal.* **25,** 1156–180 (1988).

10. Greenbaum, Anne. "Analysis of a multigrid method as an iterative technique for solving linear systems." *SIAM J. Numer. Anal.* **21,** 473–85 (1984).

11. Young, David M., and Vona, Bi R. "Parallel multilevel methods." Report CNA-243. Center for Numerical Analysis, Univ. of Texas at Austin (March 1990).

8

Using Algebraic Geometry for Multivariate Polynomial Interpolation

Chandrajit L. Bajaj

1. INTRODUCTION

Interpolation provides a direct way of fitting analytic functions to sampled data. Chapter 8 is motivated by computational efficiency and deals with polynomials rather than arbitrary analytic forms. We distinguish between multivariate polynomial functions

$$\mathcal{F} : x_n = f_1(x_1, \ldots, x_{n-1})$$

multivariate rational functions

$$\mathcal{R} : x_n = \frac{f_1(x_1, \ldots, x_{n-1})}{f_2(x_1, \ldots, x_{n-1})}$$

and polynomial algebraic functions or implicitly defined hypersurfaces

$$\mathcal{H} : f_1(x_1, \ldots, x_n) = 0$$

where all f_i are multivariate polynomials with coefficients in $\mathbb{R}$. While prior work on interpolation has dealt with multivariate polynomial functions $\mathcal{F}$ and rational functions $\mathcal{R}$, see for example References 1–5, little work has been reported on interpolation with implicitly defined hypersur-

Chandrajit L. Bajaj • Purdue University

Studies in Computer Science, edited by John R. Rice and Richard A. DeMillo. Plenum Press, New York, 1994.

faces $\mathscr{H}$. See References 6 and 15 which summarizes prior work on implicit surface interpolation in three dimensions and provides several additional references.

Chapter 8 presents a form of multivariate Hermite interpolation that generalizes the usual curve fits through points in the plane and surface fits through both points and curves in space to general hypersurface fits through points, curves, surfaces, and any subvarieties up to dimension $n-2$ in n-dimensional space and matches of specified derivative information along the subvarieties. We show that even implicitly defined hypersurfaces $\mathscr{H}$ lend themselves quite naturally to Hermite interpolation in any dimension. This chapter improves the bounds over earlier results of Reference 16 on the sizes of the linear systems that the multivariate interpolation problem reduces to for all dimensions.

2. PRELIMINARIES

In this section we review some basic definitions and theorems from algebraic geometry that we use in subsequent sections. These and additional facts can be found for example in References 7 and 8. The set of real and complex solutions [or *zero* set $Z(S)$] of a collection S of polynomial equations

$$\mathscr{H}_1 : f_1(x_1, \ldots, x_n) = 0$$
$$\vdots$$
$$\mathscr{H}_m : f_m(x_1, \ldots, x_n) = 0 \tag{1}$$

with coefficients in $\mathbb{R}$ is referred to as an algebraic set. The algebraic set defined by a single equation ($m = 1$) is also known as a hypersurface. A algebraic set that cannot be represented as the union of two other distinct algebraic sets, since neither one contains the other, is said to be irreducible. An irreducible algebraic set is also known as an algebraic variety V.

A hypersurface in $\mathbb{R}^n$, an n-dimensional space, is of dimension $n-1$. The dimension of an algebraic variety V is k if its points can be put in $(1, 1)$ rational correspondence with the points of an irreducible hypersurface in $(k+1)$-dimensional space. An algebraic set $Z(S)$ on the other hand can have irreducible components or subvarieties of different dimension. An algebraic set is called unmixed if all of its subvarieties are of the same dimension, and mixed otherwise. The dimension of the algebraic set $Z(S)$ is considered the maximum dimension of any of its subvarieties. An algebraic variety of dimension 1 is also called an algebraic space curve, an algebraic variety of dimension 2 is also called an algebraic surface. The following two lemmas summarize the resulting dimension of intersections of varieties and subspaces of different dimensions.

Lemma 2.1: In an n-dimensional space $\mathbb{R}^n$, a variety V_1 of dimension k intersects a general subspace $\mathbb{R}^{n-k+h}$, with $k > h$, in a variety V_2 of dimension h.

Lemma 2.2: In $\mathbb{R}^n$, a variety V_1 of dimension k intersects a a variety V_2 of dimension h, with $h \geq n - k$, in an algebraic set $Z(S)$ of dimension at least $h + k - n$.

In Lemma 2.2, the resulting intersection is termed proper if all subvarieties of $Z(S)$ are of the same minimum dimension $h + k - n$. Otherwise the intersection is termed excess or improper.

    The degree of an algebraic hypersurface is the maximum number of intersections between the hypersurface and a line, counting both real and complex intersections and infinity. This degree is also the same as the degree of the defining polynomial. A degree 1 hypersurface is also called a hyperplane. The degree of an algebraic space curve is the maximum number of intersections between the curve and a hyperplane, counting both real and complex intersections and infinity. The degree of a variety V of dimension h in $\mathbb{R}^n$ is the maximum number of intersections between V and a subspace $\mathbb{R}^{n-h}$, counting both real and complex intersections and infinity. The degree of an unmixed algebraic set is the sum of the degrees of all its subvarieties.

    The following theorem, perhaps the oldest in algebraic geometry, summarizes the resulting degree of intersections of varieties of different degrees.

Theorem 2.1 (Bezout): A variety of degree d that properly intersects a a variety of degree e does so either in an algebraic set of degree at most $d * e$ or infinitely often.

The normal or gradient of a hypersurface $\mathscr{H} : f(x_1, \ldots, x_n) = 0$ is the vector

$$\nabla f = (f_{x_1}, f_{x_2}, \ldots, f_{x_n}).$$

A point $\mathbf{p} = (a_0, a_1, \ldots, a_n)$ on a hypersurface is a regular point if the gradient at $\mathbf{p}$ is not null; otherwise the point is singular. A singular point $\mathbf{q}$ is of multiplicity e for a hypersurface $\mathscr{H}$ of degree d if any line through $\mathbf{q}$ meets $\mathscr{H}$ in at most $d - e$ additional points. Similarly a singular point $\mathbf{q}$ is of multiplicity e for a variety V in $\mathbb{R}^n$ of dimension k and degree d if any subspace $\mathbb{R}^{n-k}$ through $\mathbf{q}$ meets V in at most $d - e$ additional points. It is important to note that even if two varieties intersect in a proper manner, their intersection in general may consist of subvarieties of various multiplicites. The total degree of the intersection however is bounded by Theorem 2.1. Finally we note that a hypersurface $f(x_1, \ldots, x_n) = 0$ of degree d has $\binom{n+d}{n}$ coefficients, one more than the number of independent coefficients.

3. LAGRANGE INTERPOLATION

Our first problem deals with constructing C^0 interpolatory hypersurfaces.

Problem 3.1: Construct a single real algebraic hypersurface $\mathscr{H}$ in $\mathbb{R}^n$ so that C^0 interpolates a collection of l_1 points $\mathbf{p}_i$, and l_k subvarieties V_{j_k} of dimensions k, $k = 1 \cdots n - 2$ and degree $e[k]_{j_k}$.

Since a point is a variety of dimension 0 and hypersurfaces in $\mathbb{R}^n$ are of dimension $n - 1$, we note from Lemma 2.2 that a hypersurface in general does not contain a given point. However the hypersurface $\mathscr{H} : f(x_1, \ldots, x_n) = 0$ of degree d can be made to contain, that is C^0-interpolate, the point $\mathbf{p}_i$ if the coefficients of f satisfy the linear equation $f(\mathbf{p}_i) = 0$.

From Lemma 2.2 we note that a hypersurface in $\mathbb{R}^n$ always intersects all subvarieties of dimension h, for $h = 1 \cdots n - 2$. To increase the dimension of the intersection or more precisely to ensure that the hypersurface $\mathscr{H} : f(x_1, \ldots, x_n) = 0$ of degree d completely contains (that is C^0-interpolates) a subvariety V of dimension h and degree $e[h]$, we use the following algorithm:

Algorithm 3.1: Select a linear sub-space $W = \mathbb{R}^{n-h+1}$ which is not completely contained in $\mathcal{H}$ nor contains V. A randomly chosen set of $n - h + 2$ points in $\mathbb{R}^n$ will suffice [17]. Select any set L_V of $n_V = (d*e[h]+1)$ points on $V \cap W$,

$$L_V = \{ \mathbf{p}_i = (x_i[i], \ldots, x_n[i]) | i = 1, \ldots, n_V \}$$

The set L_V can be computed by a straightforward generalization of the method for computing random points on algebraic curves and surfaces. See Reference 9 for a discussion of such techniques. Next consider the intersection of $\mathcal{H}$ and W. Since W is a linear sub-space spanned by $h - 1$ linear equations $y_i = \sum_{j=1}^{n} a_i x_i = L(\mathbf{p})$, with $i = 1 \cdots h - 1$, $\mathbf{p} = (x_1, \ldots, x_n)$, it is straightforward to compute the intersection with $f(x_1, \ldots, x_n) = 0$ to yield a modified equation $\hat{f}(y_1, \ldots, y_{h-1}) = 0$. Then set up n_V homogeneous linear equations $\hat{f}(L(\mathbf{p}_j)) = 0$, for $\mathbf{p}_j \in L_V$. Any nontrivial solution of this linear system will represent an $\mathcal{H}$ which interpolates the entire subvariety V.

Correctness Proof: The proof of correctness of the above algorithm follows from several invocations of Bezout's theorem 2.1. By Bezout's theorem W intersects $\mathcal{H}$ in a sub-variety of degree d and dimension $(n - h + 1) + (n - 1) - n = n - h$, and intersects V in a sub-variety of degree $e[h]$ and dimension $(n - h + 1) + h - n = 1$ (a curve). By making $W \cap \mathcal{H}$ contain $n_V = d*e[h] + 1$ points of $W \cap V$ implies from Bezout that $W \cap \mathcal{H}$ intersects $W \cap V$ infinitely often and because of the generic selection of W implies that $\mathcal{H}$ must intersect V infinitely often, i.e. $\mathcal{H}$ must contain V.

The irreducibility of the subvariety is not a restriction, since an algebraic set can be handled by treating each irreducible component separately. The situation is more complicated in the real setting if we wish to achieve separate containment of one of possibly several connected real components of a single subvariety. There is first of course the nontrivial problem of specifying a single isolated real component of the subvariety. One solution to the problem of interpolating with only a single real component, given in Reference 10, uses weighted least squares approximation from additional data. See also Reference 11, where a solution to isolating real components of varieties is derived in terms of a decomposition of space into sign-invariant cylindrical cells.

For the collection of l_1 points $\mathbf{p}$ and l_k subvarieties V_{j_k} of dimension

$k, k = 1 \cdots n - 2$ and degree $e[k]_{j_k}$, the preceding C^0 interpolation with a degree d hypersurface $\mathcal{H}$ yields a system $\mathbf{M}_I$ of

$$\sum_{k=1}^{n-1} l_k + \sum_{k=2}^{n-1} \sum_{j_k=1}^{l_k} (d*e[k]_{j_k} + 1)$$

linear equations. Remember that $\mathcal{H} : f(x_1, \ldots, x_n) = 0$ of degree d has $K = \binom{n+d}{n} - 1$ independent coefficient unknowns. C^0-interpolation of the entire collection of subvarieties is achieved by selecting an algebraic hypersurface of the smallest degree n such that $K \geq r$, where $r(\leq k)$ is the rank of the system $\mathbf{M}_I$ of linear equations.

4. HERMITE INTERPOLATION

An algebraic hypersurface $\mathcal{H} : f(x_1, \ldots, x_n) = 0$ is said to Hermite interpolate or C^1-interpolate a subvariety V with associated derivative or normal information

$$\mathbf{n}(\mathbf{p}) = [(n_{x_1}(\mathbf{p}), \ldots, n_{x_n}(\mathbf{p})],$$

defined for points $\mathbf{p} = (x_1, \ldots, x_n)$ on V if

- $f(\mathbf{p}) = 0$ for all points $\mathbf{p} = (x_1, \ldots, x_n)$ of V (containment condition)

- $\nabla f(\mathbf{p})$ is not identically zero and $\nabla f(\mathbf{p}) = \alpha \mathbf{n}(\mathbf{p})$ for some $\alpha \neq 0$ and for all points $\mathbf{p} = (x_1, \ldots, x_n)$ of V (tangency condition)

Our second problem then deals with constructing C^1 interpolatory hypersurfaces.

Problem 4.1: Construct a single real algebraic hypersurface $\mathcal{H}$ in $\mathbb{R}^n$ so that C^1 interpolates a collection of l_1 points $\mathbf{p}_i$ with associated normal unit vectors $\mathbf{n}_i(\mathbf{p}_i)$ and l_k subvarieties V_{j_k} of dimension k with $k = 1 \cdots n - 2$ and degree $e[k]_{j_k}$ together with associated normal unit vectors $\mathbf{n}[k]_{j_k}$ for all points on each subvariety of the given collection.

In the previous section, we showed that the containment condition reduces to solving a system of linear equations. We now prove that meeting the tangency condition for C^1-interpolation reduces to solving an additional set of linear equations.

A hypersurface $\mathcal{H} : f(x_1, \ldots, x_n) = 0$ of degree d, satisfies the tangency condition at the point $\mathbf{p}_i$ if the coefficients of f satisfy, without loss of generality, the $n - 1$ homogeneous linear equations

$$n_{x_1} \cdot f_{x_j}(\mathbf{p}_i) - n_{x_j} \cdot f_{x_1}(\mathbf{p}_i) = 0 \qquad j = 2 \cdots n \qquad (2)$$

For the preceding equations we assumed, without loss of generality, that $n_{x_1} \neq 0$ as the given normal $\mathbf{n}$ is not identically zero at any point. To verify that these equations correctly satisfy the tangency condition, it suffices to choose $\alpha = f_{x_1}/n_{x_1}$, since then each of the $f_{x_j} = \alpha n_{x_j}$. Also note that for the choice of $n_{x_1} \neq 0$, it must occur that $f_{x_1}(\mathbf{p}_i) \neq 0$ and hence $\alpha \neq 0$, for otherwise the entire $\nabla f(\mathbf{p})$ is identically zero.

To ensure that a hypersurface $\mathcal{H} : f(x_1, \ldots, x_n) = 0$ of degree d meets the tangency condition for C^1-interpolation of a subvariety V of dimension h and degree $e[h]$, we use Algorithm 4.1.

Algorithm 4.1: Similar to algorithm 3.1, select linear sub-spaces $W_j = \mathbb{R}^{n-h+1}$ which are not completely contained in $\hat{G}_j$ (below) nor contains V.

Select a set of L_{NV} of $n_{NV} = (d - 1)*e[h] + 1$ point-normal pairs $[\mathbf{p}_j, \mathbf{n}[h]_j]$ on $W_j \cap V$ where $\mathbf{p}_i \in L_V$, with point set L_V on $W_j \cap V$ computed to meet the containment condition.

Substitute each point-normal pair in L_{NV} into the $n - h - 1$ equations of $\hat{G}_j = W_j \cap G_j$

$$\hat{G}_j : n_{x_1} \cdot \hat{f}_{x_i}(\mathbf{p}) - n_{x_i} \cdot \hat{f}_{x_1}(\mathbf{p}) = 0 \qquad i = 2 \cdots (n - h) \qquad (3)$$

to yield additionally $(n - h - 1)*n_{NV}$ linear equations in the coefficients of the $f(x, y, z)$. The defining partial derivative equations $\hat{f}$ of $\hat{G}_j = W_j \cap G_j$ are obtained by intersecting with the defining linear equations of W_j and is similar to the process in Algorithm 3.1.

Correctness Proof: The proof of correctness of the above algorithm follows from the following. We first note that even though each of the equations 3 above is evaluated at only $n_{NV} = (d - 1)*e[h] + 1$ points of $W_j \cap V$ it holds for all points on V. Each equation (3) defines an algebraic hypersurface T of degree $(d - 1)$ which intersects V of degree $e[h]$ in a subvariety of degree at most $(d - 1)e[h]$ and dimension $h - 1$. Invoking Bezout's theorem as in the correctness proof of the earlier subsection, it follows that V must lie entirely on the hypersurface T. Hence each equation (3) is satisfied along the entire sub-variety V.

We now show that the $n - h - 1$ equations (3) satisfies the tangency condition as specified earlier. Again we assume, without loss of generality, that $n_{x_1} \neq 0$ as the given normal $\mathbf{n}$ is not identically zero at along V_h. Note that the containment i.e. C^0 interpolation of the dimension h variety V_h by the hypersurface $\mathcal{H}$ already guarantees that the h tangent directions on V_h at each point $\mathbf{p}$ of V_h are identical to h tangent directions of $\mathcal{H}$ at $\mathbf{p}$ on $\mathcal{H}$. Hence h components of the given normal vector $\mathbf{n}(\mathbf{p})$ (orthogonal to the tangent directions of V_h) are already matched with h components of the gradient vector $\nabla f(\mathbf{p})$ (orthogonal to the tangent directions of $\mathcal{H}$). Assume, without loss of generality, that these vector components are $f_{x_i} = \alpha n_{x_i}$, $i = (n - h + 1) \cdots n$, for any non-zero α. The remaining $n - h$ components of $\nabla f(\mathbf{p})$ of $\mathcal{H}$ are then matched up with the $n - h - 1$ equations 3 as follows. Let $\alpha = f_{x_1}/n_{x_1}$. Then from the $n - h - 1$ equations 3 we note that each of the $n - h - 1$ $f_{x_i} = \alpha n_{x_i}$, $i = 2 \cdots (n - h)$ as required. Hence the entire vector $\nabla f(\mathbf{p}) = \alpha \mathbf{n}(\mathbf{p})$. Also note that for the choice of $n_{x_1} \neq 0$, it must occur that $f_{x_1}(\mathbf{p}_i) \neq 0$, and hence $\alpha \neq 0$, for otherwise the entire $\nabla f(\mathbf{p})$ is identically zero.

For the collection of l_1 points $\mathbf{p}$ and l_k subvarieties V_{j_k} of dimension k, $k = 1 \cdots n - 2$ and degree $e[k]_{j_k}$ to achieve the tangency condition with a degree d hypersurface $\mathcal{H}$ requires satisfying an additionally system of

$$(n - 1) * l_1 + \sum_{k=2}^{n-1} \sum_{j_k=1}^{l_k} (n - k - 1) * [(d-1) * e[k]_{j_k} + 1]$$

linear equations. For C^1-interpolation we obtain a single homogeneous system $\mathbf{M_I}$ of linear equations consisting of the linear equations for C^0-interpolation of Section 3 with the preceding linear equations. Any nontrivial solution of this linear system $\mathbf{M_I}$, for which additionally ∇f is not identically zero for all points of the collection (that is the hypersurface $\mathcal{H}$ is not singular at all points or along any of the subvarieties V_k) represents a hypersurface that Hermite interpolates the collection.

5. CONCLUSION

There are numerous open problems in the theory and application of multivariate interpolation. The primary problem among these stems from the nonuniqueness of interpolants in two and higher dimensions. There is an acute need for techniques for selecting a suitable candidate solution for the given input data from the $K - r$ parameter family of C^1-interpolating hypersurfaces of degree d in n-dimensional space. Here $K = \binom{n+d}{n} - 1$ and r is the rank of the system $\mathbf{M}$ of linear equations. One difficulty of the selection problem arises when a certain choice of the free parameters of the interpolating surface family yields a degenerate blending solution in real space. Other difficulties arise from ensuring that the selected solution is also smooth (nonsingular) in the domain of the input data. One possible selection technique involves using weighted least-squares approximation on additional constructed data and interpolating the given input data set (see references 13 and 14). These and related problems involving low-degree, piecewise polynomial interpolation are what we are currently pursuing in our study of multivariate Hermite interpolation.

ACKNOWLEDGMENT. I thank Susan Evans and Insung Ihm for the efficient implementation of the interpolation and display algorithms. This research was supported in part by NSF grants CCR 90-02228, DMS 91-01424, and AFOSR contract 91-0276.

References

1. Alfeld, P. "Scattered data interpolation in three or more variables," In *Mathematical Methods in Computer Aided Geometric Design,* T. Lyche, and L. Schumaker, eds. 1–34. Academic Press, New York.
2. deBoor, C.; Hollig, K.; and Sabin, M. "High-accuracy geometric Hermite interpolation." *Computer Aided Geometric Design* **4,** 269–78 (1987).
3. Chui, C. *Multivariate Splines.* Regional Conference Series in Applied Mathematics, 54 Philadelphia: SIAM (1988).
4. Dahmen, W.; and Micchelli, C. "Recent progress in multivariate splines." *Approximation Theory IV,* vol. 3, no. 2, ed. Chui, C., Schumaker, L., and Word, J., 27–121 (1983).
5. Hollig, K. "Multivariate splines." *SIAM J. Numer. Anal.* **19,** 1013–31 (1982).
6. Bajaj, C. "Surface fitting using implicit algebraic surface patches." In *Topics in Surface Modeling,* H. Hagen, ed. Philadelphia: SIAM Publications, 23–52 (1992).
7. Semple, J.; and Roth, L. *Introduction to Algebraic Geometry.* Oxford University Press, New York (1949).
8. Zariski, O.; and Samuel, P. *Commutative Algebra,* Vols 1, 2. Springer Verlag, New York (1958).
9. Bajaj, C. "Geometric modeling with algebraic surfaces." In *The Mathematics of Surfaces III,* D. Handscomb, ed. Oxford University Press, Oxford, (1988). 3–48.

10. Bajaj, C.; and Ihm, I. "Algebraic surface design with hermite interpolation," *ACM Transactions on Graphics* **11**(1), 61–91 (1992).
11. Arnon, D.; Collins, G.; and McCallum, S. "Cylindrical algebraic decomposition 1: the basic algorithm," *Siam J. Comput.* **13**(4), 865–89 (1984).
12. Golub, G., and Van Loan, C. *Matrix Computations.* Baltimore: Johns Hopkins Univ. Press, (1983).
13. Bajaj, C.; and Ihm, I. "Smoothing polyhedra with implicit algebraic splines." *Comput. Graphics* **26**(2), 79–88 (1992).
14. Bajaj, C.; Ihm, I.; and Warren, J. "Exact and least squares approximate C^k fitting of implicit algebraic surfaces." *ACM Transactions on Graphics* Vol 12, No. 4, (1993), 327–347.
15. Bajaj, C. "The Emergence of Algebraic Curves and Surfaces in Geometric Design" *Directions in Geometric Computing,* R. Martin, ed., Information Geometers Press, U.K., (1993) 1–29.
16. Bajaj, C. "Multi-dimensional Hermite Interpolation and Approximation for Modeling and Visualization", *Proc. of the IFIP TC5/WG5.2/WG5.10 CSI International Conference on Computer Graphics,* ICCG93, (1993), IFIP Transactions B-9, North Holland, (1993) 335–348.
17. Schwartz, J. "Fast Probabilistic Algorithms for Verification of Polynomial Identities," *Journal of the ACM, 27, 4, 701–717 (1980).*

9

Object-Oriented Design with Box Structures

Alan R. Hevner and Harlan D. Mills

1. OBJECT-ORIENTED DESIGN METHODS

There are many discussions in the literature today about object-oriented designs but few about systematic methods for object-oriented designing. There is a profound difference between a syntax correct object-oriented design and a sound engineering process for achieving one, often it is the difference between heuristic invention and systematic derivation. In either case the syntactic result is an object-oriented design, but practical results can vary widely in effectiveness.

Several methods for object-oriented design have been proposed. One of the most popular of these methods has been developed by Booch.[1] The Booch method begins with a data flow diagram of the intended system, then a five-step object-oriented design method is defined:[2]

- Identify objects and their attributes.

- Identify operations affecting each object and operations that each object must initiate.

- Establish the visibility of each object in relation to other objects.

- Establish the interfaces of each object.

- Implement each object.

Alan R. Hevner • University of Maryland   Harlan D. Mills • Florida Institute of Technology

Studies in Computer Science, edited by John R. Rice and Richard A. DeMillo. Plenum Press, New York, 1994.

A necessary final step involves designing and implementing the portion of the system that ties the objects together into a functional system. This portion of the system is called the set of transformational functions.[3] Other object-oriented design methods have been proposed that extend this basic approach, for example methods presented in References 3–5. There are several significant difficulties with the object-oriented design approach proposed by Booth;[1,2] for example there is a serious gap between the requirements and analysis phases of systems development and the object-oriented design and implementation phases. Using block diagrams, such as data flow diagrams, has a number of weaknesses as a starting point for object-oriented design because block diagrams coalesce the uses of system transactions into single nodes and the usage relations among transactions into arcs between nodes. Thus such diagrams irreversibly summarize information needed to develop good object-oriented designs.[6]

The object-oriented design approach in References 1 and 2 provides no systematic means of intellectual control over the growth of a complex system. Thus there is little clear discipline or order to discovering, designing, and implementing objects. In particular discovering embedded objects (that is, objects within objects) and inheritance opportunities are not addressed.

Since the object-oriented design approach depends on the heuristic invention of objects, there is no formal, mathematical basis for evaluating the correctness or quality of design decisions. Object-oriented designs are often presented as complete in data flow diagrams, thereby skipping important analytic steps. In small problems such lacunae may be possible, but in larger ones, it becomes difficult and even painful to determine if the leap was due to inspiration or ignorance. As complex as large problems are, and as numerous as design alternatives, it is risky to leap from data flows to object stimuli and responses without considerable engineering analysis. Typically, designing and implementing the transformational functions that tie together objects are left as exercises for the programmer once the objects have been completed. Programmers not involved in the design process may not understand the design and produce an incorrect system implementation.

Many of these problems arise because of the widely held misconception that top-down functional decomposition is inappropriate and even contradictory to an object-oriented design process. Instead it is our premise that with the correct concepts and techniques, the advantages of both system decomposition and object composition can be combined into a rigorous object-oriented design process.

The box structure concepts and techniques support a rigorous yet practical set of methods for the development of systems.[6,7] Chapter 9 shows that box-structured system design provides a systematic process for creating object-oriented designs. In Section 2 we review box structure concepts to show that box structures are in fact representations of objects. Section 3 presents a complete object-oriented design process with box structures. Section 4 provides a discussion of such object-oriented concepts as inheritance and reusability and their implications in the design process. An example of a box structure system design is given in Section 5, and a set of observations completes the chapter.

2. RELATIONSHIP OF BOX STRUCTURES TO OBJECTS

This section examines the relationship between box structures and the object concept in system design.

2.1. Box Structure Overview

Box-structured system design is a stepwise refinement and verification process that produces a system design. Such a system design is defined by a hierarchy of small design steps that permit immediate verification of their correctness. Three basic principles underlie the box-structured design process:[6]

1. All data to be defined and stored in the design are hidden in data abstractions.
2. All processing is defined by sequential and concurrent uses of data abstractions.
3. Each use of a data abstraction in the system occupies a distinct place in the system's usage hierarchy.

Box structure methods define a single data abstraction in three forms to isolate the creative design steps involved in building the abstraction. A *black box* gives an external description of data abstraction behavior in terms of stimulus histories to responses. A black box is the most abstract description of system behavior, and it can be considered as a requirements statement for the system. A *state box* includes a designed state and an

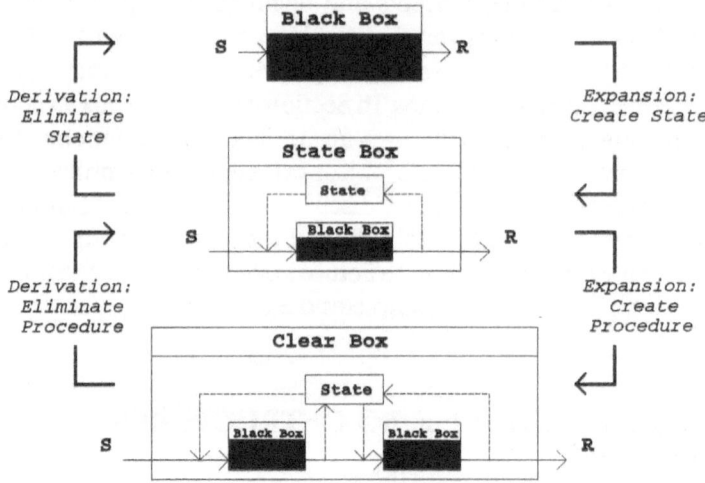

Figure 9.1. Box structure derivation and expansion.

internal data abstraction that transforms the stimulus and an initial state into the response and a new state. The state is designed from analysis of the required stimulus histories and responses for the system. Finally a *clear box* replaces internal data abstraction with the designed sequential or concurrent use of other black boxes. These other black boxes are new data abstractions that will be expanded at the next level of the system box structure hierarchy into state box and clear box forms. Reference 6 presents the formal mathematical definitions and relationships of the three box structures. Figure 9.1 shows relationships among the three views of a single data abstraction. The creative design steps on the right-hand side of the figure are called expansions. The design verification steps on the left-hand side of the figure are called derivations. A given black box (state box) can be expanded into many correct state box (clear box) designs. Conversely a state box (clear box) defines a unique black box (state box) by derivation.

To have intellectual control over the development of a complex system, we must be able to decompose the system into smaller, more manageable parts. A box structure hierarchy represents black box data abstractions at a higher level, clear box data abstraction. A hierarchy of data abstractions provides referential transparency among all black boxes within a clear box.[8] Thus each black box can be designed independently of the others.

2.2. Box Structures as Objects

Similarly to box structures, the object concept can be seen as an extension of abstract data types in programming languages.[9] A precise mathematical definition of an object has not been widely used; it is informally defined as a unit of information and descriptions of its manipulations. In describing what it means to support object-oriented programming, several concepts are presented as critical to the object-oriented paradigm. These concepts include information hiding, data abstraction, inheritance, dynamic binding, and automatic storage management.[10]

For the purpose of system design, box structures contain all of the integral aspects of objects (see Section 4 for a discussion of how box structures support inheritance); in fact box structures provide important design extensions for object-oriented design. These extensions include isolating and verifying all creative design steps in small units and systematically deriving the design in a top-down hierarchy for intellectual design control. Another major benefit in viewing box structures as objects is that all system design units, from the top-level, complete system to the smallest subsystem components and down to simple variables, are viewed and described as box structure objects. Thus there is no need to develop transformational functions to tie objects together, which is required in traditional object-oriented design methods.

3. BOX STRUCTURE OBJECT-ORIENTED DEVELOPMENT PROCESS

The object-oriented design process discussed here integrates and extends the following ideas.

- The spiral development process, as described in Reference 7, is an iterative, flexible schedule of investigation, specification, and implementation steps that more accurately models the process of systems development than do traditional life cycles based on the waterfall model.

- In Reference 11 box structures and the box structure hierarchy provide the unifying concepts for achieving a truly integrated development environment across the complete systems development process. No artificial bridges nor intermediate data representations are needed to exchange information from one step of the development process to the next. All information from requirements to detailed designs are recorded and stored in box structure formats.

- Reference 6 presents an 11-step procedure for producing a box structure expansion. Each expansion of a box structure is an exercise in designing internal-state data and the internal procedure. Since each expansion requires considerable invention, it helps to break the expansion into smaller steps, leaving design trails that permit more objective engineering inspections.

We propose a general systems development process consisting of five phases. The order of performance of these phases during system development is based on the spiral paradigm in which the next phase of development is determined by previous phase results. This requires definite result milestones and strict management control of the development process. The five development phases are

1. Problem definition: A clear problem statement must be generated to provide a basis for system development.
2. Requirements determination: Requirements are elicited from the system domain experts and system users. Requirements are represented in formats to facilitate review and feedback.
3. Systems analysis: System requirements are analyzed, and information is gathered to support subsequent design decisions.
4. Systems design and verification: Definitive design decisions are made, and the systems design is grown via top-down functional decomposition. Each creative design step is verified to be a correct expansion of the existing design.
5. Systems implementation: Systems design is transformed into an operational system. The final system is a combination of hardware, software, firmware, and or human behavior components. Boundaries and interfaces among these components must be specified in the final system design.

Our emphasis in this section is on detailing the processing found in Phases 2–4 and demonstrating the inherent object orientation of the box structure development process. Requirements determination phases, systems analysis, and systems design and verification are performed as a tightly integrated iterative process. The ability to achieve this tight integration results from the unifying box structure concepts and representations. (In the following discussion, the term box structure refers to a component in the system hierarchy; however the term object could be used with identical meaning.)

3.1. Determining Requirements

Input in the requirements determination phase is a complete problem statement, typically presented as a structured English document. Investigation tasks precisely determine the requirements of a system to solve the presented problem. Note that the requirements determination phase is performed for each box structure (that is object) in the box structure hierarchy. Requirements for any system object level can be represented in a box structure format. The ultimate goal is to state all requirements in a state-free, procedure-free black box. Defining requirements solely as a black box places no constraints on the eventual design. The first two steps of the Mills box structure expansion process are performed as follows:[6]

1. Define black box stimuli, determining all possible stimuli to the box structure.
2. Define the black box requirement, determining all required responses from the box structure.
3. Define transactions mapping stimulus histories into responses.

Black box transactions are defined as mathematical functions for deterministic behavior or mathematical relations for nondeterministic behavior. For high-level, complex box structures, it may be necessary to state the function or relation in the natural language of the problem domain, which is often a mixture of formal and informal language. Whatever the notation, the black box description is a set of mathematical functions.

Systems requirements often contain design constraints on such things as the availability and use of data or the need to conform to a defined procedure. Such requirements cannot be recorded in a black box; thus state box and clear box formats must be used to express such constraints. In addition certain nonfunctional requirements, such as performance and documentation standards, can be stated in structured English forms. During requirement reviews it is important for system owners to understand that any requirements beyond a black box are constraints on the system's design freedom. In this way many nonessential requirements can be discovered and eliminated.

Results from the requirements determination phase are a precisely defined black box with accompanying state box, clear box, and nonfunctional design constraints. This box structure requirement is stored in a repository as the initial definition of this system object.

3.2. Systems Analysis

Systems analysis tasks are performed to support decisions that must be made during systems design. The box structure requirement is analyzed, and information is gathered to enable one or more of the following types of activities:

- Feasibility studies are performed to determine the feasibility and cost/benefit of potential designs.

- Reuse opportunities are explored. Repositories of system objects from this project or existing systems are investigated for requirements matching. The cost/benefit of reusing existing objects, along with any required modifications, are analyzed at this point. Reuse is a potential major benefit of object orientation discussed in Section 4.

- Prototyping is done to evaluate design alternatives. The prototype development process takes on a life of its own with the five development phases performed in an iterative manner. Objects developed in the prototype may be candidates for reuse and modification in the principal system.

- Trade-off studies evaluate advantages and disadvantages of designing and implementing the current box structure as hardware, software, firmware, human behavior, or some combination thereof. Such decisions impact reuse opportunities and interface designs.

- Reuse potential should be analyzed for the current box structure. If the decision is made to design the box structure as a reusable object, then reuse standards may dictate certain design decisions (for example interface standards).

The preceding types of analyses are essential for supporting high-quality system designs. Information, analysis, and conclusions from these studies are recorded in the evolving box structure in the system repository. Some analysis discoveries may cause changes in the system requirements, thus iteration between the phases of requirements determination and systems analysis is to be expected.

3.3. Systems Design and Verification

This phase uses the box structure requirement and the analysis results to produce a complete design specification of the box structure (Steps 3–10 in Mills box structure expansion process).[6,7]

3. Discover state data requirements for each black box transaction. For each transaction encapsulate its required stimulus history into a state data requirement.
4. Design state data for the box structure. Integrate state data requirements for all transactions into a single data design. This is a critical creative design step.
5. Design the state box. For the designed state, determine the internal black box requirement to map mathematically (stimuli, current state) into (responses, new state) for each box structure transaction.
6. Verify the state box. Using the formal derivation from state box to black box, verify the correctness of the state box with respect to the required black box behavior. The completed state box is stored in the repository. The clear box can now be designed.
7. Discover transaction and state relationships. Determine all possible accesses of each state item by each transaction.
8. Design data abstractions. Organize state data into abstractions for effective access. This is the creative design step that determines data abstractions (that is objects) defined at the next level of the system hierarchy. This design decision uses relationships discovered in Step 7 and performs state migration of appropriate state data into lower level box structures.
9. Design the clear box. Given the data abstractions from Step 8, sequential and/or concurrent uses of data abstractions are de-

signed. This is a creative design step that produces the procedural
design to replace the nonprocedural internal black box in the
state box. The clear box completely defines communication and
coordination among its internal black boxes (that is data abstractions).
10. Verify the clear box. Using the formal derivation from clear box
    to state box, verify the correctness of the clear box design with
    respect to the existing state box.

Designing the clear box completes the detailed design of the current
box structure. The complete specification of the box structure object—
from the black box requirement, through the intermediate state box, to
the final clear box design—is stored in the system repository. Then the
final step of the Mills expansion process is

11. Repeat the stepwise expansion of the system until the design is
    complete. For each new black box designed in Step 8, repeat
    Steps 1–11 recursively.

The procedural clear box design, developed in Step 9, ensures that
each black box is referentially transparent from all other peer black boxes
and can be designed independently. Thus for each black box requirement,
the development process of requirements determination, systems analysis, and systems design and verification begins. Note that much of the
work performed, and dutifully recorded in the repository, for higher level
box structures in the hierarchy can be used to analyze and design lower
level box structures. The desired system is complete when no black box
requirements exist in the box structure hierarchy. The detailed design
of the complete system is then ready for the final phase of systems
implementation.

4. OBJECT-ORIENTED DEVELOPMENT CONCEPTS

Although described in terms of box structure concepts, the systems
development process just presented is in essence a formal development
process for object-oriented systems. In this section we discuss and clarify
the application and implications of object-oriented concepts in this development process.

4.1. Systems and Software Development

A comprehensive systems development methodology should support analysis, design, and implementation of the complete system; and integration of hardware, software, firmware, and human behavior. Objects have traditionally referred to software components designed and programmed in object-oriented languages. We support a broader view of the object-oriented development paradigm where all components of a system are modeled as objects, and decisions on the physical representation of the objects are delayed as long as feasible in the development process. Note that reuse opportunities and trade-off studies impact these design decisions. This broad system perspective for object-oriented development is one of the main motivating principles in the Department of Defense STARS program.[12]

4.2. Object Decomposition and Object Composition

There has been considerable debate over the advantages and disadvantages of decomposition versus composition as competing techniques for object-oriented design. We believe that with the correct development concepts, both techniques can be used to advantage. Decomposition and composition of objects are employed in the systems development process in Section 3.

Top-down systems decomposition enables an essential intellectual control in development, since the system grows one level at a time, and mathematically structuring systems in hierarchies of objects allows formal verification methods to be used. The referential transparency of objects in a clear box also grants design independence to each object. But in this framework of an object hierarchy, the advantages of object composition come into play. An object requirement, stated as a black box, can be matched with existing object types stored for reuse in a repository. During the systems analysis phase, benefits and costs of object reuse and modification can be studied. Another opportunity for object composition occurs while designing the clear box. Knowledge of existing object types or insight into desired object types influence the use of data abstractions as black boxes at the next level in the object hierarchy.

4.3. Reusing Objects

Reuse is a fundamental concept in object-oriented development.[13] Reusing objects within and among systems has the potential of significantly raising systems development productivity, and box structure methods support a high level of object reuse.

In a top-down approach, each object in the systems hierarchy is stored in its three box views in a system design repository. Certain of these objects, usually the smaller objects at lower levels in the hierarchy, are selected for reuse, and special design requirements are then imposed on the objects, such as interface and documentation standards. These reusable objects migrate to large organizational repositories as object types for potential reuse across all development projects. By including all three box views of the object in the reuse repository, a verified design trail of the object from requirement to detailed design is available for evaluation and use during reuse decisions.

During the systems analysis phase, reuse decisions are made for a given black box requirement. A reusable object type can be found in the reuse repository to meet the requirement. We recognize several forms of object instantiation for reuse during systems development, such as:

- Organizationwide object instantiation to encapsulate information and operations used by many systems; these objects include database and file systems, common user interfaces, and sensors maintaining physical properties (for example temperature and pressure).

- Systemwide object instantiation to encapsulate information and operations used in several different places in the systems uses hierarchy but not outside of the system; examples include commonly used data structures (for example files, stacks, and queues) and monitors for critical sections of the system.

- A one-time object instantiation to allow information and operations reuse without information sharing; this would primarily be beneficial for reusing existing program code.

The first two forms of object instantiations are termed common service box structures in Reference 7.

4.4. Inheritance

Inheritance has been firmly established as a criterion for judging the completeness of an object-oriented programming language or development method. Inheritance is the process by which one object type, the subclass, inherits the information and operations of another object type, the superclass. The subclass object type is then modified by adding or deleting information and/or operations of its own.

Inheritance is exhibited in the box structure development process by building new object types from existing object types during systems development. After an object type has been instantiated in a systems design, the designer can modify the object design by altering the state design of the state box and the procedure design of the clear box. If the modified object is designated for reuse, then a decision must be made about its representation in the reuse repository. The complete object type from black box to clear box can be stored as a unit, or the new object type (subclass) can be stored as a set of modifications with a pointer to the existing object type (superclass). Thus inheritance is a representation issue based on the structure and size of the reuse repository.

4.5. Object-Oriented Design Languages

The search for appropriate design languages for object-oriented development has led to graphics-based aids, such as Smalltalk icons,[14] Booch diagrams,[1] and syntactical forms, such as Ada PDLs.[15] Box structures have both a graphic notation and a syntactic notation, the box description language (BDL).[7] While graphics may be appropriate for small-system designs and high-level presentations, we see no alternative to using a syntactically complete design language for large-scale object-oriented systems development. An Ada design language (ADL) provides a complete basis for object-oriented development, and it is consistent with BDL, which adds box structure capabilities to the design process.

5. DESIGNING A MASTER FILE–TRANSACTION FILE SYSTEM

We demonstrate the application of object-oriented design with box structures to a simplified version of the classic example of a master file—transaction file system. In our example, a supply business maintains a master file of parts inventory with attributes (PARTID, QOH). Each day parts are received and shipped. For each transaction, a record is added to a transaction file with attributes (PARTID, ACTION, QTY), where ACTION has the value of in or out. We wish to develop a system that transfers transactions to the master file at the end of each day and produces a management control report showing the disposition of each transaction record and its effect on the master file.

We develop the top level of this system using box structure BDL. The BDL notation is similar to standard Program Design Languages (PDLs) and should be self-explanatory.

5.1. Requirements Determination

We begin by listing all of the stimuli and responses of the desired inventory system; these are stimuli: transaction file and master file; and responses: master file and management report. System requirements should indicate omissions and necessary extensions of the problem statement. For example what are the correct actions to take when unusual or erroneous conditions arise? We deal with two such conditions here: (1) If the transaction file is empty, the management report notes this and the system finishes; (2) if the PARTID in the transaction file does not match any record in the master file, the transaction record is written with an error message. All pertinent conditions and contingencies should be studied during requirements determination.

The black box BDL for the inventory system requirement follows

define BB INVENTORY

  stimulus
    Transaction_file : file of records
      record
        PARTID : integer,
        ACTION : type of ('in', 'out'),
        QTY : integer
      endrecord.
    Master_file : file of records
      record
        PARTID : integer,
        QOH : integer
      endrecord.

  response
    Master_file : file of records
      record
        PARTID : integer,

```
        QOH : integer
     endrecord.
Report :
   record
        HEADER : report_header,
        BODY : report_body
   endrecord.
```

transaction

If the transaction file is empty, then write the management report and end. Else, for each record in the transaction file, match the PARTID value in the master file. If a match exists, then modify the QOH value by adding (ACTION = 'in') or subtracting (ACTION = 'out') the value of QTY; and write the transaction record and new master record in the management report. If no match is found, write the transaction record and an error statement in the management report.

end transaction.

Note that the transaction statement in the black box is in structured English for exposition purposes. We could also present a mathematical representation of conditional algebraic assignments for the transaction.

5.2. Systems Analysis

We concentrate our analysis of the example on discovering reuse opportunities. We assume that a File_manager object type exists as a box structure design in the business's reuse library. The object type is designed to encapsulate a file of arbitrary design and size. Visible operations on the file include typical file operations, such as:

- OPEN: Establishes a currency pointer at the first record of a file and checks access rights.

- ISEMPTY: Checks if file is empty; returns a boolean value.

- READ: Reads the record at the currency pointer and moves the pointer to the next record.

- ATEOF: Checks if the currency pointer is at EOF; returns a boolean value.

- WRITE: Overwrites a given record at the currency pointer.

- FIND: Given a primary identifier value, this file operation finds the first record with that identifier; if no match is found, a STATUS value is returned. [1]

- ADD: Given a record with a valid identifier, this file operation places the record in the file in correct order.

- DELETE: Given a record identifier, this file operation finds a record and deletes it from the file.

- CLOSE: Establishes file integrity and update commitments; releases any file locks.

We assume that two object instantiations of File_manager encapsulate the master file and the transaction file. Since these files are also used by other systems in the business, these objects are organizationwide common services. We term the objects Master_file and Trans_file.

5.3. Systems Design and Verification

State box design of the inventory system reveals the need to store the evolving management report as an intermediate state. Thus the state box design is given as follows:

define SB INVENTORY

    common services
      Master_file.
      Trans_file.

    stimulus

    response
      Report :
        record
          HEADER : report_header,

```
        BODY : report_body
    endrecord.
```

state
```
    Report :
        record
            HEADER : report_header,
            BODY : report_body
        endrecord.
```

transaction

If the transaction file is empty, then print an empty Report and end. Else, for each record in Trans_file, match the PARTID value in Master_file. If a match exists, then modify the QOH value in Master_file by adding (ACTION = 'in') or subtracting (ACTION = 'out') the value of QTY in Trans_file; and write the Trans_file record and new Master_file record in Report. If no match is found, write the Trans_file record and an error statement in Report.

end transaction.

The state box can be verified as a correct design of the black box requirement in a straightforward manner. Although we do not present all of the details here, the critical tasks involve verifying the correct uses of Master_file and Trans_file objects and the Report state in the state box transaction.

During the clear box design, an important design decision has to be made: Should Report remain a global state in the system, or should it be encapsulated into a data abstraction with visible operations? We choose to develop a systemwide common service object called Mgmt_report with Report as encapsulated data with four visible operations:

- NEW: Initializes Report with defined header information, such as date, time, titles, and column headings.

- ADD: Adds correctly processed Trans_file record and new Master_file record to the body of Report.

- ERROR1: Adds a Trans_file record and error statement to the body of Report when no match is found in Master_file.

- PRINT: Prints the current state value of the Report.

The Mgmt_report object will be completely developed and verified, from black box requirement to clear box design, and used in the inventory system as a common service object.

The clear box design of inventory can be presented as follows:

define CB INVENTORY

   common services
      Master_file. (* organization-wide common service *)
      Trans_file. (* organization-wide common service *)
      Mgmt_report.   (* system-wide common service *)

   stimulus

   response

   state

   transaction
   data (* temporary data *)
      TEST1 : boolean,
   proc
      use Mgmt_report(in: NEW);
      use Master_file(in: OPEN);
      use Trans_file(in: OPEN);
      use Trans_file(in: ISEMPTY, out: TEST1);
      if NOT TEST1 **then** use Update_master;
      use Mgmt_report(in: PRINT);
      use Master_file(in: CLOSE);
      use Trans_file(in: CLOSE)
   corp
   end transaction.

Again the clear box can be verified, but that is not shown here.

The only new object at the second level of the system hierarchy is the Update_master black box. We iterate the development process for this object, defining the black box and performing systems analysis, and finally designing the state box and clear box. We show the final clear box design.

define CB Update_master

   common services
      Master_file. (* organization-wide common service *)
      Trans_file. (* organization-wide common service *)

Mgmt_report.   (* system-wide common service *)

stimulus

response

state

transaction
data (* temporary data *)
  TEST2 : boolean,
  T_REC :
    record
      PARTID : integer,
      ACTION : type of ('in', 'out'),
      QTY : integer
    endrecord.
  M_REC :
    record
      PARTID : integer,
      QOH : integer
    endrecord.
proc
  use Trans_file(in: ATEOF, out: TEST2);
  while NOT TEST2
  do
    use Trans_file(in: READ, out: T_REC);
    use Master_file(in: FIND, out: M_REC, STATUS);
    if STATUS = NOT_FOUND
    then use Mgmt_report(in: ERROR1, T_REC)
    else
      if T_REC.ACTION = 'in'
      then M_REC.QOH < -- M_REC.QOH + T_REC.QTY
      else M_REC.QOH < -- M_REC.QOH − T_REC.QTY;
      use Master_file(in: WRITE, M_REC);
      use Mgmt_report(in: ADD, M_REC, T_REC)
    fi;
    use Trans_file(in: ATEOF, out: TEST2);
  od
corp
end transaction.

Since there are no undefined black boxes in Update_master, no further design work is needed, and the inventory system is completely specified as a hierarchy of object uses.

6. CONCLUSIONS

Our goals in Chapter 9 were to discuss and demonstrate the use of box structures in a rigorous and systematic object-oriented systems design process. The following observations support and summarize our discussion.

- Box structures define data abstractions and objects in three mathematical views.

- The box structure hierarchy allows intellectual control over the development process.

- Each box structure in the system hierarchy is an object.

- All design inventions are separated into clearly identified small steps, so that at each step of design, information and procedure are handled with equal concern within an object.

- Design verification is performed at each design step to provide a systematic basis for inspection.

- An object is stored in the system repository in all box structure views, from black box requirement to clear box detailed design.

- Certain objects can be designated and designed for reuse. Such objects are stored in special reuse libraries.

- Object inheritance is provided by reusing and modifying existing superclass object types. Representation of the new subclass object type is a system efficiency question.

- Box structures support an integrated development process, since there is no need to transform the representation or content of development information from one phase to another.

- The systems development process is completely flexible between development phases. The next phase to be performed is based on feedback from previous work results. Developing a systems box structure hierarchy provides discipline and assures sound and complete design.

References

1. Booch, G. "Object-oriented design." *IEEE Trans. Software Eng.* **SE-12** (2) 211–221 (1986).
2. Booch, G. "Object-oriented design with applications." Benjamin Cummings Pub. Co., Redwood City, CA (1991).
3. Jalote, P. "Functional refinement and nested objects for object-oriented design." *IEEE Trans. Software Eng.* **15**(3) 264–270 (1989).
4. Seidewitz, E.; and Stark, M. "Towards a general object-oriented software development methodology." *Proc. of the 1st International Conference on Ada Programming Language Applications for the NASA Space Station* (1986).
5. Ward, P. "How to integrate object orientation with structured analysis and design." *IEEE Software* (March 1989).
6. Mills, H. "Stepwise refinement and verification in box-structured systems." *IEEE Computer.* **21**(6) 26–36 (1988).
7. Mills, H.; Linger, R.; and Hevner, A. *Principles of Information Systems Analysis and Design.* Academic Press, Orlando, FLA, 1986.
8. Parnas, D. "On a 'buzzword' hierarchical structure." *Proc. of the IFIP Congress 1974,* North-Holland (1974).
9. Danforth, S.; and C. Tomlinson. "Type theories and object-oriented programming." *ACM Computing Surveys* **20**(1) 29–72 (1988).
10. Pascoe, G. "Elements of object-oriented programming." *Byte* (August 1986).
11. Hevner, A. "An integrated systems development environment with box structures." *Proc. of the INTEC Symposium on Systems Analysis and Design Research,* Atlanta (November 1988).
12. Software Technology for Adaptable, Reliable Systems (STARS). "Statement of work." STARS Joint Program Office (October 1987).
13. Meyer, B. "Reusability: the case for object-oriented design." *IEEE Software* 50–63 (March 1987).
14. Goldberg, A.; and Robson, D. *Smalltalk-80: the Language and Its Implementation.* Addison-Wesley, Reading, NH, 1983.
15. IEEE. "Ada as a design language." Ada as a PDL Working Group (P990) of the Tech. Comm. on Software Engineering of the IEEE Computer Society (1985).

10

Toward Formalizing Control System Simulation Software

Joseph E. Hollingsworth

1. INTRODUCTION

The job of a control engineer is to build controllers for physical systems. Traditionally this has been done by creating a mathematical model of the system using differential equations. With the model the engineer designs a controller and analyzes the new model (original model and the controller) for proper control and stability.

Before the advent of digital computers, the control engineer used analog computers to perform simulations of the model. The natural correspondence between mathematical functions in the model (addition, integration, and so forth) and their analog computer counterparts made model simulation by the computer easy. Even though simulation by digital computer has generally replaced simulation by analog computer, the control engineer's approach to modeling the physical system mathematically remains the same: to identify a reusable software component for simulating a control system design. The obvious candidate is a component that captures the essence of an analog computer. Attention has been focused on identifying and formally specifying the conceptual basis of analog computation.

Section 2 of Chapter 10 provides necessary background and terminology, while Section 3 introduces a specification for the signal template, a module providing an abstract data type that models an analog computer's signal, Section 4 discusses future work.

Joseph E. Hollingsworth • Ohio State University

Studies in Computer Science, edited by John R. Rice and Richard A. DeMillo. Plenum Press, New York, 1994.

2. BACKGROUND

The main focus of our overall research effort is software reuse by developing formally specified software components that are modular, efficient, and certified to be correct. Currently we are developing a programming system called RESOLVE (*re*usable *so*ftware *l*anguage with *ver*ifiability and *e*fficiency) that supports the development of such software components.

2.1. Separating Specification from Implementation

A central doctrine of RESOLVE is separating specification from implementation. Because of this, a RESOLVE module has two separate parts: conceptualization and realization. Conceptualization formally specifies the types and operations the module provides; realization contains the actual code and data structures used to implement the module. Since Chapter 10 is concerned with the formal specification of an analog signal and operations on it, we limit our discussion to conceptualizations. For a more thorough treatment of RESOLVE conceptualizations and realizations, see Reference 1.

2.2. RESOLVE Conceptualizations

Writing a conceptualization involves setting up an explicit mathematical model for the programming objects of interest. Specifications are expressions that mathematically describe a data type and operations. Conceptualization constitutes the official interface between the implementer and the module's client; therefore it must be an abstract, complete, and unambiguous statement of what the module does. Conceptualization is abstract because it reveals nothing about the underlying implementation (in observation of accepted software design principles.[2] It must be complete and unambiguous, since it is the only interface between implementer and client. An added advantage of mathematical specifications is that these can be used as a basis for rigorously verifying and testing both implementations and client programs.[3]

The RESOLVE specifications are written as assertions using mathematical types, functions, and predicates associated with a relatively small class of existing mathematical theories, such as string theory, number theory (integers), set theory, functions, and relations. Consequently when writing a conceptualization for a type, we first identify the conceptual nature of the type and then identify an existing mathematical theory in which to model the type. Then we create the conceptualization by writing mathematical assertions from the theory that describe the behavior of the type and the operations provided.

3. SIGNAL TEMPLATE SPECIFICATION

This section provides an operational analysis of an analog computer, identifying the type and operations that should be provided by a RESOLVE module that captures the concept. An application followed of a module design guideline that aids identification of primary operations (those to be included in the most reusable module that provides the basic type) and secondary operations (those to be left for an enhancement to the module). Finally we present the conceptualization for the analog template.

3.1. Operational Analysis of an Analog Computer

Analysis of an analog computer is based on how a control engineer uses it to perform control system simulation. The first step is to create a mathematical model of the system using differential equations. With the model the engineer designs a controller and analyzes the new model (original model and the controller) for proper control and stability. Analysis involves simulating the model on the analog computer. Simulation uses wires and a plug board to interconnect the computer's adder, multiplier, integrater, and so forth, components. Simulation is then driven by a function generator that models an input to the system. Output is usually presented in the form of graphs of variables of the model. Thus there are three different kinds of tasks being performed: (1) model simulation by math components, (2) function generation by function generation components, and (3) output presentation by graphing components. The rest of chapter 10 focuses on model simulation by math components, with some discussion of function generation components; output is not considered.

The general analog computer has a basic set of components for model simulation:[4] adders, inverters, multipliers, and integraters. Each takes a signal (possibly more than one) as input and produces another signal as output. For example an inverter takes a signal as input, then produces the same signal with its sign inverted as output. In the analog computer a signal is a continuous function from time to voltage where the voltage remains within a fixed range.

What mathematical theories are used to explain the analog computer's signal and components? First of all since passage of time is viewed as continuous, mathematical real numbers are used to represent time. The same argument applies for voltage. Mathematical function theory is needed to model the signal; the function is from real numbers (time) to real numbers (voltage). The type signal and operations on signals can be formally specified based on this abstract mathematical model.

3.2. Identifying Primary and Secondary Operations

An important result of our research on reusable software components has been the development of module design guidelines. One module design guideline seeks to separate operations that must have access to the underlying representation of a provided type from those that do not. Operations given access to the underlying representation are called primary operations, and those that are not given access are called secondary. One of the deciding factors is whether the operation can be implemented efficiently without access to the underlying representation; if this is the case, then it is probably a secondary operation. Another factor is that primary operations must provide sufficient power to support implementation of all secondary operations.

The choice of signal's primary operations also depends on the initial value of variables of type signal. When a new type is specified in RESOLVE, an initial value must also be specified for variables of that type. This initial value is automatically assigned to new variables as they are declared. The initial value chosen for signal is the ideal impulse function: a signal that is zero everywhere except at zero and whose integral from negative infinity to positive infinity has value one.

Primary operations are chosen so that a rich set of signals can be built from the initial value and primary operations. The operations needed certainly include add, scale, integrate and eval(uate). With add, scale, and integrate, polynomials can be built. For example a unit-step function is obtained from integrating a variable set to the initial value; a unit-ramp function is obtained from integrating the step function; a square function from a ramp, a cubic from a square, and so forth. By applying the scale and add functions to these signals, we can build polynomial signals. Eval gives us the capability of examining the signal at any time t, which is useful for displaying the output of a simulation.

3.3. Signal Template Conceptual Module

The following signal template illustrates our discussion

conceptualization Signal_Template
  parameters
    facility Signal_Real_Facility **is** Real_Template
      renaming
        Signal_Real_Facility. Real **as** Signal_Real
      end renaming
    facility Time_Real_Facility **is** Real_Template
      renaming
        Time_Real_Facility.Real **as** Time_Real
      end renaming
  end parameters

  auxiliary
    math facilities
      Real_Theory **is** Real_Theory_Template
        renaming
          Real_Theory.Real_Number **as** Real_Number
          Real_Number.* **as** *
          Real_Number.+ **as** +
          Real_Number.= **as** =
          Real_Number.< **as** <
          Real_Number.≤ **as** ≤
        end renaming

      Function_Theory **is** Function_Theory_Template
          (Real_Number, Real_Number)
        renaming
          Function_Theory.Function **as** Signal_Model
        end renaming
    end math facilities
  end auxiliary

  interface
    type Signal **is modeled by** Signal_Model
      exemplar s
      initially "∀t : Real_Number,
        $t \neq 0 \Rightarrow s(t) = 0$ and
        $\int_{-\infty}^{\infty} s(t)dt = 1$"

lemma "$\forall t :$ Real_Number, $t < 0 \Rightarrow s(t) = 0$"
end Signal

function Add **returns** s : Signal
  parameters
    preserves x : Signal
    preserves y : Signal
  end parameters
  ensures "$\forall t :$ Real_Number, $s(t) = x(t) + y(t)$"
end Add

function Scale **returns** s : Signal
  parameters
    preserves x : Signal
    preserves y : Signal_Real
  end parameters
  ensures "$\forall t :$ Real_Number, $s(t) = x(t) * y$"
end Scale

function Integrate **returns** s : Signal
  parameters
    preserves x : Signal
  end parameters
  ensures "$\forall t :$ Real_Number, $s(t) = \int_{-\infty}^{t} x(r)dr$"
end Integrate

function Eval **returns** y : Signal_Real
  parameters
    preserves x : Signal
    preserves t : Time_Real
  end parameters
  ensures "$y = x(t)$"
end Integrate

  end interface
end Signal_Template

    The parameters section lists parameters to the module, in this case two instances of the Real_Template—one for signal, the other for time. (Facility parameters are module instances. Types provided by a facility may also be parameters to modules.) These instances are parameters so can have different realizations.

    The auxiliary section declares any mathematical machinery needed to write the specifications that follow. In this case Real_Theory is declared an instance of the mathematical theory of real numbers. Real numbers are used from the Real_Theory instance in the specifications to discuss both signal and time values. Along with Real_Theory come the mathematical types and functions defined therein (mathematical type Real_Number and addition and multiplication functions, for example).

Function_Theory is also declared here, and this declaration is the core of the specification for the type signal. This declaration creates an instance of the mathematical theory of functions with two arguments of type Real_Number (from the Real_Theory instance). The product of this instantiation is a mathematical module providing a mathematical type that is a function from Real_Number to Real_Number. In the renaming section it is given the name Signal_Model to signify that we are modeling an analog signal with this mathematical abstraction.

The interface section specifies the external interface of every realization of Signal_Template. It provides a program type called signal that is modeled by the mathematical type Signal_Model. The exemplar keyword introduces a mathematical variable of type Signal_Model to be used in the following specifications. The initially clause describes the initial condition for every variable of type signal. The lemma clause notes that variables of type signal have a value of zero for time $t \leq 0$, an invariant preserved by all the operations. This is a standard control engineering view of analog signals.

The remainder of the interface section contains specifications for procedures and functions provided by the module. For example the add operation has two signal parameters, (whose values are not changed; they are preserves mode parameters). The ensures clause is a postcondition for the function that says, on completing add, s (the returned variable) equals the sum of the two input signals x and y for all time t. Other operations are specified similarly.

4. FUTURE WORK

The Signal_Template provides a good foundation for both implementation of the module and client applications of the module. Future work will focus on implementation issues and simulating mathematical models that contain feedback loops. Work will also concentrate on multiple implementations of signal. The appeal of multiple implementations arises because some simulations are more efficient with one implementation than another. Some standard implementations for signal would be polynomial interpolation, piecewise-polynomial approximation, and so forth.[5]

ACKNOWLEDGMENTS. I thank members of the Reusable Software Research Group at The Ohio State University for their discussions on the content of this chapter.

References

1. Weide, B. W., Ogden, W. F., and Zweben, S. H., "Reusable Software Components," *Advances in Computers* **33**, 1–65, M. C. Yovits, ed., Academic Press, 1991.
2. Parnas, D. L. "A technique for software module specification with examples." *Comm. ACM* **15**(5) 571–585 (1972).
3. Gourlay, J. S. "A mathematical framework for the investigation of testing." *IEEE Trans. Software Eng.* **SE-9**(6) 686–709 (1983).
4. Truitt, T. D.; and Rogers, A. E. *Basics of Analog Computers.* New York: John F. Rider, 1960.
5. Conte, S. D.; and de Boor, C. *Elementary Numerical Analysis, an Algorithmic Approach.* New York: McGraw-Hill, 1980.

11

Sensitivity of Differential Equations

R. V. M. Zahar

1. INTRODUCTION

Although it had received little attention until recently, the sensitivity of two-point boundary value problems in differential equations is the subject of much current study (see, for instance Reference 1). The question of how the solution of a differential system depends on its data is not only fundamental in analyzing differential models for physical processes, but it is essential for understanding numerical methods for solving the system. Indeed the sensitivity of the difference systems that approximate differential systems must depend in one way or another on the sensitivity of the original problem. Thus it is mathematically convenient to present a conditioning analysis that applies to both the differential and the difference systems. Chapter 11 develops the basis for such a uniform analysis.

We consider the separable linear two-point differential boundary value problem given by

$$y_1(0) = \alpha_1 \tag{1a}$$

$$y'(t) = A(t)y(t) + b(t) \qquad 0 \le t \le T \tag{1b}$$

$$y_2(T) = \alpha_2 \tag{1c}$$

where $y(t)$, $b(t)$ are complex vectors of dimension n; $b(t)$ is a continuous function; $A(t)$ is an $n \times n$ matrix of continuous functions; and vectors y

R. V. M. Zahar • University of Montreal

Studies in Computer Science, edited by John R. Rice and Richard A. DeMillo. Plenum Press, New York, 1994.

are partitioned as $y^T = [y_1^T, y_2^T]$, with y_1 of dimension k and y_2 of dimension $n - k$. When it exists, the unique solution vector in Equation 1a–c is denoted by f, and we assume that $f(t) \neq 0$ for all $t \in [0,T]$. We examine this simplest form of the two-point boundary value problem instead of one with the more general boundary condition $M_0 y(0) + M_T y(T) = \alpha$ to demonstrate the main principles in the development. In fact we believe that the clearest way of treating the conditioning of the more general problem is to reduce its analysis to that of the separable case.

The framework for our discussion is as follows. First we suppose that the data α, $A(t)$, and $b(t)$ are subject to relative errors of magnitudes less than or equal to the positive constant ε. We consider relative instead of absolute errors because the data are often given to a fixed number of significant figures rather than decimal places and because floating point computation is generally employed in the numerical solution of Equation 1a–c. Next we consider continuous perturbations of the data. The justification for doing so is based on the idea that the numerical solution of Equation 1a–c by a finite method on a discrete subset of $[0,T]$ can always be embedded in a continuous problem on the entire interval. Finally we measure the relative error in the resulting solution. We appreciate the fact that most authors consider absolute perturbations in the solution, but we feel that an initial understanding of the concepts is more easily obtained by examining the relative error. (Although the absolute error analysis should perhaps be performed separately, some intuition about absolute conditioning can be gained from the relative analysis by a continuous mapping of the desired solution to a function of unit norm.)

Thus we suppose that Equation 1a–c is perturbed to a continuous problem of the form

$$\hat{y}_1(0) = \alpha_1 + \eta_1 \tag{2a}$$

$$\hat{y}'(t) = [A(t) + E(t)]\hat{y}(t) + [b(t) + e(t)], \qquad 0 \leq t \leq T \tag{2b}$$

$$\hat{y}_2(T) = \alpha_2 + \eta_2, \tag{2c}$$

where

$$\|\eta_1\| \leq \|\alpha_1\|\varepsilon \qquad \|E(t)\| \leq \|A(t)\|\varepsilon \qquad \|e(t)\| \leq \|b(t)\|\varepsilon \qquad \|\eta_2\| \leq \|\alpha_2\|\varepsilon$$

and the L_∞ vector norm and its subordinate matrix norm are employed.

If Equation 2a–c possesses a solution, then we denote it by $\hat{\mathbf{f}}$, and we measure the conditioning of Equation 1a–c by the error function

$$r(t) \equiv \sup_{\substack{\|E(t)\| \leq \|A(t)\|\varepsilon \\ \|e(t)\| \leq \|b(t)\|\varepsilon \\ \|\eta_1\| \leq \|\alpha_1\|\varepsilon \\ \|\eta_2\| \leq \|\alpha_2\|\varepsilon}} \frac{\|\hat{\mathbf{f}}(t) - \mathbf{f}(t)\|}{\|\mathbf{f}(t)\|} \tag{3}$$

The condition number is defined as $c(t) \equiv \lim_{\varepsilon \to 0} r(t)/\varepsilon$ or in other words, the factor of ε in a convergent perturbation ε-series for $r(t)$ when such a series exists. We say that Equation 1a–c is well conditioned if and only if $\sup_{0 \leq t \leq T} c(t)$ is bounded by a specified constant that of course depends on the context. Our goal is therefore to derive upper and lower bounds for $c(t)$. To introduce the techniques, we consider the case $k = n$ first.

2. INITIAL VALUE PROBLEMS

When $k = n$ and Equation 1a–c reduces to an initial value form, the existence of solutions to both Equations 1a–c and 2a–c follows from the continuity of the data. If we let $\eta_1 = \eta$ and subtract Equation 1a–c from Equation 2a–c, we see that the difference $\delta(t) \equiv \hat{\mathbf{f}}(t) - \mathbf{f}(t)$ is the unique solution of

$$\delta(0) = \eta \tag{4a}$$

$$\delta'(t) = A(t)\delta(t) + E(t)[\mathbf{y}(t) + \delta(t)] + e(t) \qquad 0 \leq t \leq T \tag{4b}$$

Taking $H(t)$ to be a fundamental matrix of complementary solutions for $\mathbf{y}'(t) = A(t)\mathbf{y}(t)$, it follows from the variation-of-constants formula that $\delta(t)$ satisfies the implicit integral equation

$$\delta(t) = H(t)H^{-1}(0)\eta + H(t)\int_0^t H^{-1}(s)\{E(s)[\mathbf{f}(s) + \delta(s)] + e(s)\}ds$$

By repeated substitution of this same expression for $\delta(s)$ on the right-hand side, we obtain the formal series, or matrizant (Reference 2) given by the three infinite sums

$$\Omega(t) = H(t)H^{-1}(0)\eta + H(t)\int_0^t H^{-1}(s)E(s)H(s)H^{-1}(0)\eta ds$$

$$+ H(t)\int_0^t H^{-1}(s)E(s)H(s)\left\{\int_0^s H^{-1}(s_1)E(s_1)H^{-1}(0)\eta ds_1\right\}ds + \cdots$$

$$+ H(t)\int_0^t H^{-1}(s)E(s)f(s)ds + H(t)\int_0^t H^{-1}(s)E(s)H(s)$$

$$\times\left\{\int_0^s H^{-1}(s_1)E(s_1)f(s_1)ds_1\right\}ds + \cdots$$

$$+ H(t)\int_0^t H^{-1}(s)e(s)ds$$

$$+ H(t)\int_0^t H^{-1}(s)E(s)H(s)\left\{\int_0^s H^{-1}(s_1)e(s_1)ds_1\right\}ds + \cdots \quad (5)$$

We now show that this series converges and $\Omega(t) \equiv \delta(t)$ as expected. Because of the definition in Equation 3 for the error function $r(t)$, it is convenient first to divide Equation 5 by $\|f(t)\|$. We introduce the notation

$$F(s,t) \equiv \|H(t)H^{-1}(s)\|\frac{\|f(s)\|}{\|f(t)\|} \quad (6)$$

and as in Reference 3, we call $F(s,t)$ the amplification factor. Taking norms in Equation 5 we obtain

$$\frac{\|\Omega(t)\|}{\|f(t)\|} \le \varepsilon F(0,t) + \varepsilon^2\int_0^t F(s,t)F(0,s)\|A(s)\|ds + \varepsilon^3\int_0^t F(s,t)\|A(s)\|$$

$$\times\int_0^s F(s_1,s)F(0,s_1)\|A(s_1)\|ds_1ds + \cdots$$

$$+ \varepsilon\int_0^t F(s,t)\|A(s)\|ds$$

$$+ \varepsilon^2\int_0^t F(s,t)\|A(s)\|\int_0^s F(s_1,s)\|A(s_1)\|ds_1ds + \cdots$$

$$+ \varepsilon\int_0^t F(s,t)\frac{\|b(s)\|}{\|f(s)\|}\|ds + \varepsilon^2\int_0^t F(s,t)\|A(s)\|$$

$$\times\int_0^s F(s_1,s)\frac{\|b(s_1)\|}{\|f(s_1)\|}\|ds_1ds + \cdots \quad (7)$$

Thus if we define

$$M(t) \equiv \sup_{0 \leq s_1 \leq s \leq t} F(s_1, s) \qquad K_1(t) \equiv \sup_{0 \leq s \leq t} \|A(s)\| \qquad K_2(t) \equiv \sup_{0 \leq s \leq t} \frac{\|b(s)\|}{\|f(s)\|} \qquad (8)$$

then because of continuity, all three functions are bounded for $t \in [0,T]$ when T is finite, and it follows from Equation 7 that

$$\frac{\|\Omega(t)\|}{\|f(t)\|} \leq \varepsilon M(t) e^{M(t)K_1(t)t\varepsilon} + \left[1 + \frac{K_2(t)}{K_1(t)}\right] [e^{M(t)K_1(t)t\varepsilon} - 1] \qquad (9)$$

if $K_1(t) \neq 0$ and that $\|\Omega(t)\|/\|f(t)\| \leq \varepsilon M(t)[1 + K_2(t)]$ if $K_1(t) = 0$. Because of Equation 9 the series in Equation 7 therefore converges absolutely and uniformly for all t belonging to any finite interval [0,T]. Moreover by differentiating Equation 5 term by term with respect to t, it follows that $\Omega(t)$ satisfies Equation 4b, and therefore $\Omega(t)$ is equivalent to the unique solution $\delta(t)$ of Equation 4a–b because $\Omega(0) = \eta$.

To show that the bound given in Equation 7 is realistic, we consider two special cases. First suppose that Equation 4a–b is a scalar equation with $\alpha_1 \neq 0$. Then by Equation 5, we see that equality is attained in Equation 7 if $|\eta|$, $|E(s)|$, and $|e(s)|$ all reach their maximum values with appropriate signs for each s. Similarly if $A(t)$ is a diagonal matrix such that for a fixed I, $\|A(t)\| = |a_{II}(t)|$ for all t, and if in addition $\|b(t)\| = |b_I(t)|$ for all t, then equality is attained in Equation 7 when $\eta \neq 0$.

Since the error function $r(t)$ is the supremum over all possible perturbations, it also follows from Equation 5 that when $\eta \neq 0$, its minimum value is $\varepsilon F(0,t)$. Using Equation 7 to bound the condition number, which depends only on the first terms in each of the three infinite sums, we obtain the following theorem.

Theorem 1. When $n = k$ and Equation 1a–c is an initial value problem, its condition number satisfies

$$c(t) \leq F(0,t) + \int_0^t F(s,t) \left[\|A(s)\| + \frac{\|b(s)\|}{\|f(s)\|}\right] ds \qquad (10)$$

where $F(s,t)$ is the amplification factor in Equation 6, and where the bound is achievable. Moreover if $\alpha_1 \neq 0$, then $c(t) \geq F(0,t)$.

To demonstrate Theorem 1, we consider the academic example of Equation 1a–c (1.1) with $k = n$,

$$\mathbf{y}'(t) = \begin{bmatrix} -8 & 9 \\ -18 & 19 \end{bmatrix} \mathbf{y}(t) + \begin{bmatrix} 4 \\ 4 \end{bmatrix} e^{5t} \qquad 0 \le t \le T \tag{11}$$

and $\mathbf{y}(0) = \alpha = [1 \quad 1]^T$, for which $\mathbf{f}(t) = e^{5t}[1 \quad 1]^T$ and

$$\mathbf{H}(t) = \begin{bmatrix} e^t & e^{10t} \\ e^t & 2e^{10t} \end{bmatrix}$$

$$\mathbf{H}(t)\mathbf{H}^{-1}(s) = \begin{bmatrix} 2e^{(t-s)} - e^{10(t-s)} & -e^{(t-s)} + e^{10(t-s)} \\ 2e^{(t-s)} - 2e^{10(t-s)} & -e^{(t-s)} + 2e^{10(t-s)} \end{bmatrix} \tag{12}$$

It follows from Equation 6 that $F(s,t) = 3e^{-4(t-s)} + 4e^{5(t-s)}$ and from Theorem 1 that

$$3e^{-4t} + 4e^{5t} \le c(t) \le 3e^{-4t} + 4e^{5t} + 41 \int_0^t [3e^{-4(t-s)} + 4e^{5(t-s)}]ds$$

so that the problem is ill conditioned for large t because of the term e^{5t}, which results from the ratio of the second complementary solution (the second column of $\mathbf{H}$) over $\|\mathbf{f}(t)\|$. Indeed since $\|\mathbf{H}(t)\mathbf{H}^{-1}(s)\|$ is a measure of the maximum growth of the complementary solutions from s to t, Equation 6 shows that $F(s,t)$ is the ratio of that maximum growth to the growth of $\mathbf{f}$ over the same interval. We remark that in this example, the size of the condition number depends principally on the value of the amplification factor $F(s,t)$. Indeed for typical linear systems, $F(s,t)$ is exponential, whereas $\|\mathbf{A}(t)\|$ and $\|\mathbf{b}(t)\|/\|\mathbf{f}(t)\|$ are polynomial. By Equation 10 therefore $F(0,t)$ is often a sufficiently accurate indication of the size of $c(t)$.

Before discussing the full boundary value formulation, we consider the case $k = 0$ in Equation 1a–c, that is an initial value problem with initial point T instead of 0. By interchanging the roles of 0 and T in Theorem 1, we obtain

$$F(T,t) \le c(t) \le F(T,t) + \int_t^T F(s,t)\left[\|\mathbf{A}(s)\| + \frac{\|\mathbf{b}(s)\|}{\|\mathbf{f}(s)\|}\right]ds \tag{13}$$

when $y(T) = \alpha \neq 0$. Thus for the same differential equation as Equation 11 and with $\alpha = [1 \quad 1]^T$ as the given condition at $t = T$, it follows that

$$c(t) \geq 3e^{4(T-t)} + 4e^{-5(T-t)}$$

so this time it is the ratio of the first complementary solution of H in Equation 12 to $\|f(t)\|$ that causes the ill conditioning, whereas the second complementary solution contributes little to $c(t)$. Rephrasing the problem in boundary value form can be regarded as an attempt to incorporate the best behavior of each of these two initial value problems.

3. BOUNDARY VALUE PROBLEMS

We now consider Equation 1a–c when $k \neq n$ and $k \neq 0$. It is convenient to have the following notations: for $n \times n$ matrices we employ the partition

$$H = \begin{bmatrix} H_{11} & H_{12} \\ H_{21} & H_{22} \end{bmatrix}$$

where H_{11} is $k \times k$ and other submatrices are of consistent dimensions. We also use the partition $H = [H_1 \quad H_2]$, where H_1 is of dimension $n \times k$ and H_2 is $n \times (n - k)$. If the matrix has an inverse sign, we write

$$H^{-1} = \begin{bmatrix} [H^{-1}]_1 \\ [H^{-1}]_2 \end{bmatrix}$$

where $[H^{-1}]_1$ is of dimension $k \times n$ and $[H^{-1}]_2$ is $(n - k) \times n$. Therefore it follows that

$$H(t)H^{-1}(s) = H_1(t)[H^{-1}(s)]_1 + H_2(t)[H^{-1}(s)]_2$$

a simple expression demonstrating that the Green's function for Equation 1a–c can also be partitioned as the sum of two separate reduced functions of similar structure. We remark, however, that the two terms on the right of the Green's function expansion depend on the column order in H, whereas the Green's Function itself is independent of that order.

We analyze the existence of a unique solution to Equation 1a–c briefly, as follows. Let $\mathbf{g}$ be the solution of Equation 1b, which is defined by the initial condition $\mathbf{g}(0) = [\alpha_1^T \quad \mathbf{0}]^T$, so that it also satisfies Equation 1a. A unique solution $\mathbf{f}$ to Equation 1a–c exists therefore if and only if it can be written as $\mathbf{f}(t) = \mathbf{V}(t)\mathbf{d} + \mathbf{g}(t)$, where $\mathbf{V}$ is the fundamental matrix for Equation 1b specified by $\mathbf{V}(0) = \mathbf{I}$, the identity. Solving for $\mathbf{d} = [\mathbf{d}_1^T \quad \mathbf{d}_2^T]^T$ from the boundary conditions, we obtain $\mathbf{d}_1 = \mathbf{0}$ and the expression

$$\mathbf{V}_{22}(T)\mathbf{d}_2 = \alpha_2 - \mathbf{g}_2(T)$$

Thus a unique $\mathbf{f}$ exists if and only if $\mathbf{V}_{22}(T)$ is nonsingular.

Under the assumption that $\mathbf{V}_{22}^{-1}(T)$ exists, we can express the solution for Equation 1a–c in a convenient form as follows. Let $\mathbf{G}$ to be any fundamental matrix for Equation 1b that satisfies $\mathbf{G}_{12}(0) = \mathbf{0} = \mathbf{G}_{21}(T)$ and is normalized so that $\mathbf{G}_{11}(0) = \mathbf{I} = \mathbf{G}_{22}(T)$. At least one such fundamental matrix exists because we can take

$$\mathbf{G}(t) = [\mathbf{V}_1(t) - \mathbf{V}_2(t)\mathbf{V}_{22}^{-1}(T)\mathbf{V}_{21}(T) \qquad \mathbf{V}_2(t)\,\mathbf{V}_{22}^{-1}(T)]$$

Then by direct differentiation, the function

$$\mathbf{f}(t) = \mathbf{G}_1(t)\alpha_1 + \mathbf{G}_2(t)\alpha_2 + \mathbf{G}_1(t)\int_0^t [\mathbf{G}^{-1}(s)]_1\mathbf{b}(s)\mathrm{d}s$$

$$- \mathbf{G}_2(t)\int_t^T [\mathbf{G}^{-1}(s)]_2\mathbf{b}(s)\mathrm{d}s$$

satisfies Equation 1b. But because of the partitioned form of $\mathbf{G}$, this function also satisfies Equations 1a and 1c, and thus it is the unique solution of Equation 1a–c.

Consequently we can express the difference $\delta(t) = \hat{\mathbf{f}}(t) - \mathbf{f}(t)$ between the solutions of Equations 1 and 2 in the similar form

$$\delta(t) = \mathbf{G}_1(t)\eta_1 + \mathbf{G}_2(t)\eta_2 + \mathbf{G}_1(t)\int_0^t [\mathbf{G}^{-1}(s)]_1\mathbf{p}(s)\mathrm{d}s$$

$$- \mathbf{G}_2(t)\int_t^T [\mathbf{G}^{-1}(s)]_2\mathbf{p}(s)\mathrm{d}s$$

where $\mathbf{p}(t) = \mathbf{E}(t)[\mathbf{y}(t) + \delta(t)] + \mathbf{e}(t)$. Substituting for the $\delta(s)$ occurring in the terms $\mathbf{p}(s)$, we can develop a convergent series of six infinite sums for

$\delta(t)$ just as we did for Equation 5. However only the first term in each sum is of order ε. Thus if we divide by $\|\mathbf{f}(t)\|$ in the last expression and take bounds, we obtain the following result by the same arguments as those used for Theorem 1 and Equation 13.

Theorem 2. Suppose that a unique solution to Equation 1a–c exists. Then the relative condition number of Equation 1a–c satisfies

$$c(t) \leq F_1(0,t) + F_2(T,t) + \int_0^t F_1(s,t)\left[\|\mathbf{A}(s)\| + \frac{\|\mathbf{b}(s)\|}{\|\mathbf{f}(s)\|}\right]ds$$

$$+ \int_t^T F_2(s,t)\left[\|\mathbf{A}(s)\| + \frac{\|\mathbf{b}(s)\|}{\|\mathbf{f}(s)\|}\right]ds \quad (14)$$

where $F_1(s,t)$ and $F_2(s,t)$ are the amplification factors defined by

$$F_1(s,t) \equiv \|\mathbf{G}_1(t)[\mathbf{G}^{-1}(s)]_1\| \frac{\|\mathbf{f}(s)\|}{\|\mathbf{f}(t)\|} \qquad F_2(s,t) \equiv \|\mathbf{G}_2(t)[\mathbf{G}^{-1}(s)]_2\| \frac{\|\mathbf{f}(s)\|}{\|\mathbf{f}(t)\|} \quad (15)$$

and where $\mathbf{G}$ is any fundamental system such that $\mathbf{G}_{12}(0) = \mathbf{0} = \mathbf{G}_{21}(T)$. The bound of Equation 14 is achievable. Moreover if $\alpha_1 \neq \mathbf{0}$ and $\alpha_2 \neq \mathbf{0}$, then $c(t) \geq F_1(0,t) + F_2(T,t)$.

The governing principle of the boundary value formulation therefore becomes perfectly clear on examining Equation 14. Since the first integrand varies from 0 to t and the second from t to T, the boundary value problem is well conditioned if there exists a partition $\mathbf{G} = [\mathbf{G}_1 \quad \mathbf{G}_2]$ such that none of the solution columns of $\mathbf{G}_1(t)$ dominate $\mathbf{f}$ in norm and such that $\mathbf{f}$ does not dominate any of the solution columns of $\mathbf{G}_2(t)$. Thus for a large class of equations, the conditions for the boundedness of all terms in Equation 14 can be met if the number k of initial conditions is properly chosen.

In the elementary system in Equation 11 for example, it is clear that $k = 1$ should be chosen. A fundamental matrix $\mathbf{G}$ satisfying $\mathbf{G}_{12}(0) = \mathbf{0}$ and $\mathbf{G}_{21}(T) = \mathbf{0}$ can easily be constructed from the matrix $\mathbf{H}$ in Equation 12 as

$$G(t) = [H_1(t) - H_2(t)H_{22}^{-1}(T)H_{21}(T) \qquad H_2(t) - H_1(t)H_{11}^{-1}(0)H_{12}(0)]$$

$$= \begin{bmatrix} e^t(1 - e^{-9(T-t)}/2) & e^{10t}(1- e^{-9t}) \\ e^t(1 - e^{-9(T-t)}) & 2e^{10t}(1 - e^{-9t}/2) \end{bmatrix}$$

It follows after some calculation, that approximately $F_1(0,t) \doteq e^{-4t}$ and $F_2(T,t) \doteq e^{-5(T-t)}$ so that $F_1(s,t) \le 3e^{-4(t-s)}$ and $F_2(s,t) \le 4e^{-5(s-t)}$. For this example therefore we have

$$c(t) \le e^{-4t} + e^{-5(T-t)} + 123 \int_0^t e^{-4(t-s)}ds + 164 \int_t^T e^{-5(s-t)}ds \le 66$$

demonstrating that the partition of solutions is correct when k is appropriate.

4. DIFFERENCE SYSTEMS

The solution of Equation 1a–c by a finite difference method can lead to a boundary value difference system of the form

$$z_1(0) = \alpha_1 \tag{16a}$$

$$z(i) = B(i)z(i - 1) + d(i) \qquad i = 1, 2, \ldots, N \tag{16b}$$

$$z_2(N) = \alpha_2 \tag{16c}$$

Since the theory of linear differential systems parallels that of linear difference systems, the analysis presented in this chapter can easily be adapted to the latter context. In fact the variation-of-constants formula for the solution of Equation 16b in terms its fundamental matrix $K(i)$ and the initial condition $z(0) = \alpha$ is

$$z(i) = K(i)K^{-1}(0)\alpha + K(i) \sum_{s=1}^{i} K^{-1}(s)d(s)$$

Since its counterpart was the only formula used to prove Theorem 1, that theorem applies equally well to difference systems of the Equation 16a–c type if A is replaced by B, b by d, and the integral by the sum. With the same notation change, the analysis presented in Section 3, and in particular Theorem 2, applies to Equation 16a–c. Therefore for a concurrent analysis of a differential boundary value problem and its finite difference approximation and a proof of the compatibility of the difference scheme with the original problem, it is necessary only to establish an isomorphism between the solutions of Equation 1a–c and those of Equation 16a–c. Such a technique was used in Reference 4 to design a semi-implicit step-by-step series method for stiff differential systems.

5. References

1. Lentini, M.; Osborne, M. R.; and Russell, R. D. "The close relationships between methods for solving two-point boundary value problems." *SIAM J. Numer. Anal.* **22,** 280–309 (1985).
2. Ince, E. L. *Ordinary Differential Equations.* Dover, London 1926. 408.
3. Gautschi, W. Zur Numerik rekurrenter Relationen. *Computing* **9,** 107–26 (1972).
4. Jalbert, F.; and Zahar, R. V. M. "A highly precise Taylor series method for stiff O.D.E.s." *Cong. Numer.* **46,** 347–58 (1985).

Published Works of Samuel D. Conte

1. "The circular plate with eccentric hole." *Q. Appl. Math.* IX(4), 435–41 (1952).
2. "On the reduction of shadowgrams." BRL Report no. 786 (January 1952).
3. "Eigenfunction expansions." Oak Ridge National Laboratory Report (1953) (with W. C. Sangren).
4. An Asymptotic solution for a pair of first order equations. *Proc. Am. Math. Soc.* October, 1953, 696–702 (1953) (with W. C. Sangren).
5. "On some nonlinear partial differential equations." *Industrial Mathematics* 1954, 17–23 (1954).
6. "An expansion theorem for a system of first-order equations." *Canad. J. Math.* **6,** 554–60 (1954) (with W. C. Sangren).
7. "A convolution theory for Gegenbauer transforms." *Quart. J. Math Oxford 2* (March 1955) 48–52.
8. "On the new integrating procedure." Ordinance Computer Research (October 1955).
9. "A Kutta third-order procedure for solving differential equations requiring minimum storage." *JACM* 22–26, (January 1956) (with R. Reeves) pp. 22–25.
10. "The operational calculus of Gegenbauer transforms." Zeitschrift für Angewandte Mathematik und Mechanik (March 1956) 1–3.
11. "Convergence of finite difference solutions to a solution of the equation of the vibrating rod." Proc. Amer. Math. Soc., 742–49 (August 1945) (with W. C. Royster).
12. "A study of finite difference approximations to a fourth-order parabolic differential equation." Ballistic Research Lab Report No. 959 (October 1955).
13. "An equiconvergence theorem." *Industrial Mathematics* **6** (May 1956) 27–38.
14. Solid Geometry for Colleges. Ronald Press, New York. 1957 (with H. Mandelbaum).
15. "A stable implicit finite difference approximation to a fourth-order parabolic differential equation." *J. Assoc. Comp. Mach.* **4** 18–24 (1957).
16. "Numerical solution of vibration problems in two-space variables. *Pac. J. Math.* **7** (1957) 1535–1544.
17. "An alternating direction method for solving the biharmonic equation." *Math. Tab. Aids Comp.* **12** (1958) (with R. T. Dames) 264–273.

18. "On the numerical integration of the Orr–Sommerfelt equation." *Society for Industrial and Applied Mathematics* 7 361–67 (1959) (with J. W. Miles).

19. "Eigenvalues in modern industry—problems involving differential operators." *Proc. of the Symposium on Digital Computing in the Aircraft Industry.* NYU–IBM (1959) New York, (with D. M. Young).

20. "Computer programs for space missions." In *Space Trajectories,* Chap. 9. Academic Press, New York, 1960.

21. "On an alternating direction method for solving the plate problem with mixed boundary conditions." *JACM* 7 (1960), (with R. T. James) 198–225.

22. *The Plasma Dispersion Function.* Academic Press, 1961 (with Burton D. Fried), New York.

23. "Computational procedures for orbital problems." In *Flight Performance Handbook for Orbital Operations,* Appendix F. TRW Inc., Los Angeles, CA.

24. "The numerical solution of axisymetric problems in elasticity." *Proc. Fifth AFBMC Symposium, Space Technology Labs.* Academic Press, 1961 (with K. L. Miller and C. B. Sensenig), New York.

25. "On the computation of missile and satellite trajectories." In *Advances in Computers,* vol. 3. Academic Press, 1962, New York.

26. "Education in the computer sciences." *Proc. Assoc. for Computing Machinery* (1964).

27. *Elementary Numerical Analysis. An Algorithmic Approach.* McGraw-Hill, 1965, New York.

28. "Graduate education in computer sciences." *Proc. Assoc. for Computing Machinery* (1965).

29. "The numerical solution of linear boundary value problems." *SIAM Rev.* (July 1966) 309–321.

30. "The solution of simultaneous nonlinear equations." *Proc. Assoc. for Computing Machinery* (August 1967) (with K. M. Brown) 111–114.

31. "Satellite, interplanetary, and tracking programs at Space Technology Laboratories." *Proc. NASA Symposium on Space Trajectories* (1968) (with L. Wong).

32. "Education in the computer sciences." *Proc. of the Park City Conference.* Academic Press, 1969, New York.

33. "An experiment in an automated instructional system for numerical methods." *Comm. Assoc. Comp. Mach.* (October 1971) 643–649.

34. Elementary Numerical Analysis, 2d ed. New York: McGraw-Hill, 1972 (with C. deboor).

35. "The technology of computing center management." *Comm. Assoc. Comp. Mach.* (July 1976) (with M. H. Halstead) 369–370.

36. "The projection and employment of Ph.D.s in computer science." *Comm. Assoc. Comp. Mach.* (June 1976) (with O. Taulbee).

37. "Numerical analysis." In *Encyclopedia of Computer Science.* New York: Petrocelli Charter, 1976.

38. "The production and employment of Ph.D.s in computer science." *Comm. Assoc. Comp. Mach.* (June 1977) 311–313.

39. "Operating budgets for computing centers." *Encyclopedia of Computer Science and Technology* 1978 (with B. Rhoads) 359–374.
40. "Computer science and numerical analysis: the interface." *Proc. Assoc. for Computing Machinery* (December 1978) 25–26.
41. "Historical development of computer science at Purdue." TR 197 (1979) New York.
42. "Mathematics of computing." In *Taxonomy of Computer Science and Engineering.* AFIPS Press, 1979.
43. "Estimating software effort." *Proc. of AIRMICS Workshop on Performance Management* (November 1979) (with V. Shen).
44. Elementary Numerical Analysis, 3d ed. New York: McGraw-Hill, 1980 (with C. deBoor).
45. "Software science." In *Encyclopedia of Computer Science and Technology.* New York: Petrocelli, 1982 (with V. Shen).
46. "Effort minimization based on hierarchical modularization." CSD-TR-347. Computer Sciences Department, Purdue University.
47. "The software science language level metric." CSD-TR-373. Computer Sciences Department, Purdue University.
48. "On the effect of different counting rules for control flow operators on software. *Science Metrics, PER* **Y.11** (1982) (with V. Y. Shen and K. Dickey).
49. "Software science revisited: a critical analysis of the theory and its empirical support." *IEEE Trans. Software Eng.* **SE-9**(2), 155–65 (1983) (with V. Y. Shen and H. E. Dunsmore).
50. "A comparison of a few-effort estimation models." *J. of Parametrics* (March 1984) (with V. Y. Shen and H. E. Dunsmore).
51. "Software effort estimation and productivity." *Adv. Comp.* (July 1984) (with V. Y. Shen and H. E. Dunsmore). pp. 1–60 Academic Press, New York.
52. *Software Engineering Metrics and Models.* Benjamin Cummings Press, 1985 (with V. Y. Shen and H. E. Dunsmore).
53. "A software cost prediction model." Software Engineering Research Center TR-1-P (March 1987).
54. "Early prediction of software size and effort." Software Engineering Research Center TR-10-P (March 1988) (with M. K. Rathi and R. L. Campbell).

Index